"Based on his days as a fly in the mosh pit of the nascent punk scene in Toronto and decades of drumming for some of my favorite beat groups, you would think that Don Pyle has a lot of great stories to tell, and insight to share. You are not wrong. Come for the Guelph Riot, and then see if you can guess which Shadowy Man tossed a lovingly compiled Grateful Dead cassette from a moving vehicle."

— Ira Kaplan (Yo La Tengo)

"A big-city-art-punk-music-dream recounted from the first row, backstage, on stage, and under the carpets. A marvel of memory and identity entangled in sound and vision across decades, it's also an emotional and intimate travelogue of revelation, transformation, and the power of creativity and community."

— Patti Schmidt (*Brave New Waves*)

"What can't Don Pyle do? He's dazzled us with his drumming, documented Toronto's punk history with intimate verve, and (for a lucky few) styled our hair. Now, he's written the most affectionate, insightful and tender music memoir I've ever read. Like the sweetest, sweatiest moshpit hug, you'll never want it to end."

— Jason McBride (author of *Eat Your Mind: The Radical Life and Work of Kathy Acker*)

ROUGH DESCRIPTION

love letters and ghost stories from a life in music

DON PYLE

Published by ECW Press
665 Gerrard Street East
Toronto, Ontario, Canada M4M 1Y2
416-694-3348 / info@ecwpress.com

Editor for the Press: Michael Holmes / a misFit Book
Copy editor: Michael Barclay
Cover design: David A. Gee
Front cover image: Heather Cameron
Back cover image: Don Pyle

Unless otherwise specified, all photographs are the author's.

To the best of his abilities, the author has related experiences, places, people, and organizations from his memories of them.

LIBRARY AND ARCHIVES CANADA CATALOGUING IN PUBLICATION

Title: Rough description : love letters and ghost stories from a life in music / Don Pyle.

Names: Pyle, Don, 1961- author

Identifiers: Canadiana (print) 2026011572X | Canadiana (ebook) 20260115800

ISBN 978-1-77041-713-7 (softcover)
ISBN 978-1-77852-588-9 (PDF)
ISBN 978-1-77852-587-2 (ePub)

Subjects: LCSH: Pyle, Don, 1961- | LCSH: Rock musicians—Ontario—Toronto—Biography. | LCSH: Sound recording executives and producers—Ontario—Toronto—Biography. | LCGFT: Autobiographies.

Classification: LCC ML419.P996 A3 2026 | DDC 781.66092—dc23

This book is funded in part by the Government of Canada. *Ce livre est financé en partie par le gouvernement du Canada.* We acknowledge the support of the Canada Council for the Arts. *Nous remercions le Conseil des arts du Canada de son soutien.* We would like to acknowledge the funding support of the Ontario Arts Council (OAC) and the Government of Ontario for their support. We also acknowledge the support of the Government of Ontario through the Ontario Book Publishing Tax Credit, and through Ontario Creates. This book was produced with the support of the City of Toronto through Toronto Arts Council.

Ontario

ONTARIO CREATES

FUNDED BY THE CITY OF TORONTO
TORONTO ARTS_COUNCIL

CERTIFIED CANADIAN PUBLISHER

PRINTED AND BOUND IN CANADA

PRINTING: MARQUIS 5 4 3 2 1

CONTENTS

PREFACE

AFTER THE RELEASE OF EACH OF MY TWO OTHER BOOKS, I DID A series of talks, using the photographs contained in them as prompts. It was a great pleasure to explore more deeply some of the things I was thinking or feeling about the images, connections I was making to other events, and details a viewer wouldn't know without context. It was the kind of storytelling that I respond so positively to when I hear others speak. I love hearing the cultural context of a photograph, or a song, and what was going on with the artist when they created a particular work, what was going on in their background or the world at large when you look at a picture or an event.

My book *Shot in a Mirror* is a small collection of fifty portraits, most of them quite intimate. Unless I had a particular narrative I wanted to share specifically about a photograph, I avoided writing too much text, not wanting any person to be reduced to a caption that was incapable of summarizing them, and in a way that they themselves would perhaps not use to self-define. Their most known moment is not who they were.

One of the photographs is of artist Wendy Coburn. I projected so many feelings and thoughts onto my picture of her that I started to be preoccupied with what I was interpreting from the image. There were so many things about her story that I wanted to talk about. Reflecting on and speaking about that one photo became the impetus for this book. I made a "set list" of things and people about which I felt I had something to say, mostly based on a photo or two.

Although *Rough Description* is a memoir of sorts, it's as much about other people who've affected me as it is about me. While there are millions of people in bands, and who did other creative things, my circumstances are uniquely my own, as are all of ours. I've been very fortunate to have had some of the experiences I've had, and with that comes stories that have made a few jaws drop, made people recoil in horror or just laugh at the absurdity. I've had, and am still enjoying, what I'd call a successful career, in that I've been able to do most things on my terms, and have always been able to pay my rent.

From first band at sixteen to a life-long entanglement as drummer and co-founder of Shadowy Men on a Shadowy Planet, detours through being a member of eminent groups Fifth Column, King Cobb Steelie, and Phono-Comb, taking up photography in the earliest moments of punk rock and the attendant lifetime of negatives and photo files that come with that, scoring the *Kids in the Hall* series and a few feature films, criss-crossing the continent, and beyond playing shows, there are situations and feelings imprinted on me that I've tried to share. I write about my mother, a childhood car accident I was in, going to hair school, and, well, you'll find out if you read it. It's not just about music, even though that's been a significant motivator in my life. What's contained here is as much about the people and experiences that make up a rich journey, with lots of bumps to make it interesting and provide perspective on the best or worst days.

It isn't chronological but is arranged like a set list, not unlike the thousands of those I've made up in my life. There is somehow a correlation between each chapter, and I guess the commonality is me and my interpretation of the experiences I've had. It's incomplete, as all life stories are, but it is not intended as an autobiography. I describe people and situations as accurately and selectively as I wanted to.

There wasn't a way to work it into the events I was writing about but, despite what I say about Mickey DeSadist, I believe that he's a character invented by Mike Grelecki. Part of Mickey's punk agenda was to be as offensive as possible, something I certainly enjoy when the moment is right. I don't experience Mike to be racist or homophobic.

I am eternally grateful to Michael Holmes, Michael Barclay, Ira Kaplan, and Jason Winkler for their thoughtful reading and feedback in the process of writing this book. Each of them has helped in some significant way to make this collection better, and I thank them.

Posthumous dedications often read to me like posthumous pardons for criminal convictions. Like why the fuck didn't you do that when they were alive? Not having written this book yet is one excuse. I lovingly dedicate this book to Shirley Pyle, Dallas Good and Reid Diamond, and to Jason Winkler, who is very much alive.

THE BEGINNING

FREDDY POMPEII, BASS PLAYER OF THE VILETONES, AND HIS partner, Margarita Passion, ran a little punk shop in Toronto called New Rose, on Queen Street East by Parliament, in what then felt like a pretty rough spot. At fifteen, having grown up in the west-end Junction neighbourhood, I didn't know the east side very well. New experiences were taking me to different parts of the city, and it's funny to think now that I thought of this shop, maybe just twelve blocks from Toronto's main north-south road, Yonge

Street, as being the east *end*. Other than visiting my grandparents and great-grandparents, we barely went east of the Don River, that valley being the city's dividing line.

Walk two blocks east from Yonge and you encountered the strip where all the pawnshops in the city were, museums filled with other peoples' fascinating old things; so many desperate and aspirational stories tied up in the belongings there, waiting for the owner to abandon and the shop to resell. I regularly found all kinds of great treasure: books, records, camera equipment. There would be stationery from the Second World War, with encouragement on the package to write to the boys overseas, with suggested topics: *Don't say anything negative, it's all about morale.*

The first of many beer halls that lined Queen East was at the same intersection, Church and Queen. These bars were alluringly tragic, places populated almost exclusively by men spending not just nights but days drinking. Everyone smoked. The smell of stale beer and cigarettes would hit you through the open door as you passed, catching a glimpse of a small TV, eternally on, perched on a little corner shelf ten feet up.

I was so into the Viletones, their dangerousness, their ability to rumble for minutes on end on one looping riff as the theatre of vocalist Steven Leckie played out. He would writhe on the floor, or drag broken beer bottles across his arms and chest as we'd all heard Iggy did. New Rose was kind of the band's clubhouse. Freddy was goofy, silly, sweet, and welcoming, the antithesis of the band's public image, and he was the only Viletone I befriended. Margaret too. I'd go there to buy records or clothes, and Freddy often gave me beer, something that, at fifteen years old, made me hyper-aware of the age gap between us, and concerned that Freddy might get in trouble. Not quite belonging in this adult situation, but somehow here. In 1977, punk was a sort of scene already and only a relatively small number of people were into this burst of new bands. People were generally inviting and warm to others they sensed were in the same tribe.

I'd taken many photos of bands by then, and my first experiments in printing resulted in me giving New Rose a few large prints for their wall, one of the Dead Boys and one of the Viletones. I still get a bit of a thrill seeing them hanging in the shop in Suzanne Naughton's Super-8 verité film *An Afternoon with the Viletones at New Rose*. In it, visibly self-conscious punks hang around, taking too many sips on their beer to occupy their hands, trying to look poised while simultaneously trying to fit in and stand out.

At some point, I took a course at Visual Arts Ontario, a membership collective you had to join if you wanted to access their colour photocopier. There were only two such machines in the city, and of course, many of the art-scene punks were excited by this new medium. Colours on the output were vibrant — but way off, and you always had to manually adjust the colour balance to get something closer to what you were after. The "off-ness" was part of the appeal though, the machine's uncanny ability to turn any ordinary picture into art.

The photocopier accepted a finicky kind of heat-transfer paper, but it always jammed. It's kind of unbelievable now to think that part of the mandatory course you had to take before using the machine included its general maintenance. Users were constantly trying to fix different aspects of this sophisticated machine that was constantly breaking down, and that none of us were remotely qualified to repair. I started making my own T-shirts with the transfer paper, prompting Freddy to ask me where I got the unique John Cale shirt I was wearing. When I told him, he asked if I'd make some shirts for the shop. It was an invigorating process, making designs for bands I liked.

I went to Honest Ed's and bought up a bunch of plain white T's. Things were already cheaper at Ed's, and even cheaper if you bought seconds, as I did. You'd have one with a sleeve sewed closed, or misshapen angles making the shirt wonky, or with little holes and missed seams. I didn't mind, and neither did the shop. I made a Clash shirt, a Heartbreakers one using my own Johnny Thunders photo, one of the Jam's debut album, and, my favourite, a Viletones shirt using an outtake photo from their first seven-inch that Freddy had given me. I scorched the first shirt using my mom's iron to melt the images onto the shirts, before she showed me her trick for ironing her pantyhose: put a tea towel over the transfer to diffuse the heat.

One day, I mentioned to Freddy that I was going to Calgary to visit my brother and his family. He said, "Hey, we just got a letter from a guy in Calgary. You should write him and see if there are any punk shows happening when you're out." He copied the address down and, not long after, I wrote to Steve Koch.

Steve's reply came quickly: "Don't come. It's terrible here, I can't wait to get out." I was going anyway, and the idea that there would be even one punk band in Calgary hadn't even occurred to me. This guy seemed smart and interesting, so we immediately started writing back and forth. I kept those letters for years and one day gave them back to Steve, after rereading them. He quoted *Les Chants de Maldoror* and asked if I knew where he could find a dog collar like Leckie's. He told me that the only thing close to a punk band was his brother's group, Buick McKane. That they were named after a T. Rex song was promising. He explained that they were sort of a bar band but moving more toward punk, doing a mix of originals and covers. They did "Vambo," by the Sensational Alex Harvey Band, and that was enough to interest me.

Not long after, a letter arrived from Alex Koch, Steve's brother. I now had two pen pals! We talked about the Runaways a lot, and he told me about his band, inviting me to come to a rehearsal, as they didn't have any live dates while I was there. It was unlikely I'd get into a bar in Calgary anyway, still a few years away from legal drinking age.

My brother drove me out to where they rehearsed on the opposite side of the city, in a planned community near a fake lake, in the basement of the guitarist's childhood home. The guitarist was Brian Connelly; the bassist was Reid Diamond. The band had their own room, with huge amps big enough for an arena, and played at full volume. I was going out to see a lot of bands by this point, including what I thought was the loudest show I'd ever heard, the Dead Boys at the New Yorker Theatre for their first headlining show in Toronto. It may have been the same volume, but inside a small room the sound was blistering. As kids, my friend and I would kneel in the alleyway between houses to watch a couple of neighbourhood bands practise in basements. Seeing a real band rehearse at this point was novel and thrilling. They weren't dressed like punks, more like the teens I went to high school with, with shag rocker hair, extra tight T-shirts and a mix of high-waisted wide and tight pants.

When I went upstairs at some point, I encountered Brian's parents sitting in the living room reading newspapers, the TV on silently in the background. I was shocked at how loud it was up there too. Not only were they tolerating it, his mom cheerfully asked if I'd like something to drink. I talked to them briefly and they showed me some relics of the times they'd spent in the Far North. I had no relationship to the North, and found their old artifacts like something I only connected to history class or museums, not to actual people and places.

Buick McKane sounded really good. Other than my pen pals Alex and Steve, who I met that day for the first time, the others were aloof. When they heard there was a Toronto punk coming to rehearsal, they probably didn't expect a sixteen-year-old with Coke-bottle glasses and a degree of self-consciousness. But I would soon form a band with three of them, called Crash Kills Five, and two of them I'd spend most of the rest of my life entangled with in Shadowy Men on a Shadowy Planet. I know now that the exact date I met them was March 22, 1978.

Reid Diamond was a huge fan of the Jam, and gasped incredulously when I told him that they were, in fact, playing Toronto that very night. He couldn't believe that I would leave town while they were there, but Toronto had mind-opening bands every week at this time. The other event that night was the premiere of *All You*

Need Is Cash, the TV special about the Rutles, a Beatles spoof by Monty Python's Eric Idle. After band practice was over, I stood there as Reid and singer Scott argued, annoyed about who would have to drive me home because none of them wanted to miss any of the Rutles special. I felt bad, but needed a ride. There was no public transit that went anywhere near where I was coming from or going — typical of Calgary for years to come. Reid grumbled all the way to Bowness, but was friendly too. There were no home VCRs yet, so I couldn't blame him for being bummed about potentially missing the Rutles.

Steve was the first to get out of Calgary, landing in Toronto not long after my visit. After a few days staying in my mother's basement, as many émigrés from Calgary would in the future, he found a spot in a rooming house. We immediately bonded, going to shows and hanging out. Steve tells me that I talked our way into the Horseshoe one evening, saying we were in local band Johnny and the G-Rays, reasoning that nobody would know what they looked like. Together we saw L.A.'s the Screamers and were blown away by the intensity, frequency, and dynamic of the band, completely awed by their lead singer, Tomata DuPlenty. They were extreme and radical, unlike anything we'd heard before. We went to their van with them after the show to chat, so captivated by their personas and the astonishing music we had just heard.

Steve and I also saw the first Toronto show by the Police at the Horseshoe, one of those events that hundreds claim to have been at but only about forty really were. Years later, one friend said I was the only person he believed — because I was the only one who thought they were terrible, singing in fake Jamaican accents and bringing out an inflatable sex doll to serenade. So boring, conventional, and contrived.

Steve was an exceptionally talented guitarist. He was maybe five or six years older than me and knew a lot of music outside my realm of knowledge, so we immediately talked about starting a band together. I'd wanted to do so for a couple of years, but not playing any instrument, I knew I'd have to be the singer — something I didn't relish, but it didn't matter, that was all I thought I could do then. We asked two friends from the scene to play with us. One was a lanky, slow-talking guy known as Boring Bill, not by his choice. Years later, I felt bad that we called him that, his name really being Bill Kirby. He played bass. Mohamed Nagdee, aka Eddy Dent, was the guitarist in the Dents, who I think were still going at that point, and he wanted to play drums. We started rehearsing in a friend's furnace room up in North York. Steve was adept at everything: playing Eddie Cochran riffs, and slashy guitar figures lifted from metal, English folk, and our favourite new bands. He'd written me once after he'd been to England to tell me about some of the bands he had seen. He was electrified by Wire, who I wouldn't hear until they started making records. He expressed excited disbelief at a band whose songs were sometimes only twenty seconds long! This idea alone inspired us, and we wrote a couple of songs that short.

We picked the name Crash Kills Nine, after seeing a headline and laughing that it sounded like a fucked-up version of John Barry Seven, or Count Five. For our first show, we played to some friends who hung around at the house where we rehearsed, a short fifteen-minute set with a few originals and a couple of covers, including the new Adverts single that had just come out, "Bored Teenagers."

Our first show out was on a cold Sunday night in December at the Turning Point, one of the lively clubs where punk bands played. It was an easy club to get into if you were underage because the headlining band ran the door, so policing entry was counterproductive. Later, my younger sister even worked the door there — and she was only fourteen. Their policy was that you couldn't come in unless you were drinking.

We sort of crashed the stage for our third performance. The Sofisticatos, a blazing new band out of Milton, a small town west of Toronto, put on a show there in a quonset hut. Some of the best new groups in the city played. We asked some others if we could use their equipment and did an impromptu set. Viletones were also on the bill, and were in flux. The original musicians had all quit, leaving just the singer, Steven Leckie, to carry on with the name. He was on maybe his third or fourth line-up when he saw Steve Koch play and asked him to join. He did, and that was the end of Crash Kills Nine.

That ended our friendship for years to come. I was hurt that Steve had jumped ship so easily. We avoided each other for a few years after that, but crossed paths regularly. Even though I was wounded at the time, years later I totally knew this was the right thing for Steve to do. He'd moved to Toronto idolizing the Viletones, and his punk dream was coming true. Steve subsequently did time in a number of other bands after he departed from the Viletones, as every musician inevitably did before and after him.

Our animosity softened over the years. Playing with the Demics, the Handsome Neds, and the Ugly in subsequent years, Steve once said to me, "I was in all the best bands in Toronto — after they were good." That wasn't true in all cases, but something about that was petty validation.

Meanwhile, back in Calgary, Reid, Brian and drummer Alex plotted moving east. Calgary bars had extreme and violent racial divisions within them, and prevailing redneck attitudes would not allow them to be the band they wanted to be. You could get beat up for wearing a cardigan. Besides, with stories from me and Steve about what was happening in Toronto, they wanted to get here quickly and revel in the punk rock fantasia of the moment. Right before they were about to move, Alex went on a bender, stealing a city bus and spray-painting his name all over his former high school. Needless to say, he was busted and had to stay behind to deal with the fallout.

Reid and Brian packed up Reid's white Econoline and started the long journey east. Bored while driving across the Prairies, they were pulled over by cops who asked where they were going and if they'd been drinking. "No sir," they replied — before the officer held up an empty beer box, asking how they'd explain this. Claiming they didn't know anything about it, they asked where he got it from. It was an Alberta brand on an Alberta van and had lodged itself on the back of the van, stuck behind the spare tire after being chucked from the window of the moving vehicle.

They finally arrived in Toronto and were eager to go out on the town. The day they made it was a Monday, not exactly a premium night for choices. We went down to the only club that had something happening that night, the Beverly Tavern. All the art-school bands played the Bev, mostly due to its proximity to the Ontario College of Art right around the corner. The side entry door for the upstairs venue was separated from its neighbour by a laneway, slick with blood and grease from the chicken slaughterhouse mere feet away. We tiptoed around the muck and got a table. The band playing that night, the Biffs, were a bouncy, campy and kitsch outfit that used props and sardonic humour, basically the antithesis of the heavy thrash the Calgarians hoped for. After a few songs and a drink, Reid, visibly discouraged, restlessly asked if there was somewhere else to go. Uh, no. Toronto wasn't really a punk wonderland where you could frolic from place to place on any given night, spoiled for choices. Some nights it was a feast, other nights it was, well, freshly slaughtered chicken. You had to pay attention to who was playing where, and go where the action was on that particular night.

A couple nights later it was up to a tavern called Nags Head North. This club was part of the shitty circuit that typical bar bands would cycle through, catering more to hard-rock cover bands and orthodox working outfits. Before any kind of "alternative" club situation was established, these were the bread-and-butter locations for bands of that ilk. It was horribly unappealing to my snobbish attitudes, and my opinion of local punk bands who entered into this world diminished. Having started club-going at the beginning of punk in 1976, I was more familiar with bands in live spaces being an event, a spectacle where you were much more likely to see and hear something mind-blowing that had never been seen or heard before. With bouncers, ladies' nights, and long hair, bars like the Nags Head were common, boring, and sometimes dangerous with their anti-punk agendas. Other than the usual drunk-guy bar fights, these places had no element of boundary-pushing or unexpected progressive ideas. The only thing "progressive" in bars like this was that genre of music. FM and Max Webster were two of the better bands in this circuit, far more interesting than who you were more likely to see.

Reid wanted to go see a band he was really into, the Battered Wives. A few other friends and I referred to them as the Buttered Knives, not wanting to even say their casually sexist, violent name. Their first album cover reinforced the business-as-usual conventional, pedestrian rock tropes that I loathed, with its chick-as-object photo, and band logo showing a lipsticked mouth impression on a fist. After a few songs, I went and hung out at the pizza joint next door while my two friends watched the band. A little too close to the situations they had left behind in Calgary, it wasn't long before they joined me.

Buick McKane's singer, Scott, was a '70s belter in the vein of Loverboy and Foreigner, the dominant sound of the era that punk, Alex, Brian and Reid were eager to escape. I heard years later that, after not hearing from his bandmates for a while, Scott called up Brian's parents to ask about their next practice. Brian's mom said, "Oh no, they moved to Toronto!"

After a few days in the same basement where Steve Koch had stayed, Brian and Reid found a flat by Dufferin Mall. Having an open apartment, without a door to close, the place was not ideal from the start. Barely out of their teens and living on their own for the first time, they were totally incompatible with their landlady, an elderly woman who constantly came up to complain about everything they were doing, mostly playing records and walking from room to room. The final straw was when a surprise houseguest arrived: Alex, freed from Calgary after dealing with his legal consequences. She told them to leave. They then found a basement apartment down the street from my mom's house, right across the road where I went to public school.

It was a bad situation from the first moment they moved in. While playing the Dickies' revved-up version of Black Sabbath's "Paranoid," there was banging on the door and wall, people yelling for them to play the record at the right speed. These weird Calgary punks, who were as normal-looking as could be, caught the attention of neighbourhood trouble, including a kid named Billy, who had been the playground bully when I was at school. He was probably nineteen now, and every inch the redneck they had hoped to never see again. These twerps knew my friends were in a band after spotting them moving their laughably oversized amps in and out. Reid had an SVT bass head and two massive speaker cabinets, each containing eight 10-inch speakers, standard for Calgary bar bands but out of place in the streamlined situations punk bands played here. They were so large that some days it was unbearable to move them. Reid would just put a blanket over the amps and leave them in the van.

Of course, one morning they came out to find the van doors wide open, the cursed cabinets gone. Billy and his pals stood smirking, half a block away. It was all weird for me to see. The area I'd grown up in was calm, a regular leafy neighbourhood of streets with nothing like crime or gangs, the worst misdemeanour being some kid stealing another's hockey stick. Suddenly the place seemed different, as seen from an odd-looking outsider's point of view.

There was a very large church next door, and a couple of times after too much drinking, we wandered over to listen to the incredible voices coming from the windows open in the summer heat. People invited us in and were so friendly and welcoming. It was incongruous to me that this was where hospitality was to be found on the street I grew up on.

The three of them rented rehearsal time in the Lansdowne Artists' Cooperative, an arts warehouse near Lansdowne subway station. I knew the couple of guys who ran it from their time in the band Tyranna. I'd go hang out with them while they rehearsed and auditioned singers. The space was totally dumb, not at all conducive to a band rehearsing, partly because almost all the other tenants were painters or sculptors, but primarily because the individual spaces were only cubicles, a small area of the room partitioned with two partial walls that met the brick exterior wall. Each artist's cubicle was U-shaped, open on one side to the common room and opened to the ceiling. You were on display in every way to everyone who walked by, and your gear was vulnerable when you weren't there.

After asking me to fill in at rehearsals until they found someone, it wasn't long before Alex, Brian and Reid invited me to be the singer in their new band. It was so easy to step into. They had some songs I knew already and was comfortable with, but I had no idea what my singing voice really sounded like, so there was nothing to be self-conscious about. Yet. Singing aloud felt great, not only as a physical feeling but as an inhibition-reducer.

We started practising regularly, me not even thinking that the end goal was to play shows. Many days we'd arrive to find the band in the next cubicle, Drastic Measures, also rehearsing. It quickly became a stupid battle of the bands. Reid and Brian's huge amps and Alex's powerful whack easily drowned out the meticulous working out of musical arrangements going on on the other side of the wall. It's hilarious to even think of now, a situation that could have no resolution. Their singer, Tony Malone, argued with Reid pointlessly. A compromise was struck. We'd play a song, they'd play a song, but that only lasted for a few takes before the battle was on again. They were understandably pissed as they were there first; we were crashing their good thing.

The LAC was throwing a party and asked if we'd perform. We were far from ready, but sure, we didn't even have to move any gear: our cubicle was already open to the main room. The space was an old factory that had been repurposed at different times, so across from us was a wall with open window frames that had once been an exterior wall but was now part of the warren of hallways that made up the interior. We started playing, and almost immediately most of the attendees left, but laughably went into the next room and watched us through the window frames. That cracked us up and encouraged us even more. People sniffed past us, sneering as they did. We concluded our short set after Brian did a quick turn and smashed the headstock of his Gibson SG on a brick pillar, causing the neck to snap off. Patsy Poison, drummer for the Curse, a band I loved dearly, made a face and called us buggerheads, adding, to an already upset Brian, "I'm glad you broke your guitar." Ouch! We just laughed, and for the next couple of weeks referred to our new band as the Buggerheads.

We were unreasonable brats and were shown the exit, or rather showed ourselves the exit, after a late-night snowball battle royale resulted in broken windows, up and down the fire escape, into parts of the darkened building and through the hallways, where sculptors' and painters' works were out in the open.

We had to come up with a name. Thinking no one would know Crash Kills Nine anyway, we should use that name but change it to Crash Kills Five, a tasteless jerk take on the Dave Clark Five. Just yesterday a friend sent me a photo of the front page of the newspaper in Milton, Ontario, with the headline "Crash kills five." My first reaction was to giggle, the headline to me so disconnected from its morbid and tragic meaning, and always first seen as a band name.

Real estate was still plentiful enough in the late '70s, and there were a multitude of odd factories and warehouses repurposed as live/work spaces by and for artists and bands. If you had some kind of unusual enterprise, it was fairly easy to find an affordable spot to do your business.

Our next rehearsal space was in one of these buildings, a factory on the Esplanade at the bottom of downtown. It was another fiasco waiting to happen. The room itself was massive, a brick corridor that was very old and bare, but the quirk about it was that it had no door, only a freight elevator at one end with a wooden gate that you'd raise and lower manually. The units off the freight elevator were staggered, the floors offset just enough so that the next unit up or down was half a floor away and on the other side of the elevator shaft. A dumb rock band moving in meant that our oversized volume spilled into the elevator shaft, disturbing everyone who shared it with us.

Angriest of all was the mime school that was our closest neighbour. Every day outraged mimes would come and yell at us, and we'd reply with a silent finger to our lips. We didn't make any friends there. Without a door to lock, we took turns living in the space for security. It was a really stupid situation. The neighbourhood was desolate after dark, and there was nowhere to go for food or anything.

The freight elevator would only operate if the gates on both sides were fully closed. It was a regular occurrence for someone to forget or not fully close the gate, so residents would call into the shaft for whoever could hear to close the gate. The mimes started using this against us, effectively locking us in our space, by deliberately leaving the old wooden gate open. The situation couldn't last.

One day, promoter Gary Topp called me and asked if Gang of Four could use our gear. Theirs had been stopped at the border, and ours was a close match as far as Gary knew. Gang of Four only had one or two singles out at this time, and I don't think we'd heard them yet, but I'd probably have said yes to anything Gary asked. It was him and his business partner Gary Cormier who had been the primary support for all the earliest out-of-town punks and innovative music coming to Toronto, booking most of the best shows I'd seen up until that point. We moved our equipment over and were put on the guest list for later that night.

For some reason, Brian and I were back at our rehearsal space before showtime, and when we went to leave, the elevator was stuck on the main floor, stranding us three storeys up, calling down to the empty building. With no one to close the gate, we knew the only way out was to climb down the dark elevator shaft, which we did. We arrived at the Edge club covered in grease and dirt, and were startled by the intensity and radical new sound Gang of Four were sending out. Even on the tiny club stage, singer Jon King and guitarist Andy Gill raced from side to side, their body motions expressing the anxiety and tension in their slashing sounds, their bodies colliding, electricity sparking the whole venue. We were in shock. Neither of us had ever heard a band that sounded like them.

Our next practice space was in one of the purpose-built rehearsal joints starting to sprout here and there. This was a popular one at the moment, right next to the Spadina Hotel and its Cabana Room, where we played regularly. The warehouse building had been renovated into a floor of maybe a dozen small rooms for bands to practise in, but had clearly been designed by someone who didn't know or didn't care how loud music worked. There was no insulation, just drywall. When the band next to us, the Hi-Fi's, were blasting just as loud as we were, neither one of us could hear ourselves. The hotheads from each band met angrily in the hallway and almost came to fisticuffs over who had more right to make noise, a useless conflict that should have been addressed to our landlord instead. They got along a lot better when they re-met years later through our new bands, Shadowy Men on a Shadowy Planet and Blue Rodeo.

Crash Kills Five played out a lot, pretty much anywhere we could, whenever we could. We wanted to keep doing it all the time, but there was hardly enough money in it to do that. I was still in high school, Alex was working restaurant jobs, Brian in the warehouse of Capitol Records out by the airport, and Reid at various odd jobs. I thought the three of them were fantastic musicians, and I loved watching each of them play. They were distinct and skilled. We spent most of our time together, hanging out at the house where they all rented rooms on Glen Road, listening to records, drinking, going to see bands and practising. It felt important to me.

When Brian announced that he was going away for a summer job, it was gutting. With each passing year, months pass at an ever more breakneck speed. But three months at eighteen years old felt like an eternity, and we were bummed he was going to be gone for so long. We wanted to keep playing, so we thought we'd get a temporary guitar player. Naive to how long it takes to gain cohesion in any new band, we thought three months was a whole career. We'd make a new record, write a ton of new songs. Reality hit when guitarists actually came to audition. We played briefly with one guy, someone who went on to become a successful artist and director, but he was fairly new to guitar, whereas Brian could play almost every record in his collection handily.

Years later Brian told me about his job in the Far North, cleaning up oil drilling and research sites. It was one of those jobs that pays ridiculously well for treacherous work, and can buy you freedom in the future. The rest of the band were too young, dumb and selfish to appreciate this. He and another guy would be dropped by helicopter on vast ice sheets and have to gather up mechanical debris. Some days they dropped them at different sites, leaving Brian alone, something that blows my mind now to think of the unprepared twenty-one-year-old I knew to be put in that situation. Polar bears were a real concern where he was.

Happy to have him back, we carried on after his return, making plans to record. Brian had quit the band a couple of times, but we didn't really know what was going on with him. The final time he quit was on stage, during a show at the Edge. I don't know exactly what was happening, but being in front of people was already nerve-wracking for him, and not being able to tune his guitar one night caused him to explode, busting his guitar into pieces and storming off, saying, "I quit." It seemed pretty obvious that he didn't want to be in the band, so the three of us decided on the spot to ask Mohamed "Eddy" Nagdee to join; he was there at the show. Mohamed's band, the Dents, had been the youngest of the first wave of punk bands. We loved him and he'd been in Crash Kills Nine.

Forty years later, I was going through some of Reid's papers that I'd been given after he died. There was an unsent letter to his best friend expressing his concern about Brian, afraid that Brian would be no more one day. Reid knew him much better than I did, knew his behaviour. I related to Brian's reclusiveness and thought that I might be as solitary if I had my own place to live. I never once thought about anyone's mental health, just their behaviour on display. I'm not sure if I even knew that "mental health" was a thing.

Our sound immediately changed, from Brian's winding and enthralling expressive guitar that played three parts at once to Eddy's propulsive Ramones power-chording with minimal leads. Eddy wrote cool leads, one of which Teenage Head lifted from a part he wrote in the Dents. I was with him the first time we saw Teenage Head do their then-new song, "Infected." When Gord Lewis's lead started in the instrumental outro of the song, Eddy and I turned to each other and burst out laughing. It was his solo from the Dents' song "Who Needs Love." When the band finished, we were standing around talking when Gord walked over. "Holy shit, that was my lead," Eddy said. Gord smiled and agreed, "Yeah, I know." Eddy didn't mind.

We somehow found a little eight-track studio called Pyramid Sound and booked time to record a single. The place was named after the roof of the garage the studio occupied, and was run by engineer Gerry Fielding. Gerry had long straight hair and reminded us of bassist Dennis Dunaway on Alice Cooper's *Love It to Death* album cover, so we thought he was cool. We'd cross paths with Gerry years later when Shadowy Men began working on the *Kids in the Hall* series. He was one of the audio engineers on the show, so we got to know him more and learned he had been in the band Fat Mouth, the house band at legendary Queen Street East venue Electric Circus. His band had opened for the original Alice Cooper group, and he's mentioned in Geddy Lee's autobiography as having been close to being asked to join Rush before that band met Neil Peart.

It was a one-room space, with Gerry tucked in a corner at his mix console. Like so many recordings from 1980 and before made with eight or fewer tracks, he captured a dynamic and exciting few takes. Audio engineering then required a far greater commitment, resulting in more engineers really knowing what they were doing. The band played instrumentally while I mouthed the words for reference.

Then it was my turn. Gerry set up a mic in the centre of the room, facing the couch where the other three knuckleheads sat and watched. They squirmed in anticipation at the very exposing situation. I don't think any of us had *really* heard what my singing voice was like. The first instrumental take played back in my headphones while they could only hear my voice. I started singing and they all immediately broke out laughing. I don't remember being self-conscious at all. I knew what I was doing and was ready. When the vocals were double-tracked, they sounded alright, tolerable even.

I was determined to have my first record out while I was still eighteen. In the summer of 1980, we released our one seven-inch record.

Our last and longest-term rehearsal space was on Baldwin Street, sharing the basement with the Demics, whose singer Keith Whittaker lived upstairs. It was a pretty, clean street, a leafy downtown oasis. One of the oldest and oddest used record stores was directly adjacent, and probably half of the food we ate came from the Chinese bun place right across the road. If we didn't eat there, lunch would be in one of the hospitals that lined University Avenue a block away. Ridiculously bargain hospital cafeterias were the cheapest place to eat, and not bad for kids with not much in the way of knowledgeable palates or money. For under two dollars, we'd have roast beef, mashed potatoes, some frozen mixed vegetables, and a piece of pie, seated next to families numb from some awful hospital situation. The clientele was staff, visitors to the ill — and us.

We played numerous shows with the Demics all around southern Ontario. It was them who introduced us to their hometown of London, Ontario. We had enough of a foothold there that we booked a three-night stand at the Cedar Lounge, one of the few clubs in that city. They gave each of us our own room in the fleabag rooming house above the bar. I'd never had my own room in a hotel before, and my standards for accommodations were exceedingly low. This was a step above sleeping on someone's floor, and it was fun to stay there as a band. Old men haunted the halls at night, wandering and moaning restlessly like ghosts. We were told to always keep our doors locked. No problem.

This run of shows fell in the middle of my high school's final exams, my exit from grade twelve and this high school. My grades had already plummeted from a pretty high previous average once I started playing in a band. I was half out the door already. I had a job in a record store and was playing in a band, who needs school?! I took the train back to Toronto each morning to write exams and scooted back to London afterward to play shows. I passed, but just barely, and not with the ease I had in previous grades.

During our time with the Demics, their original guitarist quit — and who should join the band but Alex's brother, Steve. Even though we were around each other a fair bit, we avoided talking, something I later recognized as a pattern in most young guys and that I experience over and over, to this day. Many people don't know how to communicate — and when I say "people," I'm being generous, as this is vastly more common with guys. It took years for me to appreciate Steve Koch as much as I do.

We were on the scene for the Demics negotiating and subsequently recording their album, with producers who wanted to make them big by polishing them up. It's tough when you know a band deeply from their live shows, know every song like an album you've owned for ages. We'd literally heard these songs a hundred times or more, so when we heard the first neutered mixes we avoided talking with them about the album. Like so many Canadian bands from this period, I think the album hurt them more than it helped.

We had a lot of fun travelling around with the Demics. Their singer, Keith, was a total alpha, a charming and smart character who still had a deep cockney accent inextricably tied to his persona, despite having lived in Canada most of his life. All eyes would be on him in a room. He was a funny, lively guy, until he wasn't. Years later when Shadowy Men were having some degree of success, I ran into Keith on a late-night drunken streetcar. When he would drink to obliteration, his bitterest impulses would come to the surface. When he was straight he was loud, boisterous, and a clever raconteur. When drunk, he was venomous and would beat his beautiful girlfriend. He had jealous rage for old Crash Kills Five making good, and let me know it in an ugly way. I'd grown up with an alcoholic bully and loathed being around any of that loutish behaviour.

The fun was starting to wear off Crash Kills Five. When I began singing, I didn't think about what the actual words were so much. The songs at the start of the band were already written; I was delivering words written by Reid, words I became increasingly uncomfortable with over time. Many of the songs were boy-meets-girl and about relationship things I didn't relate to.

I wasn't out to the band yet, and didn't feel comfortable coming out to them, even though they later said that they all knew. In a typical guy way, I avoided rather than confront my reality with them. Near the end of the band, I was secretly dating my first boyfriend and going to gay bars and dance clubs.

So many gays had been involved at the beginning of punk. For half the people that started the scene, it was an art movement, and a revolution of radically restructuring music norms. For others, it was the menace, intensity, speed, and dumb thrills that were most electrifying. I was living both sides of this divide. The black leather, aggressive, and heavy punk scene was homophobic; coming out didn't feel safe. It wasn't just the music scene, it was everywhere, a message delivered over and over in ways those who aren't the target don't even see.

At the end of grade twelve, someone handed me their yearbook and asked me to sign it. I turned to the page where my photo was and written across my face was the word FAGGOT. I have a recording of the Viletones from a show I was at in which Leckie rages at someone with whom he's picked a fight: "You know what I think of you, I think you're a fucking faggot." Hamilton band Forgotten Rebels already seemed anachronistic in 1979, a cornball, lowest-common-denominator costume punk band with loads of homophobic and racist "ironic" lyrics that, with their hoser-punk demeanour, went over my head. I missed the joke. At the Turning Point one night, they sang their new song "Third Homosexual Murder": "I got away with third homosexual murder, and the fourth one might be you" as singer Mickey DeSadist spun around and pointed directly at me.

One of the British music weeklies had a regular feature called Embarrassment Corner, or something like that, in which they presented pics of punks before they'd cut their hair short, or rockers who'd appeared in some dorky situation. Gene October, singer of 1976 UK punk band Chelsea, had been targeted with a still from a gay porno he'd done. When the band played Toronto's Edge club not long after its publication, in a particularly silent moment between songs someone shouted out, "Faggot." I watched October wince painfully and sort of smile uncomfortably, putting his head down and holding on to the mic stand, not making eye contact until the band kicked in. The audience didn't respond. Maybe most of them thought nothing of it, but in the glaringly elongated moment of silence after the heckle, I connected the dots to that magazine picture. It was hardly an embracing environment for a gay kid, but at the same time, was so normalized — just as being in the closet was. There was less and less space for me in this scene. I wanted to withdraw.

I was listening to Joy Division and many bands whose words enveloped and stimulated me, caused me to take apart their meaning or feeling. Although I started writing words and music toward the end of the band, my sudden self-consciousness about what I was doing made singing really uncomfortable. Coupled with this, we began recording songs for a new record. We'd booked studio time at a religion-based Yonge Street Mission, an odd setup I never quite figured out. To save money, we'd record at night, but this became almost impossible as Alex would spend the day bored and drinking, waiting for night to arrive and recording to commence. One night he was so out of it that he wasn't even able to remain on his drum throne, falling off it continually. Some nights were a waste of time, and we'd have to abort before we'd even really begun. Despite that, he played remarkably well on what we did put down, but I found the sound of my own voice unbearable. I hated all the recordings and didn't want to use them. When I hear the songs now, they're not as bad as I remember them being.

Things had gotten dark in the punk scene. So many people I'd known as dazzling, untamed youth were now heroin addicts in despair. I was having way more fun dancing at Stages to Kraftwerk and Soft Cell than seeing formulaic groups at the Turning Point. It was time to leave the band and ultimately quit being the guy out front singing.

THE CAR ACCIDENT

SUMMER HOLIDAYS OF 1972 HAD JUST BEGUN, THAT INFINITE stretch of time that takes forever to arrive. I'd just finished grade five and was going up to Innisfil, a small beach town between Toronto and Barrie. My brother, his wife, and their one-year-old daughter — my first niece — had just moved there, into a ranch-style bungalow at the edge of development. All around them were forests and gravel roads.

Besides getting to be with my brother, the draw of Innisfil was the mini-golf, where I'd spend so much time that I actually started getting hole-in-ones. There were a couple of beaches, one for locals and the public one with a launching dock and pier. When I was maybe eight, my sisters and I dove off the pier, picking up parts of the lake bed and throwing them at each other, laughing and playfighting. My sister-in-law's brother had recently died in a bike accident, and she had distributed his ashes off the end of the dock. We were clueless to adult feelings regarding what we were touching.

There was the bakery where every morning the aroma of bread made the whole neighbourhood smell heavenly. We called it Murder Bakery, because the owner had just killed his wife, but that didn't stop us from going there for butter tarts.

My sister-in-law picked me up in Toronto, my one-year-old niece strapped in a baby seat in front. I was in back with Fred, their beautiful collie–German shepherd mix, who I really loved. He always looked like he was smiling, and I believed he was. He had a pretty good life. They had a light blue Beetle, a car I thought was really cool because of its round shape, engine in back and its starring role in the Herbie movies we'd seen at the Parry Sound drive-in. A heavy downpour was the only time we went there, so *The Computer Wore Tennis Shoes* and *It's A Mad, Mad, Mad, Mad World* were viewed through a distorted waterfall streaming down the windshield, interrupted regularly by wiper blades.

It was a clear summer's day as we headed north on Highway 400. My brother and his wife were always insistent on passengers wearing seatbelts, even though that was uncommon then. Some cars didn't even have seatbelts. We were cruising along at the speed of the other cars. Not too far out of the city, pretty much where a giant theme park now stands, my sister-in-law suddenly went off the road into the tall grasses and weeds beyond the soft shoulder. I was startled and didn't know what was happening. I shouted to her from the back, and she replied calmly, "It's okay, don't worry." The look on her face was so poised, unafraid, as we continued hurtling at full speed, grasses whipping past the side windows. She told me to hold on as she then veered the car back toward the road.

As we reached the asphalt of the highway, the car's wheels lifted. I entered into an unknowable blank space, all memory of what happened over the next few minutes gone, or at least buried somewhere inaccessible.

I opened my eyes and saw the guardrail above my head. There were intense noises all around, but with a calm silence superimposed over them. Loudest of all was my breathing and the sound of Fred barking. A detached sound came from inside me, as if from another place that wasn't my body. I tried to raise my head or get up, but couldn't. There were people around me, but at a distance as Fred barked at them and protected me. People were trying to get Fred away so they could get at me. I had a hazy distant sense of there being an ambulance in view. Everything was a jumble. The quiet air smelled like sweetgrass and the summer mash of hot insect splatter on the car's windshield and grill, a distinct scent I've smelled a couple more times since then that has taken me right back to that moment. All traffic was stopped, but I don't remember seeing a line of cars waiting for the accident on the highway to clear.

A couple of men got to me, trying to calm me down. I didn't know what had happened to the others in the car, where they were. I don't even remember seeing the car. I was put onto a stretcher and felt the odd floating sensation of being lifted into the air and through open ambulance doors. A loud sound came out of me each time I inhaled or exhaled. One of the men in the back with me placed a mask over my face and tried to get me to concentrate on making the sound stop. In and out of consciousness as we drove to a local hospital, I had a vague sense of the flurry of activity around me. I have only murky images of moments at that hospital, enough to understand that my injuries were too serious for this place to treat me. Somehow we were back in the ambulance and driving again, to another hospital.

When we arrived, I was upset and tried to stop them from cutting my baby blue corduroy pants off me. I think they even cut my shoes. I was worried about how I'd get home without shoes or pants.

Time moved differently from how I'd always known it. I don't know how much it passed in reality. I can't even say "for the next several days or weeks," because it wasn't a space that had movement. It was dark and cool, with lights intruding the dark void I floated in. Sometimes they were shone into my eyes as an outer presence lifted my lids, other times it was the blinking red and white lights of the machines that lit the dim room. My eyes would open briefly now and again as I forced myself into a more alert state of consciousness, wanting information. I don't remember anyone telling me what had happened, but I think I knew. Voices came and went from my side, but the wail of people in tears, in pain and fear, were all around me all the time. I don't know if I knew at the time that they were all children.

From things people were saying, I could tell they didn't think I could hear, that I wasn't taking any of it in. Tubes went in and out of my body, feeling so many of them that I couldn't even tell where they were. I couldn't move and only felt the sensation of things moving around me, or of being moved.

I stayed in this twilight state that eventually started to have a rhythm of interruption, of people doing various things to my body. I had casts on both arms, something holding my head, and gauze tape all over me. My back had been skinned off, something that happened as I was ejected from the back window of the car as it rolled, sliding along the highway until I came to rest under the guardrail. I don't know how they cleaned it or changed the bandages.

The first time I had a continuous sense of what was happening was a time when they cleaned a wound on my left arm. I knew from the sensations that it had been done to me previously, but for the first time I had an awareness and watched some of what they did. My arm was laid out with a frame of bandage and paper surrounding a pink mess of flesh. It looked like a grotesque portrait, a picture in a frame that wasn't me, didn't feel like part of me. I couldn't speak because of tubes down my throat, or a mask. I felt unmovable, a block held in place by hospital mechanics. A woman told me she was cleaning the wound. This happened daily for a while, until one day I was able to watch it from beginning to end, feeling completely detached but knowing it was still my body. For years after, I'd feel a tiny bump near my scars and watch over time as a grain of sand grew closer through my layers of skin until it exited back into the outer world it came from.

After what seemed like weeks, the tubes came out of my throat and I could have Jell-O and liquids. My brother snuck in a milkshake from our favourite burger joint, its coldness giving such relief to my burning throat.

Once I was more coherent, I was moved to a new room, a general ward with five other beds in it. Curtains surrounded all the beds, creating some sort of illusion of privacy, even though the sounds were more disturbing than anything I might have seen. Activity happened around the clock, with nurses and doctors doing their jobs without any thought of being quiet, because it was really the middle of the night. In these small hours, the sounds of crying — and sometimes screaming — made sleep distressing, but there was nothing else to do but sleep. After long stretches of darkness punctuated by harsh hospital lights, the sun rose. The room had windows, and I made small steps back toward the living, where people did things and could get up and walk around.

Eventually I saw and understood the full extent of my injuries. My back had been skinned off and remained a giant scab for ages. I had a severe concussion, and a puncture in my chest that went all the way deep inside, probably the point of impact that had broken my ribs and punctured my lung. My left arm was mangled, ripped open in a way I didn't know was possible for a human. At some point I was aware that my arm had stitches all up and down it, holding half my arm together. Before staples were used for this kind of injury, stitches would look like Frankenstein's monster, large x's that formed odd geometric patterns along their length.

When I was coherent enough to understand, I was told what had happened. My sister-in-law had an abrasion on the top of her head from the roof smashing in. Their baby and dog Fred had no visible injuries. Since then, whenever I see a Volkswagen Beetle, I'm struck by the design flaw somehow overlooked or just accepted as part of the deal if you wanted to drive one of these snappy European vehicles. It looked like a car designed to facilitate rolling.

As I recovered, I could get up and explore the ward floor more. It was hard to walk, but I figured out that I could use my IV pole as a skateboard, standing on its tripod base. Sometime late in the summer, I was told my best friend was in the hospital. He'd crashed his bicycle into a tree while going down a hill in High Park and split his head open. I wheeled to his room. The first time I saw him, I was frightened by what I saw when I peeked through the curtain that surrounded his bed. He wasn't awake, so I left and came back later. He was never the same after that, his personality very different, someone to whom I no longer related in the same way.

As discussion began about me going home, I realized it was the end of summer and almost time to start back at school. I missed my guinea pig and dog intensely. It felt oddly stifling to step out into sunlight for the first time in two months. The air seemed aglow with dust as the golden yellow sun approached setting. I was weak; even walking down the stairs to the subway took a lot of effort. I was still in pain, and one arm remained in a cast. As we got lower underground, with each step I could feel my throat close and the horrible wheezing sound returning. I couldn't breathe in the gritty underground air, so we resurfaced, my mother distressed about what to do. We never went to restaurants and never took taxis, so it was a big deal when my mother flagged a cab to take us home. I cried when I went down to my bedroom and saw my guinea pig. On my bookshelf were my dog's collar and tags.

I had a dog named Rex and was as obsessively close to him as he was to me. A German shepherd–whippet mix, he was a beautiful, sleek, but nervous black-and-brown dog, frightened by everything. He trembled constantly. He followed me everywhere. If I went to the bathroom, he had to come too. He'd wait for me to come home from school and would run with excitement, his whippet speed making him a blur of ecstatic energy. When I asked where he was, my mother had to tell me that he'd run away from home while I was gone and been hit by a train. I burst into tears, feeling so many things at once, so hurt knowing he'd tried to find me, knowing he wouldn't understand where I was.

To this day, I have no doubt that the Hospital for Sick Children (now Sick Kids) saved my life. I had a significant chunk of muscle and tendon missing from my left arm, and for years people would recoil in horror when they saw it. I kind of enjoyed the frightened looks on their faces as they withdrew while simultaneously trying to look closer.

Years later, Viletones singer Steven Leckie noticed my arm. He had lots of scars on his arms — from slashing himself — but nothing this deep or dramatic. "Whoa, what happened to you?" I said I'd been in a car accident when I was a kid. Ever the drama queen, Leckie told me I should never tell anyone that. "Tell them it was a shark or knife fight." I never did, because nothing like that could compare to the real experience I'd had to get my scars.

Quite remarkably, my arm mostly works normally, though it's significantly weaker than the other arm. I like to credit it for my very average drumming ability, although that's about as believable as the shark business.

ALBERT

I DON'T THINK I'D HEARD OF BIG BROTHERS BEFORE MY MOTHER asked me if I might be interested in having one. *I don't know, what for, what do they do? I already have a brother.* Dressed up a little more than we usually did, we went to meet a lady at the Big Brothers of Toronto offices. I was wearing a plaid shirt and knit jacket, both made by my great-grandmother. It was my favourite outfit, one in which you might want to make an impression. I was eight and my mother had probably told me that it was something important, so I had to look nice.

We entered the mansion-type house, with dark wood and a fancy staircase. They asked me to wait in one room while my mother went into the office with the woman we were meeting. I fidgeted and tried to hear what they were talking about. When I was brought in, the woman explained to me that Big Brothers were for boys without fathers. I'd be connected to a volunteer Brother and we'd do things like go to the movies, or lunch, or just hang out, stuff like that. We rarely did either of those first two in my home, so it already sounded interesting. They asked me questions about my interests, and I'm pretty sure I said music, dogs and reading. Mostly I felt guilt that I was getting this and my sisters weren't, but like every small benefit from being a boy in a house of women, you shut up about the inequity and hope no one else notices.

They thought I might be a good connection with a young university student named Albert. The Big Brothers lady lowered her voice to quietly ask my mother if she was okay with him being Jewish. It made no difference to me. I thought Jewish would be no different than the Maltese or Italian kids in my neighbourhood, just another variety who had this designated brand assigned to them. As so-called Baptists, we only went to church when someone died or was married. I knew very little about what Jewish meant and only had positive associations, all of them about food. My mother worked weekends at a synagogue, bringing home delicious leftovers from the wedding or bar mitzvah she'd been serving. For as common as racism and xenophobia were in my family, being Jewish didn't come with stigma attached. My mother quietly replied that no, that wasn't a problem.

My first date with Albert was just meeting, walking and talking — plus ice cream. It was looking good so far. I rattled off my favourite records at the time; Albert smiled and nodded. He was a really nice guy, a mix of jazz cat and good mama's boy.

He wore dress shirts and had big, black, plastic-framed glasses. Right away we were seeing each other once a week, or every other week. We'd meet at the subway station near me. From there we'd go to the museum, the movies, bookstores and, once in a while, to his parents' place, where he still lived. His dad was a furrier with a shop on Spadina. I knew that stretch of the street from my real brother taking me to the delis that dotted the road then. Albert's father showed me how they tanned the skins of animals, and what he'd do to turn them into a coat or hand-muff.

He'd made a fox head for me, or rather fashioned one into something like a puppet, the rigid skin holding the form of the animal so you could put your hand inside its head. He'd put in fake eyes and sewed the animal's mouth shut in a permanent snarl. I loved that thing because it was great for scaring my sisters, or for having conversations with our dogs: "Hello, why are you listening to what the people say? You can be a wild animal too."

Albert's mother would make fantastic lunches for us, and then we'd go to his room to listen to records. He played trombone and trumpet and would honk along with his records, making up harmonies or new melodies along with them. This was incredible to me. I hadn't seen anyone invent music in real time before. Two albums he had were the Vince Guaraldi soundtrack to *A Charlie Brown Christmas* and Miles Davis's *On the Corner*. We talked about music a lot. Once in a while, he'd let me pick out a 45 to buy at Sam the Record Man. There was a song on the radio that I really loved, and that was what I chose: "As the Years Go By" by Toronto band Mashmakhan. He laughed when I told him what song I wanted, something I think of every time I hear that song, understanding more and more how ridiculous it is. The lyrics are a corny morality story about the feelings and obligations that come with love, accompanied by a wacky organ riff that imparts it with a veneer of serious ancient folk song.

That iconic organ riff was so comical that when Shadowy Men introduced a Farfisa to our setup, it was the first thing I remember

Brian playing on it. We laughed so much that we had to embed a snippet of it into the song we immediately wrote, thinking of it as more a salute to a significant piece of Canadian schmaltz than an attempt to pass it off as our own. Clearly some people heard it, which I found out when Mashmakhan's guitarist, Rayburn Blake, who worked at my local music gear shop, approached me, annoyed. I'd clearly been pointed out, and he huffed that we'd stolen his band's song. *Sorry, we thought we were tipping our hat for five seconds.* I liked the song so much that I eventually even bought their album!

Albert's records were mostly jazz, stuff I didn't know, but he was overjoyed for me at a Big Brothers Christmas event when I won one of the door prizes — a choice of one gift-wrapped LP, which turned out to be *On the Corner*! Even then I wondered about the appropriateness of giving an eleven-year-old an album with a short guy staring up at a cartoon of a woman with enormous breasts and butt. I felt slightly embarrassed to be seen holding it. When I got it home and took the shrink wrap off, it had the wrong vinyl inside. Oh well.

He fed my voracious musical interests, taking me to the movie of George Harrison's *The Concert for Bangladesh* and buying me the soundtrack album soon after. As one of my earliest LPs, I played it to death, including Ravi Shankar's side-one set of raga-like dhun, something that sounded radical and new to me, and that I loved so much more than Bob Dylan's moan-y set. The film was almost like attending a concert, projected oversized in one of the biggest theatres in the city, filling all of my vision with nothing but music.

I was also introduced to rep theatres and art films. We saw a Jean-Luc Godard film that engaged me, but left me with a lot of questions. It was distinctly different from *The Sound of Music* and *The Ghost and Mr. Chicken*, two movies I was much more familiar with. Another film we went to was 1972's *Under Milk Wood*, starring Liz Taylor, Richard Burton, and Peter O'Toole, based on the Dylan Thomas play. I told him afterward that I hated it and thought it was boring, although I still think that one day I'm going to rewatch it because I suspect now that I'll love it, having better context to absorb it. Just off Yonge Street was Cinecity, an art-house movie theatre long before I knew what that even was. We saw the animated French feature *Fantastic Planet* there, a fantastical abstract film that perplexed me but was beautiful and trippy to look at. And he was a great sport coming with me and eight friends to the late-night premiere of *Phantom of the Paradise*. I'd won a package of ten tickets, the soundtrack album, movie poster, badges, and T-shirts from a radio phone-in. That overkill made me obsessive about the Brian De Palma film for a couple of years.

Being introduced to arty sensibilities in movies, music, and visual art expanded my palate, nurturing what I was obviously indicating I was interested in. I was so fortunate to connect with someone so open-minded and stimulating. In retrospect, his generosity blows my mind. He was studying at University of Toronto to be a pharmacist. Only many years later did I appreciate what a demanding education program he was in, and how difficult it must have been to make time for me, a stranger, when he surely had a lot of homework and studying to do.

On weekends, he'd take me to the university labs and give me chemicals to mix that produced coloured smoke, or crazy expansion. I loved it. He followed up with gifts of chemistry sets and microscopes, causing me queasy unease with what was in even the water we were drinking. Most subversive of all though, I think, was him telling me to pick a couple of guinea pigs from the wall of cages in the lab. They came home with me, and even though they had been spared their inevitable lab fate, I always imagined what experiments had already been done on them, that they were somehow radioactive or had implants in their brains.

When Albert came to our home for Christmas, I thought my mother was doing him a favour, knowing that he didn't celebrate that holiday. Don't worry, *we* do! And I had presents for him too! He gave me my first Hot Wheels and would come over to build the longest tracks possible, through the living room, a loop through the dining room, a curve and Super Charger to accelerate through the kitchen, and down the hall back into the living room.

He would tell me about Judaism, and I asked questions, not really understanding why he did some things differently, like wearing a little hat. He introduced his girlfriend Rhonda to me when he told me they were getting married. I hadn't even heard about her before that, but I got to be part of the wild celebration. In our family, weddings would always be in a church with receptions in someone's home. They were generally celebratory, with food, fun and dancing. This wedding was a spectacular party in a synagogue. The ceremony was similar but the pageantry and rituals were different, and the ending was dynamite! The glass they had both drunk from was wrapped in cloth. I was startled when Albert stomped on it, the place erupting into cheers as he did. I'd never had a multiple-course dinner before, and with this one, I was ready to convert. In the dancing afterward, men hoisted Albert up in a chair and danced around the room holding him aloft; it was so much more joyous than what I knew weddings to be. My mother had got me a yarmulke for the wedding, a plain white one made of shiny cloth like satin. The wedding was so much fun that I wore it regularly for the next year or so, no one ever saying anything to me about it or asking me why I wore it.

Our relationship ran its inevitable course as Albert graduated, and our time included Rhonda more frequently. She was very sweet to me and was instantly as much a part of our family as Albert had been, but I became an independent teen. We saw each other less frequently until it just kind of fell away.

Once I was older and appreciated so much more what Albert had done for me, I tried to find him again but couldn't. The last I saw of him was at his father's funeral, some time in my early twenties.

How incredible that this person gave so much of himself to a kid who needed it, who was sensitive to that kids' interests and needs. What he did was so generous, so unselfish — and that in itself was an inspirational model. He made a huge difference in my life, impacted me in ways that continue to be revealed. I recently saw that it was the fiftieth anniversary of *Phantom of the Paradise*, which brought me right back to leaving the Uptown theatre on a rainy midnight, him laughing as we walked up Yonge Street animatedly reviewing the film. His care, seeing how he and his family were with each other, was my first conscious exposure to Jewish people and culture, and it created nothing but positivity and love with me. I was so fortunate to have such a kind and caring person in my life when I needed it most.

In the last twenty years or so I'd search his name and come up blank. I had a growing need to see him and thank him for what he'd done for me. On a recent purge of old stuff, I found a document that included his middle name. I immediately searched again with his full name, and discovered that he had died a few days previous. It broke my heart. I hope he knew how much he meant to me.

The Big Brothers Big Sisters organization seems quaint and antiquated now, but only because they are no longer as great a part of the public consciousness. How incredible for people to give that most precious thing: time. I have eternal gratitude toward anyone who gives of themselves to make a stranger's life better. I carry some guilt for not having that same level of commitment and generosity, reasoning that I have kids in my life to whom I already don't give as much as I wish I did.

Anyone who has given of themselves to better the life of that most selfish human, a child, is something extraordinary.

RAMONES

CONTEXT IS EVERYTHING. A FRIEND JUST A BIT MORE THAN A THIRD my age asked me to recommend some Ramones tracks, as he didn't really get what all the fuss was about. I sent him a live clip of their 1977 New Year's Eve show at the Rainbow in London, from a time when I thought they were peaking. It was a few years into their career and they were intense, young, super-tight and full of fury. Somewhere inside I can access the exhilarating rush of adrenaline I felt upon first hearing the Ramones. Nothing had ever sounded like them before, it was so radically new. In this concert film, the self-conscious '60s bubblegum of their first few albums gave way to the angry power that would drive them through the next decade or so.

The Ramones are inextricably tied to so many moments of discovery for me, of new worlds opening up and of a restless teenager diving in at full speed. They were so many people's alarm bell; the roar that signaled a new age. From this vantage point, looking back on a flattened musical landscape, it seems more subtle. But in 1976, the Ramones' debut album was the future being bust open. It was the foundation so many bands would build on, the idea of going *further* coming directly from this record. Later artists' "further" made the Ramones' first album subsequently sound relatively restrained. They invented a radical new form of music, a cartoonish meld of speed and simplicity, compared to the dreary Seals and Crofts landscape at the time, manifesting the inevitable of the moment.

Alone in my bedroom, I stared at the lyrics printed on the inner sleeve. Their simplicity was made elegant by a clean art-deco font, the words so minimal in volume that they appeared like a magician's sleight-of-hand. Where were the rest of them hiding? How could something so full contain so few ingredients?

I don't wanna walk around with you
So why you wanna walk around with me?

How could that be the entirety of a song's words, a song that is on a record you can buy in a record store? It was shocking.

Released at the same time, Gordon Lightfoot's "The Wreck of the Edmund Fitzgerald" sounded interminable on the radio, verse upon verse upon verse sailing painfully into the distance. I couldn't wait for that goddam boat to sink. "Beat on the Brat" was the exact opposite. I understand more now that magic is created by what is removed rather than added, and the Ramones were fucking next-dimension wizards at this.

My best friend and I played the Ramones' album over and over again. It was so short and the songs belonged together, like an unknown room you could step in and out of — a complete thing. On first listen, "Blitzkrieg Bop," the album opener, was level with all the other songs in terms of impact and importance, light years away from soundtracking cruise ships and beer ads, as all cultural revolution eventually does.

The album contained a feeling of dangerous sexuality too, not the David Lee Roth writhing around in spandex kind, but one that was coded and bold, furtive and transactional. It's no coincidence that the Mineshaft leather bar opened in NYC at the same time as the Ramones' arrival, that 16mm frayed-edge porno vibe being the dominant feeling in crumbling Manhattan. Bassist Dee Dee Ramone had a visibly worn and protruding crotch in his jeans. An aggressively male belt buckle, centred where jeans and T-shirt meet, fills one side of the inner sleeve and is distinctly provocative, more intriguing than alluring. It echoed the hot, druggy S&M sex implied on another New York City album jacket, Lou Reed's *Rock 'n' Roll Animal*, but without the come-on of a bulge in leather. An inch or two up from the groin and it's a different thing, a militaristic clothes-on affair. Would you be undoing your pants if you are going to slit the throat of the trick that picked you up, as Dee Dee sang about in the greatest song ever about hustling, "53rd & 3rd"?

Sometime around the Ramones' fourth album, I accidentally discovered a cruising street-beat while cycling home to my mother's place from my job downtown. Guys lined the sidewalks, loitering and staring, pretending they were waiting for something, not putting on an overt sexual show but more an apprehensive pose-and-watch under dim light. It was all covert. I connected it immediately to "53rd & 3rd." *This is what they're singing about.* The idea of gay-for-pay was foreign to me, although I knew what hustlers were. I couldn't quite understand why Dee Dee would want to kill a guy rather than have sex with him. But as you are in that age of discovery, details unfold over time, and I connected my own experiences to Ramones lyrics.

I started making that street part of my route home sometimes. It was only a block long, parallel to another also a block long, so drivers on the prowl would circle, peering out from darkened vehicles at what was on display. I recognized a guy standing at the road's edge as one of the group of fifty to a hundred people who were going to every punk show I was. After that first Ramones show, this was a thing.

I pulled over on my ten-speed and chatted with him until he eventually suggested we go someplace dark. We walked over to a University of Toronto property a block away, back when treed spaces and rolling lawns were valued as much as housing. We laid on the grass talking, both of us nervous and waiting for the other to initiate. Eventually both our pants were undone and around our ankles. He was remote, barely seeming interested at all in the affection that was probably more of what I needed at that time. As inexperienced as I was, I sensed it was perfunctory on his part, and I thought, *Why are you even doing this if you're not so interested?*

When we were done, we walked together and he asked me for money for the encounter we'd just had. I couldn't stop myself from a quick burst of laughter, the idea never vaguely occurring to me that I would ever pay for sex, or that he would be doing it with me for money. At seventeen years old, the idea of paying someone for a blowjob was preposterous. I already knew of my currency, even if I had just enough insecurity to not acknowledge it too much. I didn't pay him; that was not part of any agreement that I understood.

Previously, he and I didn't really know each other, but I could see the nervousness on his face after that as he stood with his friends, nodding to me in silent acknowledgement. After a couple years, he felt safe enough to talk with me. I'd see his band, and it was like our encounter never happened.

It didn't take much exploring to figure out, or learn, where quick anonymous sex could be had. Parks, of course, were prime spots.

From my childhood walks in High Park, I learned to identify at a distance the movement in bushes, the scanning head-turns on men shadowed in darkness.

We were pretty unmonitored as kids, free to roam and actually encouraged to go play on the train tracks, a nearby corridor unfenced and surrounded by wildflowers and tall grasses where snakes and crickets sunned. I would often take my dog Shep for hours-long walks, either down to the Humber River or to High Park, the vast estate with miles of trails through lush forests and meadows.

On one of these walks I came upon three men partially concealed by a big tree. All three were hurriedly doing their pants up, darting nervous glances at me as Shep and I passed by on the worn path. These hidden things drew me. I knew they were doing something "bad," so I mentally bookmarked the spot to investigate sometime later.

My radar was always on alert for coded information, me forming the criteria in my head about what was of use. One Christmas when I was about nine, I overheard my mother and aunt whispering that a teenage relative had been caught in the park "doing bad things with men." This was exactly the stuff my ears and eyes had superhuman powers to take in. He'd been brought home by the police. I pictured the park across from his house, next to an area of slaughterhouses and animal pens where one of our early babysitters used to take us to play. We'd walk along the tops of wooden pen fences, talking with cows held in the open-air prison, me not fully connecting why they were there. The park had an ice rink we'd go to regularly. What I imagined happening with my relative and other men was covert, needing to be hidden. It was all about looking at each other, glancing, possibly hugging.

Maybe I just wanted to be seen, but I soon went to the park to explore. It was daytime, so there were no private spots in the big, open, sunny rectangle of grass that was the entire park. As many times as I visited that park when I was between nine and fourteen, I never found any men to do bad things with.

On Carlton Street outside Larry's Hideaway, the dumpy hotel bar now hosting punk bands, I could see bodies moving about in Allan Gardens. After the show I snuck over to investigate, and it was like lifting a rock in your garden to discover there is a whole other world happening underneath. Men did a circuit around the greenhouses like scurrying flat bugs, strolling around the fountains and watching for other men on the prowl, or for dangerous intruders and cops. Heavy landscaping concealed a well-worn series of paths behind dense shrubbery, trampled hard from thousands of feet patrolling before me. From the public side of the evergreen bushes, men were invisible, hidden. Many stood around and posed, hips thrust, just waiting for someone else to get the action going so they could join in.

I saw a handsome guy in a leather motorcycle jacket with an eagle pin on it, exactly like one the Ramones wore. Like him, I wore a black leather jacket, but in 1978, a man in a black leather jacket was very rare. It was pretty much bikers, punks and gays into S&M. I was one of those, this guy another. He wanted me to describe killing someone as he sucked my dick. I didn't feel in danger because so many other people were circulating around, but I was not into his scenario at all, and told him that. He asked instead if I could describe catching a fish and then cleaning it while he was on his knees with his mouth full. My objective was that eagle pin. We started, and as I held his shoulder with one hand, the other worked his lapel, his preoccupation too thorough to notice what I was doing. I somehow got the backing off the pin and slipped it from his jacket. I snuck it into my pocket and suddenly pulled up my pants. "I've gotta go," I said as I hurried away.

From my grandfather and my mother, I knew what most of the plants and trees in the park and our garden were. Spending time lingering in parks, wandering the trails most people avoid, it all made me sensitive to the living environment around me, to the beauty of nature and the supernatural powers contained in forests and meadows. Undulating, dark-green leaves in the night breeze could be ominous or welcoming, often both.

My best childhood friend from kindergarten, Roger, shared in my music obsessions. I sometimes wonder how differently we saw things. How, at the time, each of us interpreted seeing David Bowie get on his knees and put his mouth to Mick Ronson's guitar, his hands grasping Mick's hips and satined ass. Roger had slept over at my place, something we'd often do back and forth, for us to watch the Spiders From Mars' last concert on TV, me recording it on my little Lloyd's cassette recorder. When we both graduated from seven-inch singles to full-length albums around 1972, the same albums hooked us in, enthralling us with overwhelming emotions and the feeling of newness each record revealed. Elton John's *Goodbye Yellow Brick Road*, Sparks' *Kimono My House*, Mott the Hoople's *Mott*, the New York Dolls' debut, Todd Rundgren's *Something/Anything?*, Alice Cooper's *Love It to Death*, Lou Reed's *Berlin*, Roxy Music's first album, and everything David Bowie had out to that point. We both flipped for *Ziggy Stardust* at age eleven and had only each other to share it with. No one else we knew cared about Bowie.

Roger's haircut was already sort of proto-Ramones when their first album came out. We couldn't get enough of that record, and were equally beside ourselves when we heard that the Ramones were coming to town. Roger had a T-shirt made of stark, black-flocked, blocky letters spelling out RAMONES on the tight white chest. I was envious that he'd thought of it first. When I look at photos I shot of him wearing it back then, the chasm of time is almost incomprehensible. Imagine there ever being a time when no Ramones merchandise existed — it's almost impossible. None did exist, only Roger's homemade shirt.

Their live debut in Toronto in September 1976 had us both electrified with anticipation. We were avid readers of *Rock Scene*, so we knew what they looked like and mostly understood the context they came from. Three shows were happening, two on Friday at 7:30 and 10:30 and the other at midnight the next night. We decided to get tickets for the first show so we could maybe then see them again right after if we wanted to. This was our first time at a show at the New Yorker, a nice deco-ish theatre that Gary Topp, the guy who ran the best rep cinema in town, had just opened. We went down hours early, hoping to somehow see the Ramones and get our albums signed.

I have very distinct memories of particular people from the crowd hanging around out front before the show. The influence of David, the Dolls, *Rocky Horror*, and Bob Fosse's 1972 film *Cabaret* was blatant. Everyone there seemed to be dressed in glammy satin pants and peroxide curls paired with smoking jackets and louche getups from the ridiculously abundant and cheap vintage shops, or from army/navy surplus. Three people stuck in my memory for different reasons.

Linda Lee, soon to be the drummer of the Curse, was someone I recognized from the few big shows I'd been to. Bold and attractive, her towering stature was topped by a grand inverted V of blonde curls, with spiked high heels and lurid makeup. She and a couple of other gals waited by the entrance to the backstage area, where I, a nerdy kid in thick glasses, stood with my album jackets. They always seemed to be invited backstage. I wondered how they got to be friends with all these bands.

Another was someone I later knew to be Rob Sikora, standing out among the attention-getting duds in understated '60s collegiate looks. He exuded the cool that the Velvet Underground and Jonathan Richman did, a preppiness that allowed subverts to pass, but he also stood out because everyone else was still coming back from their flares and long-hair trip. I'd see him in the art bookstore where he worked, but didn't actually meet him until years later. He was a style influence on me, as I analyzed how he could look so understated but radical at the same time.

The other one was the guy in the ticket booth, Colin Brunton. I identified him as being the ticket guy at the Roxy too, and it was him who was in the lobby the afternoon of the Ramones' second 1977 show a few months later at the same theatre. Once again, I'd taken my album jacket to sign, *Leave Home* this time, and Colin told me to just go downstairs, the Ramones are there. I nervously made my way down into the old and raw basement space, lit by bare lightbulbs. The Ramones sat in chairs against three of the walls in the dimly lit room that I guess was their dressing room. As Johnny smiled and took the album cover, Tommy got up and left the room without saying a word.

I'd later become friends with Colin; Shadowy Men on a Shadowy Planet provided our first film soundtrack for his movie *Mysterious Moon Men of Canada*. Like so many people from those earliest of days as punk began, we crossed paths again and again: meeting him as my cab driver on one of the very few taxi rides I ever took back then; at countless doors he watched over for the clubs booked by the Garys; as the co-director of the brilliant completist-indulgent Toronto punk documentary film *The Last Pogo Jumps Again*; and more recently as producer on the reboot of the *Kids in the Hall* series.

At that first show, there were shirts emblazoned with the cover of the first Ramones album being sold at the candy counter. Colin told me they were made by the New Yorker Theatre, not the band. I sometimes wonder if those shirts were actually the first manufactured Ramones merch ever made. The band didn't have any at the time, their designer Arturo Vega not producing the famous eagle-seal logo until their second album.

The eagle was a common symbol in gay leather scenes, almost every major city having a bar called either the Eagle or the Black Eagle. When coupled with their black leather jackets, this added a seedy allure to the Ramones' whole look. Their iconography had a distinct relationship to leather daddies, New York City cops, Marlon Brando, and *American Graffiti*.

The first gay bar I ever went into is now occupied by Toronto's Black Eagle, then named Tanks, a typically corny faux-macho name that all the bars had. I plotted going for ages, choosing this place for its masculine appeal and also thinking no one would be likely to see me there. As I nervously walked up its steps, a voice called down from the second-floor balcony. "Hi Don!" It was Mike, the drummer in teen punk band the Dents.

It was this Ramones shirt, size medium, snug and now dingy, that I photographed my mother wearing forty years later. My first book, *Trouble in the Camera Club*, about the beginning of punk in Toronto, had just come out and my mother, Shirl, had recently moved into a seniors residence, a situation that was painful and unwanted, and took her away from the home she had spent most of her life in. There was going to be a book signing at the Grenadier Seniors Residence, and Shirl thought I should participate in it. It was one of the few times she had any enthusiasm for the goings-on at the "wrinkle ranch." She said she'd be my cashier and sell my books as I signed them, mingling with the hordes she imagined flocking to the Grenadier to buy my book. I'd seen another sale happen in the lobby and it was nice sweaters, watercolours of birds from High Park across the road, greeting cards of sunsets and pretty flowers.

I told her, "Ma, I don't think this is the audience for my book, I don't think this is a good idea." She pressed me and clearly had a vision of us doing this together. She really wanted to do it. It took me a few minutes to realize that even if no one came, as I expected, we'd both probably have fun. But most appallingly exciting of all, I thought: How fucking ridiculously incredible would it be to have a book signing for a punk book at a seniors residence, even if only for the flyer?

I envisioned how it would look. She came to my place and I dressed her up in one of my big-lapelled, Ramones-style black leather motorcycle jackets, with the Ramones shirt underneath and a couple of pins — one being a metallic star with the word RAWHIDE in relief. My mother posed against a garage in the back lane, and up against a brick wall like the photo on her shirt. She hated the pictures when she saw them. "My hair is a disaster!" But she consented to me using one for the flyer. She changed her tune when other residents at the home told her how much they loved the picture.

I'd acquired the Rawhide pin in 1980, from the newly opened bar of the same name in New York on my second visit there. I'd won a trip to NYC in a costume contest. My friend Natalie, attending the Ontario College of Art's New York City campus, invited me to stay at her apartment on East Second Street, between B and C. It was unbelievable to see a city in such a state of decay, one that is unimaginable now given how radically gentrified those same streets have become. Lots contained the disintegrating rubble of what were once residential brownstones. Across the road from Natalie's were three- and four-storey apartments, where a bucket was raised and lowered from an upper window to a guy distributing its contents to the people waiting in line. By being there, I understood better the sound of bands like Suicide, Ramones, New York Dolls, and Wayne County.

I immediately bought a pair of black leather pants and headed uptown on the subway to the apartment of someone who sold acid; I got the number from a Toronto friend. The door opened, and before we did any other transactions, our clothes were off and we were in the bedroom. When we were done, I bought three hits and we kissed goodbye. He told me to come that night to the bar he tended, Rawhide.

My first trip to the city had been with one of my first bands, Crash Kills Five. We stayed with the drummer Alex's sweet grandmother in Yonkers and took the train to the city daily. It was ostensibly to try and get gigs, and we thought that showing up in person at a club would result in that being a more likely possibility. Among others, we went to CBGB, which by 1980 was already vacated by the names that had made the place so mythological to us. In the light of day it held no magic, the assembly line of bands on bills there looking like random and depressing buckshot, hoping for one to make a killing. It had no energy or excitement.

We went to Max's Kansas City, delivering our 45 to someone and seeing a Heartbreakers rent-money spinoff band, the Superheroes, fronted by Johnny Thunders and Walter Lure. Dee Dee sat at another table three away from us, and I recall sneaking peeks at him as much as the band, his presence adding some kind of added value to the just-okay but still-fascinating set the band played.

The whole city felt like we'd arrived twenty years or longer after they'd stopped cleaning or taking care of the place. It was in shambles. Subway-car windows were so thick with graffiti you couldn't even see out to know what stop you were at.

I somehow knew where Andy Warhol's Factory was, so we decided to go see it. We walked up a stairwell, trying a couple of the doors as we ascended. I don't remember how we knew it was the Factory when we reached it, but I pulled the door open. There stood Andy Warhol with some kind of notebook in his hand, showing it to another man. They both turned to us silently and blankly. We were so startled that he was really there that we just started laughing and quickly closed the door, hurrying out of the building. I don't know what we expected, but at that time we probably didn't know anything about Warhol being shot, so it's remarkable that the door was just unlocked. No crowds hung around, a sign of how blasé New Yorkers are to seeing celebrities.

Judging by the number of times the Ramones came to town, it was apparent Toronto was a hot spot for them. They were a band everyone in the scene loved, and the same core of people at their first shows were still there when the Ramones were at their lowest point of popularity.

When they couldn't even sell out a mid-sized bar, we would still go see them every time they played, except for that infamous 1979 show at Exhibition Stadium where Johnny and Dee Dee gave the crowd the finger and walked off after being pelted with everything that could be thrown. To me, they were an idealized modern amalgamation of top-forty radio I'd grown up with, but the audience at the Ex for Ted Nugent, Aerosmith, and Johnny Winter thought otherwise. It wasn't lost on me that Ted Nugent was actually responsible for a dividing point for me at a high school party. All the guys there trying to sing along with "Wang Dang

Sweet Poontang" let me know that the gulf between us was not one I wanted to conquer. I was already in another place, and that song pretty much marked the end of my social experiences with everyone but a few of my real friends from school.

I'm sometimes mind-boggled by how much Shadowy Men did in our original decade. In our third year, 1987, the Garys offered us a three-night stand opening for the Ramones. There were far more bands locally, good ones even, than there were headlining shows by touring bands, so these brilliant opening spots were coveted.

It just took a few years away for people to really appreciate the Ramones. The unfulfilled pent-up desire to see them built until the sold-out set of shows we played together. At this point, they'd been together for thirteen years, an experience I couldn't relate to but now understand. It's complex to navigate emotions, personality differences, and the grind of co-existing in confined quarters for long periods of time.

Most of Shadowy Men's time on tour was either spent in the van or waiting for the show to begin, the three of us almost always together. Books, stories, and the documentary about the Ramones later revealed how much loathing there was between members, how dysfunctional they were, but our naive enthusiasm couldn't stop us from gushing to them about how much we loved them. It was mostly met with blank faces. Another night on the job for them, a thrill of a lifetime for us.

Only Johnny was responsive and friendly, and he also seemed like the one who had it most together in terms of functioning in the whirl of activity and attention. He actually knew who we were and said that he really liked us. He told us he'd tried to watch some of our set the first night, but got mobbed so he had to slip backstage. Despite knowing now what a cruel prick Johnny could be, it was him who made an effort to connect, and I still appreciate that. To be fair, Richie, their drummer at the time of their most recent album, *Animal Boy*, wouldn't be around much longer, and his place in the band as "the new guy" was apparent in how he seemed like an outsider. While the others mingled in the hall with visitors and Garys people they'd known and befriended from years of playing in Toronto, Richie sat in a back corner of the dressing room, practising on a drum pad and silently observing the action around him.

I think about my experiences with different record labels over many years and relate it to my little window of interacting with the Ramones for those three days. While Johnny is villainized by most, he was clearly as much a force as the other three original members in making the Ramones one of the greatest rock bands ever. The story is never cut and dry.

I've been ripped off numerous times by independent labels and been paid fairly and regularly by major labels, and vice versa. In my mind, I still identify and relate to the independent model more, and despite, or because of my own experience, have a bias against major labels. It's sometimes hard for me to comprehend how anyone in the arts could have such right-wing leanings, but that's also a naive idealization. Any group getting attention on any level is thrown into circumstances that different members are differently equipped to handle. I feel more of a mental alliance with Joey, despite him being completely disinterested or possibly not capable of interacting with us, but feel eternal love for Johnny for his direct connection.

Even in their songs, paradoxes abound. Joey sings about being a Nazi and fighting for the fatherland despite being Jewish. And in the same song he sings that he's a little German boy, being pushed around, a simple pairing that possibly alludes to the oppressor as weakling. Is it making fun of the Nazi as a disempowered boy, acting out that resentment with his new authority? Or a metaphor for gangly, awkward Joey being teased for acting out OCD tendencies but now being the guy centre stage in one of the most important bands of the 1970s? Gratuitous violence as comedy was in full bloom with the Ramones, delinquent provocation that teenagers employ to outrage adults and embolden themselves in their ability to achieve horrified reaction. Marlon Brando did it in 1953 in that earliest projection of teenagers as a social movement, *The Wild One. Wild in the Streets* worked the same rebellious tropes in 1968; *The Texas Chain Saw Massacre* made comedy of violent murderousness the same year the Ramones played their first show, pretty much describing the plot of the film in their song "You're Going to Kill That Girl." Malcolm McLaren, Vivienne Westwood, and the Sex Pistols exploited the swastika in the same way, creating delightful terror in the general British public.

It's no coincidence that the Ramones sprung forth in 1974, at the same time as *Texas Chain Saw*. They both exemplify the mainstreaming of and early steps in normalizing violence for kicks, or the gas chambers as tongue-in-cheek fodder for a sensationalistic reaction. It's a juvenile response that had weight and value at one time, and can really only happen when you're young and ignorant. At my age, I'm overly sensitive to those tropes. They are now far beyond metaphor, and young people are too savvy to have any excuse for employing them in most ways. Now, if someone says they are a Nazi, I believe them. In some ways, the blossoming of exploitation movies and songs have led to (or perhaps just reflected) the coldness employed by those who would assassinate for kicks the starving people running toward food aid. And yet, I still sing to myself, "Gimme Gimme Shock Treatment."

Along the foot of the stage that night in 1987 were a series of bright white lights in boxes, shining up at the band, creating dramatic shadows. In front of Joey in the centre, a piece of masking tape was affixed to the inner side of the wood lightbox facing him, with the words "TORONTO. CANADA" written on it. One of the nights I was stageside, I saw Joey look down after saying, "It's great to be here in . . ."

Although we played shows with the Ramones at other, later dates, it was these three nights that made an indelible mark on us. Reid Diamond brought his Super-8 camera along and shot some choice scenes backstage; a parade of friends in Shadowy Men T-shirts waved for the camera. When the Ramones warmed up in their dressing room, they left the doors open as they played a thirty-minute unamplified set. It was as close as any of those who watched will get to that most horrid of concerts that the Ramones never succumbed to: the unplugged set. Reid sauntered past their open door, camera pointed in, right side up, sideways, upside down — the most conspicuous of spies gliding by. The band gathered in the hall in uniform as they were about to be led to the stage on the other side of the cavernous venue. They appeared like wrestlers in character preparing to make their entrances in matching leather motorcycle jackets. We later lifted a couple of filmed bits of audience mayhem and flashing lights for our "Memories of Gay Paree" music video, it being more than apparent to us and to anyone who looked even vaguely closely that it was the Ramones, not us. Somehow, the magic of editing and power of suggestion led people to believe that hullaballoo was for Shadowy Men.

Frozen in my memory is a scene I witnessed many times. It still brings a smile and a tear as I picture Reid singing "I Want You Around," extending his finger like a praying mantis in imitation of Joey in the film *Rock 'n' Roll High School*, during the character Riff Randell's stoned bedroom fantasy. Every ten years or so when I rewatch, I feel more and more gratitude for that film ever being made. It's quite astonishing that such a perfect testimonial to the band exists. It may be the greatest music film ever made.

It's also hard to reconcile with Reid now being gone, like the original Ramones, after being such a significant part of my life and of my barely teenage beginnings in music. Not just "gone" but dead. It sometimes feels harsh to say dead, even today it makes me wince to think it, but "passed away" seems too soft, too distant from the visceral reality of the gaping space their absence creates.

I've done several talks about my photographs, starting with the release of *Trouble in the Camera Club*. As I assembled that book, I was struck by the number of people shown in it who were already dead. At the end of my talks, I felt a need to acknowledge those who were no longer here. Johnny, Joey and Dee Dee were already gone when the book came out, so it felt harsh to add Tommy's name in 2014. All the original band no longer here. The reality of their death — like Reid's — is so at odds with the radiant vitality I saw in them. As selfish as it is, each of those deaths has a subtext, acknowledged or not, of myself moving closer to the front of the line. I never think I do it, but when I saw the brilliant Roz Chast cartoon of a man reading newspaper obituaries, I related. The headline of each obit reads something like "Two Years Younger Than You," "Five Years Your Senior," and "Your Age on the Dot."

When I hear someone say "Eww, that person is so old," I think, "You will be too one day, but only if you're lucky." And how old you think anybody is — that is all a matter of context.

DUMB/SMART

YOU CAN TOUR AT ANY TIME YOU FEEL LIKE IT, BUT IT SURE HELPS to have a record out. Shadowy Men hit the road with two seven-inch singles under our non-belted pants. We mailed records out to all the community and college stations across the country, and much to our surprise, they played them. Other than those radio streams, there were three significant ways people could hear a group like ours.

The Canadian national video channel, MuchMusic, started about the same time we did, but it would be a few years before we made a video. When we did, we accidentally created the perfect bonbon to fill that one-minute gap in programming. The dead time where VJs would otherwise laugh too much in an effort to fill air was snipped by showing our forty-five second or one-minute-thirty videos. We garnered a ridiculous amount of airplay from Much with our "Shadowy Countdown" clip, a video that literally cost us forty dollars to make.

But previous to that, there was Deja Voodoo's Og Records and their elemental compilation series, *It Came from Canada*. Each volume presented the scuzziest, most lo-fi, dumb/smart rock bands stirring things up, with a particular bent toward garage and shtick rock. Deja Voodoo primed the country for what was to come, creating situations that really propelled new bands along, inspiring us with a racket they wrung out of one guitar player and one drummer — and the drummer didn't even have cymbals on his kit, the guitar only four strings.

Equally inspiring was their economic motivation. They toured by hearse or public buses, Tony Dewald stuffing his drums inside each other like Matryoshka nesting dolls. The lack of cymbals cut the weight, eliminating pounds of useless metal. It also made the beat more Neanderthal: pure deranged rhythm, nothing superfluous. Singer/guitarist Gerard van Herk played through a tiny amp not much bigger than a lunch bucket, at least in my memory. Half their luggage was LPs they sold door-to-door and at shows, their load lightening with each performance.

Ultimately, a good part of their thing originated from Hasil Adkins and the Cramps, much as a lot of our thing did, but Deja Voodoo were the ugly mole growing on the Cramps' chin, willing to drive for days to play in Salmon Arm, B.C. — unlike the Cramps. Deja Voodoo paved the way into the outliers, the pockets of weirdos in the smallest hamlets across the country, and then brought us along. *It Came from Canada* was hugely unifying, identifying comrades in other cities and making us feel connected to Montreal, Calgary, Moncton, Vancouver, Halifax — everywhere that birthed another band heard on the compilations. They were LP equivalents of classified personal ads, and you might see something of your own band in the others, and be attracted to them.

We were just coming into being when *Volume 1* came out, but we were there for *Volume 2* in 1986. Over four volumes, the line-up looked like a flyer for any of our shows from that period. We shared stages with at least half the bands presented, sometimes at their Deja Voodoo BBQs. The BBQs were like an inbred family reunion. Love was all around. Mostly in their home, Montreal, and ours, Toronto, these marathon concerts presented a good five to ten bands, all culled from the compilations. The shows were a musical revue, a situation that created unity and evidence that things are better when you work together.

We flew to Calgary in 1986, and I rented a large, white drum set for our first trip west. My own kit was almost like a security blanket; I didn't think I could play on another one. I had a barely-there skill that I thought could only be conjured in optimal conditions, so these first shows away were a real challenge to that. We played a night in Calgary, where the promoter couldn't stay for our set on account of their parole terms. We loaded up my brother's station wagon and headed for the mountains. I was totally Shirley Partridge behind the wheel: Nervous Mother Driving. I'd barely had my licence for a year, only being forced to get it when my boyfriend lost his due to drunk driving. The extent of my highway driving was as sole driver on a twenty-two-hour road trip to Provincetown and back in a standard Jeep, taken within days of getting my licence.

The drive through the winding mountain roads with a heavy load of rock in the back was terrifying. We were going to play a multi-day-and-venue festival in Vancouver and one show in Victoria. We arrived at Reid's brother's beautiful west-end Vancouver apartment, knotted into anxious balls, but welcomed by the Diamond family and cocktails. I immediately knocked over my Bloody Caesar on their new white shag carpet.

The promoters had that laid-back thing that people from the east mostly dislike about people from the west, guys who, when shit needs to get done, say things like "Just chill" and "Don't worry about it." If we had any kind of money guarantee, it was maximum two hundred dollars, plus a twelve-pack of beer per show and accommodations. I did not feel at all uptight when we declined sleeping space on the floor of the booking agent's office, shared with a couple dozen other band members and one bathroom. We heard from someone later that the promoter called us the biggest prima donnas he'd ever worked with — laughable because of how polite we actually were when we asked for what we'd been promised. Reid did get demanding when even the beer didn't happen, that most transient of payments. It only made us laugh that we'd been called that, because we'd see plenty of comical pushiness during our time.

One of Shadowy Men's earliest performances was a two-song appearance at an annual event put on by Mary Margaret O'Hara and her brother Marcus, the Martian Awareness Ball. We spent weeks building a ten-foot rocket ship that we wore to enter the stage in for our allotted four minutes, but that's beside the point. There were about forty performers in all, and we shared two tiny rooms as a dressing room, upstairs from the theatre. Jane Siberry entered one of the spaces and yelled for everyone to get out. The twenty or so people in the room obeyed, with a mix of obliviousness and amused outrage at such an audacious move. Then there were thirty-nine people in one room and Jane in the other. We never did anything close to that. From then on, we called this kind of move "pulling a Siberry."

It Came from Canada Volume 2 was released before we arrived out west. We went into a Vancouver record shop and I ended up chatting with one of the staff. I found out he was in a band called Zamboni Drivers, whose cut on the compilation we shared was one of my favourites. I was so struck by how *It Came from Canada* unified us, made us instant friends. Of course, being flattered goes a long way toward being disposed to like someone, but we encountered it over and over again. Og Records had created a trans-Canada trail of bands that set the groundwork for a network of venues to play at across the country, and of bands who were disparate but had some kind of connective tissue. It was so self-contained and of a very exact time, ending when Deja Voodoo split in 1990.

The other way people heard us was on *Brave New Waves*, the all-night radio program on CBC that brought hours of what would loosely have been called underground music at the time, each passing hour had diminishing levels of commercial appeal, until the final sixty minutes would often be quite radical and extreme, particularly for the staid CBC. The show's hosts, Augusta La Paix, Brent Bambury, and then Patti Schmidt, along with a brilliant team of writers/researchers/producers behind them, were so supportive, playing our records and inviting us to create custom sessions for the show. Heard nationally, this was a show that democratized scale, that allowed people in remote northern towns of B.C., radio listeners in St. John's, N.L., and our home Toronto, to all be able to hear some of the newest ideas happening in music, and allow a band like ours to be heard anywhere the CBC was. That there is today still so much love for *Brave New Waves* is evidence of how much the show meant to people, and how it truly connected far-apart places.

We recorded a set of music for them for a Christmas concert, ostensibly taking place in the Radio Montreal cafeteria. Presented as "Velour," Brent Bambury was the host, with us as the main musical guest of the special. We played a couple of Christmas classics, a few holiday-ified originals, and a festive medley. This would later lead us to make that most awful of records, the Christmas one. Thankfully we contained it to a seven-inch, and even then had guests join us to make it more like a TV special.

We toured more and more with each passing record, further afield than we had been previously. Shadowy Men zigzagged and circled the US and Canada over and over, graduating from station wagon to minivan and eventually settling on a three-bench passenger van. Distances between places to play in Canada are staggering, the not-so-funny joke being that you have to drive for two days west just to get past your own province.

One of our first times playing in the US was a 1988 afternoon show in Reko Muse, an art gallery in Olympia, Washington. I read years later that it was co-run by Kathleen Hanna, and I wondered if it was her who made the deluxe woodcut print flyers for our show. They featured a naked mudflap woman, definitely not our style.

Before our Olympia visit, a description I read somewhere about Beat Happening intrigued me. Their music was not yet available in our neighbourhood, so I returned from a trip to Ann Arbor with their first two albums. In my mailbox, serendipitously, was a letter from the band's Calvin Johnson, who also ran K Records. How fortuitous, we were meant to be together. He said he liked our band, and upon hearing *Jamboree*, I loved Beat Happening. We toured west across the country, and upon reaching the end, went south for our first adventure with Calvin.

The K Records aesthetic was fully formed, but not many people outside the area were on to it yet. Entering downtown Olympia was like going through some sort of portal to a little village of cardigan-wearing creative idealists, people ready to put on a craft show as likely as a rock show. And the "rock" had a deliberate anti-macho stance, affected in its delightful wimpiness. We related. The town had a community-minded bent, and it seemed like everyone was working together to create some kind of teenage utopia.

A nice-sized crowd had shown up to our show, probably on account of Calvin's endorsement, but we anticipated the worst. There was no alcohol, the sun was still up, and the people in the gallery were extremely reserved and quiet. But from the first note it was like the audience became the show. The dance floor erupted in a spectacle of never-before-seen dances. They watched us play, but it felt more to me like they were the entertainment. We were startled at the instant transformation from blithe coffee-klatchers to a writhing, go-go high mass. Every single person had a unique dance, an expressive mime class gone bonkers. I watched Calvin as he did a dance that was a mix of the frug and turning on taps, testing the water temperature with all the parts of his body, his hands and feet rising and falling to gauge the flow of imaginary water. People scrubbed pots, laid bricks, and presented a catalogue of action dances in a frenzy like we'd never seen. It felt like we'd landed in some sort of behavioural case study, a game of who could be most original at playing follow the leader.

Olympia became one of our favourite places to play, the hot spot in a region where from then on we'd always do well. It was a unique community not yet brutalized by the opioid and meth epidemics that have changed every smaller city we used to regularly visit. The local department store, Yard Birds, was in a beautiful old wooden time capsule of a space, almost certainly one of the last few in the continent to have a fully stocked scouting department.

We played Olympia about five times, and I think the last one was at the 1991 International Pop Underground festival, really the ultimate ideal of a gathering of bands and people working together. So many incredible ensembles played over the course of a week, each day's activities expanding in volume and scope. Early-week shows were in cafés and to small groups, but more and more people arrived every day until the downtown was some kind of futurist society where everyone was interestingly dressed, unerringly polite, and without the stupid aggression that mars festivals — and any gathering of people over a certain number.

We saw first shows or early shows by the Spinanes, Bratmobile, and Bikini Kill, and danced to so many incredible sets by the Mummies, Nation of Ulysses, our pal Lois Maffeo, the Pastels, Jad Fair, Some Velvet Sidewalk, the Fastbacks, Beat Happening, Thee Headcoats, and so many other inspiring and exciting bands. The only negative scene I heard about was hilarious in its uptightness — when Thee Headcoats' Billy Childish scolded Girl Trouble for their "embarrassing" singer, telling them he was holding them back and they should be ashamed of him!

Over time, we were so fortunate to play many shows with Girl Trouble. Vocalist Kurt Kendall was an astonishing asset to the band, a man who internalized every teen-time dance from every '50s and '60s rock 'n' roll movie, and was the rare embodiment of pure shamelessness. Kurt's mic stand had broken early in the show, so he only used the upper part of it, Freddie Mercury–style. Something had happened to his pants too, so they were off. Kurt hitchhiked and shimmied across the stage, commanding the audience to dance. In black Speedo and boots, Kurt was a breathtakingly inspirational showman. At this time, naturalism was the standard, albeit one that in retrospect was also contrived, like all youth movements. So far, Girl Trouble was the winning set on a stacked bill with Seaweed and the Fastbacks, but was far too flamboyant for the childish trad dad leader of Thee Headcoats.

Attendees who knew how to silkscreen were helping the bands and the festival make more shirts, as all the ones on hand were flying out the doors. Either that or they were in the stacks of shirts left out at the Capitol Theatre that the house kitties had decided would be a good litter box. Different band members worked the door at the theatre, including the guys in Fugazi. It was their set on the final night to which all the energy of the week was building. The town buzzed with excitement waiting to see them.

It may have been because Brian and I took acid some time that day and were peaking during their set, but Fugazi were breathtaking and contained moments I still get goosebumps thinking about — particularly when a woman came up out of the audience to do the quiet talk-sing part of their song "Suggestion." The song is about the male gaze and unwanted touch, a push-pull dynamic of tension, release, space, nausea, anxiousness, openness. The room became a vacuum as the woman sang, sonic space opening around her to the point that a PA wasn't needed to be heard in the large movie theatre. When the band came in loud at the end of that part, it set the place into an eruption of dancing and ecstatic release. They were incredible.

After the bands were done, the dance floor was filled all night long as Nation of Ulysses members spun soul, funk and disco, and everyone got down together. Brian and I danced in a cluster with the members of Girl Trouble and Beat Happening, laughing and gyrating with our most loved comrades on the other coast. Young Fresh Fellows would later come into our family too. We had some kind of commonality that had its roots in a stick hitting a rock. We'd all made something out of a rough idea and varying degrees of ability, an alchemy of unique personalities. We related, sort of like family but actually wanting to spend time together and express our mutual love, and enjoy seeing each other's bands play.

The International Pop Underground really was a perfect event, or at least our experience of it was. No other festival we came near was ever like it. Hillside in Guelph, Ontario, had elements of that feeling, as did Sappy Fest in Sackville, New Brunswick, but without the wild abandon and craft show aesthetic.

A couple months after IPU, Nation of Ulysses came to Toronto, playing in a small café. We'd been friendly at the fest and they were sensational live, so I went to the show, bringing my visiting brother along with me. He's fifteen years older, not into heavy music, and at this time was a Jehovah's Witness. As NoU exploded in a frenzy of style, tension, and anxious riffs, my brother was aghast. He'd never seen or heard anything like it. I mean, if you want to have your mind blown by where things went after James Brown and mutant offspring the Contortions, this was the band to do it. Some of them came and sat with me after their set, and my brother was slack-jawed. "Wow! You guys have something really special! Keep at it, keep doing it. You guys are going to go far!" It was so cute to see, and they giggled, feeling it, I think. He definitely didn't have as visceral a response when I took him to see the Smiths in 1986.

We did a few clusters of shows with Beat Happening on each coast and around southern Ontario. They were so exciting and inspiring to watch, playing the moodiest, minimal theatre pieces. Only one guitar, drum kit, and voice. They were expressionistic, the catchiest, most danceable art project, each switching instruments in a way that should have seemed natural given its place in the birth of punk rock, but was somehow unorthodox and new. All of them were a thrill to watch. Calvin in highly stylized theatricality, writhing and gyrating then locking, posing, and staring directly at you, not in a confrontational way but probing, being uncomfortably direct. Heather Lewis and Bret Lunsford both looked as if they had a task to do, each of them in hyper concentration with head down as they drummed and strummed, respectively. Heather was unequivocal, almost stoic, but her body showed the rhythm when she sang. Beat Happening built big moods for a small ensemble, and it felt like something special and transient, a golden moment that can only last for a particular period of time. We were continually wowed; they always brought something unique and unrepeatable. It was important but not, and that transferred over to the series of shows Calvin organized.

They were so shockingly casual about details we liked to be pretty clear about — like, *Where's the show? And do we and the place we're playing have the equipment we need to do the thing?* We showed up at a gallery complex in Portland, Oregon, a large, hard-surfaced atrium that didn't seem to know bands were going to be playing there. There was no PA, and we were travelling light, with just guitars and a few drum bits. There were no amps, either, except the ones that belonged to the third band, Some Velvet Sidewalk, who in retrospect were probably not too happy about their amps being offered for us to use. They were kind of cold to us — maybe that's why — but they also had a deliberately intense awkwardness in their songs that was thrilling. Some Velvet Sidewalk were a fantastic band. Beat Happening were relaxed, knowing that whatever was happening, they'd adapt to it. At showtime, a few people with amps showed up, and we all played for the small crowd. With the vocal mic plugged directly into the bass amp, the groups took on an even heavier tone, a raunchy, raw sound intensified by the sound reflecting off concrete walls.

We did a few runs with Girl Trouble too, one of our other favourite bands, up and down the West Coast with Shadowy Men and later Phono-Comb, accompanying them for part of an East Coast jaunt. It was rare for them to tour so far away from home, so when their van broke down for the second time in a week, I felt for them. Kurt recently reminded me that we met at the previously mentioned Vancouver music festival, playing together at the Vogue in 1986. I still think of them as Shadowy Men's sister band. We started just months apart, but they persevered, recently playing their fortieth anniversary show. Kurt left the band briefly but returned, their run being more or less continuous and still going.

They were born in a battle-of-the-bands situation, playing songs by the Cramps. Kurt's voice was naturally in a similar register to Lux Interior's, making the comparisons inevitable. Bass player Dale Phillips was the model of the band, a fetching man, quiet and solid. He looked great in sweaters and was always suave, a debonair anchor. Each one of the members was Girl Trouble's secret weapon, each of them having a unique ability and character that led you to watch one for several songs before another caught and held your attention.

Drummer Bon Von Wheelie played very much like I did then, and we laughed when we talked about beginning playing drums, how we'd channel the Cramps' Nick Knox when we thought we couldn't keep up. Reduce it to the elements, to the simplest beat possible. It's no surprise that our playing styles were so similar. We were guided by the imperative to keep the song on track, and probably too many viewings of *A Hard Day's Night*. I always felt like I was putting everything into every song, certainly one way to approach playing, one which inevitably left me wiped out after a set, particularly in our later years when we were playing ninety-minute sets of more than fifty songs.

Bon always looked and sounded effortlessly cool, never seeming to break a sweat. She really did, and still does, seem like the mom of the band, or perhaps older sister because she actually is that to their stellar guitarist Bill Henderson, aka Kahuna. Bill weaves intricate melodic leads around the others, one of those players who knows their instrument so well that they can carry on a conversation while playing. He was astonishing to watch, sometimes using familiar riffs borrowed from others as a launching pad to play into outer space. Each of them was integral to the whole, and they created something beyond music. We loved them as people too. They were so good live that they made us better, energizing us by winning the stage night after night.

Bill, Kurt and I recorded some songs together as Black Heel Marks. On one of those I almost fell over when Bill quoted the Sex Pistols' "Pretty Vacant," but in a new, inventive way. The riff was brittle and sideways, honouring but not copying.

Not long after an East Coast tour together, Shadowy Men and Girl Trouble were to meet up again on the West Coast for a longer run. Kurt was just too good a dancer, too witty and camp, and my gaydar was going off. When we'd met in front of CBGB on the first leg of the tour, Kurt sported a Janet Jackson T-shirt — a dead giveaway! I was as out as one could be, so I had no qualms asking him if he was gay. It was complicated: he wasn't really out to too many people, including, shockingly, his bandmates.

I understood how that was. I was the same in Crash Kills Five, when I wasn't out to my bandmates or family. You don't want to damage the functioning dynamic of the situation — or at least you tell yourself something like that, because the choice is really based in fear. Coming out is incredible in that way. It lays bare and strips one of the most powerful forces in your life of its control over you. At some point, I thought of not coming out as an act of narcissism. No one was as invested as me in thinking and worrying about how my sexuality might be perceived. Letting go of those fears, even though they are always there in some minor form, was the greatest unburdening. It was a relief to not care what others thought.

I think about shame and its usefulness/uselessness so often. Having my mom buy my clothes from the "husky" department when I was a kid was totally connected to never wanting to take my shirt off in public and only wearing long pants. While so many laugh at Iggy Pop for being old, wrinkled and shirtless, I find him breathtaking and intensely powerful. He is one person always and absolutely without shame. He is overwhelmingly inspiring to me for many reasons, but that's a big one.

My coming out happened mostly in between being the singer in Crash Kills Five and the drummer in Shadowy Men. I played drums in shorts often, and when I look back, it's the rare time when I wish I had been more motivated by shame, or at least let my aesthetic senses be my guide. But starting to wear shorts was connected to coming out for me, an unburdening of restriction. Unless you are playing at being schoolboys like Scottish band Orange Juice, or AC/DC's Angus Young, there is no place on stage for shorts. I saw Peter Hook a few years back playing Joy Division songs, and was appalled that he did that in cargo shorts. Cottage or safari wear does not belong in the equation — or maybe it makes his former band's icy museum pieces feel too casual. I'm generally alright with seeing Peter Hook's legs when I run into him on the beach in Ibiza, but not in an *Unknown Pleasures* context.

Anyway, Kurt was shameless and I loved him for that. Still do. He's my age and still takes his shirt off onstage.

That I was about to start a tour with Kurt and potentially speak to him like a sister was clearly on Kurt's mind. Our first show on the tour was in Seattle, at the Off Ramp. Both bands were loading out at the end of the night, and it was this moment Kurt chose to come out to the band. As he passed each member going the opposite direction and carrying something heavy, he'd quickly blurt out, "I'm gay." It caused a bit of a shakeup in the band, not because anyone had issue with him being gay but because as a close family, he had not shared it with them before. It happens when you're ready.

The differences between the United States and Canada become more and more pronounced as years pass. I loved travelling and touring in the US, and doing it in a van means you see it evolve on the ground. You understand how accents transform from state to state, and how one extreme landscape gives way to another. There is magic in prairies becoming mountains, and of conditions for one type of cactus being so specific that they sprout for an hour's drive through Arizona but then suddenly end, only to be replaced by another variety. Barrels to arms in minutes.

A few things are always extremely striking when I cross over the border into our neighbour's home. One is a sense of despair that is much more palpable in the States. While we share a similar sense of hopefulness in many regards, it's the crueler end of the spectrum that gets more despondent the further south you travel. Of course, everything is changing as economies collapse, but I experienced so many people who were a day away from homelessness, many who did lose their home. That hopelessness was so connected to poverty, and until I went to the States, I had never witnessed such hardship. We played a venue in Little Rock, Arkansas, near the birthplace of then-president Bill Clinton. I had some letters to mail, so I went for a walk before showtime, hoping to find a mailbox. I came upon a sort of townhouse structure made of fibreboard, repeated exposure to rain making the absorbent material disintegrate into mush, peeling off in places and leaving the walls full of holes. At first it registered as a chicken coop, but as I gazed strolling past, I tried to make sense of what I was seeing. Someone walked around the structure and crawled through an opening, and I realized it was a series of homes.

Since then I've seen almost every type of dwelling, but at the time, they were the poorest living conditions I'd seen for humans. It was all the more shocking because it was the president's hometown. When I returned to the club, I spoke with someone working there. They were taken aback when I said where I'd been: "You're lucky you came back alive." No one had ever said that to me in Canada. How could this happen? How could so many people be left to fend for themselves in such a hostile environment? The first place in Canada that I saw that same level of poverty and abandonment was in Vancouver. I somehow thought that didn't happen in

Canada. As drug crises became more pervasive, these scenes are now common almost everywhere.

The other alarming thing I experienced was how deeply embedded guns are in American culture and mindset. In the '90s in Toronto, it was extremely rare to hear of anyone being shot, of anyone even owning a gun. On our West Coast jaunt with Girl Trouble, we played a club in Sacramento, California, in the shadow of a highway overpass. Tiger Trap were also on the bill, so it was a magical evening, us loving what we were getting to do and who we were doing it with. As we stood around in the parking lot after the show saying our goodbyes, I felt the wind of something whizzing past and a high-pitched but quiet squeal of a Doppler effect. "What was that?" I asked, thinking maybe it was some kind of unseen night bird. The Americans knew exactly what it was: random bullets shot from a passing vehicle on the highway above.

Later, Shadowy Men were enjoying a night off in Austin, Texas, and after seeing some fantastic bands, we walked to a pizza joint. We stood on the road in the warm summer night eating our slices. A guy who had been sitting on the curb eating then laid back on the sidewalk, not blocking the way for people passing, but maybe a bit drunk. A passing man deliberately pounded his boot down right next to his head, in a threatening way, making the motion as if he were stomping the guy's head. The guy on the ground immediately leapt up and pulled a pistol out from the waist of his pants and put it to the man's head. Having never seen anything like this in our lives, Reid ran over to them and started waving his arms: "No, no, don't do this. You don't have to do this." I could hear the panic in his voice as he tried to talk calmly to them and defuse the situation. My heart races now even thinking about it. The guy put the gun down and the two separated, going in opposite directions without a word. I don't know if it would've played out another way if Reid hadn't stepped in.

You had to keep your wits about you at all times in the US; violence could erupt at any moment. I was going downtown and staying out all night in Toronto from a very young age, and was in many situations that were potentially dangerous. But I was never afraid at home, never felt threatened. I was once attacked in Toronto, but it was random, when a mentally unstable man on Yonge Street clocked me in the head with a suitcase. It hurt and I was forced to fight to protect myself, but it didn't change my feeling of safety. Or maybe it did. Those cuts can be incremental and accumulate without you being aware.

On another occasion, Phono-Comb had played in St. Louis and stopped at a gas station on our way out after the show. In the variety store, my bandmate Beverly Breckenridge had taken a different aisle than I, heading to the fridges at the back of the shop. I saw three guys come in and fan out the way you see coyotes on the hunt do. Each took an aisle, with me in the fourth watching what was happening. They hadn't looked at me, but I hurried toward Beverly as they made their way down the aisles past chips and charcoal toward her. I grabbed her and told her we had to get out. When the guys saw that I was with her, they started swinging punches and I had to get out backwards trying to hold them at bay, yelling at Reid to start the van. We leapt in the side sliding door, kicking and punching out at them. They ran for a few steps behind the van as we quickly pulled out. I was scared but am now so relieved no guns were involved, something I didn't even think of in the moment.

Three weeks was the ideal duration for any Shadowy Men tour. Distance didn't always make that possible. If you want to play multiple places far from home, you have to add a few more days just to get to and from your destination. One six-week tour was particularly gruelling. We were exhausted all the time from not sleeping well with four to a hotel room, from the long drives between shows, and from the van we had on this trip. The back was panelled, no windows, so we were rattled in an overly hot space with not enough light to read and no view to transport you to another place. Reid was particularly not having fun, due to a recent stomach ulcer.

Before cellphones, we'd have to call our booking agent or the record label publicist every day at a designated time from a payphone. We were burnt out, but knew we still had a lot of road ahead of us. One day at a payphone I heard the news that the Pixies wanted to know our availability for a tour. My heart sank. What should have been good news was delivered at the very worst time. I went back to the van and updated the others. Reid just said, "Fuck." We couldn't do any more then.

The deepest exhaustion I've felt in my life was always upon returning home to my own bed after a tour. It was the only time I ever slept for two days straight. We were a band somewhere in the middle of the various levels of success. For a long time it was just the three of us in the van, but eventually we got help. We valued having someone on the road with us, someone whose company was more important than their touring experience or instrumental skill. That was our friend Derek von Essen, though we instantly found out he didn't know how to drive ("I thought you knew!"). He may have never set up an amp before, but he was an excellent photographer. We were so used to being completely self-contained that his inexperience didn't seem like an impediment, and we were left with some great photos — an unexpected boon for a band that avoided having their photos taken and always felt discomfort in front of the camera.

One day our excellent US booking agent asked us who we wanted to tour with in a potential opening slot. Our list was short. It was basically the bands that we shared common love for: the Ramones, the Cramps, Alice Cooper, I don't remember who else. But we got a good laugh out of him when we mentioned the Fleshtones. "Well, that's an easy one." That band's 1982 album *Roman Gods* was a record we all adored. They had history back to the beginning of punk, but with a soul and highly charged rock 'n' roll bent. We'd seen them multiple times and were always blown away. We could easily handle a week or two watching them every night. Our agent called back and told us it was there if we wanted it.

I sometimes wonder if this was a souring point with our agent: them shooting high and moving into larger bands and venues, us wanting to get out there with a band of lifers struggling to maintain the audience they had slowly built over many years. We were going to do two weeks with them, touring through the US from the middle to the East Coast, weaving around and crossing the Mississippi River multiple times.

They were friendly but casual at first, like, *Why get too close if you're only going to know each other for one day.* At the second show they were like, *Hey, it's you guys again.* We repeated that we were doing the whole tour with them, but it took maybe four shows before that seemed to sink in. We were super low-maintenance and undemanding. I don't think we even had a rider in those days, not even thinking of a bare minimum of needs like towels — we brought our own. Every night we were astonished at the variety and volume of alcohol laid out for the Fleshtones. Their drink of choice was White Russians: Kahlúa, vodka and milk. How functional and fantastic they played, considering the volume of alcohol they consumed, was staggering. Like so many other people I know on the road, they maintained fighting weight by barely eating anything else, just what their rider had provided: some fruit, cheese and crackers.

We had been doing quite well on our own. Audiences increased in size with every excursion. On numerous nights the local paper would tout us as a hot new act, not to be missed, and the Fleshtones as the party kings from the previous decade. Most nights we had good crowds coming to see us. A small part of the audience would often vacate after our set, but those who stayed were always treated to a show of masters at work. We were doing so many shows together that I expected I'd watch half of them and sit out the others, but they were so captivating, so winning that I was transfixed every night. The show might start off slow and I'd think of going out for a walk. Then at some point they'd lock in and just clean our clocks with their showmanship. They were never not great; they always won over every audience we played for. It was thrilling to watch.

One night I asked charismatic singer/organist Peter Zaremba if he had any advice for me before we went on. "Remember, nothing is too low when you're on stage." I think of that to this day, and wish I'd had that freeing insight when I'd been a singer in a band. Another time he said that a set was like a stack of pancakes: "As long as the best one is on top, it doesn't matter what the rest of them look like." Peter would direct the audience to get down on the dirty floor and do push-ups — and they would. They made brilliant dance music, perhaps designed more for the moment than for timelessness, and their recordings have certainly been spotty. Those are the only reasons I can think of why they have not attained a level of popularity to match their status as legendary and deserving troupers.

On the drive to a show in Iowa City, the Fleshtones stopped to take in some scenic caves. Drummer Bill Milhizer stayed behind in the van. When they returned from underground, they found Bill toasty from having drunk a whole twenty-six-ounce bottle of vodka left from the previous night's rider. He couldn't even stand, much less play, but he was giddy and funny when they arrived at the club, Bill dancing around and being sweet and silly, as he always was. They took him to their hotel to sleep it off before showtime. I got to play drums for their soundcheck. When Bill arrived to play the set, I was mentally preparing myself to have to step in and play songs I'd never played before. They started a bit shaky, but after the first song they'd go into a power stance, standing in formation with arms crossed, extended at chest height. Bill was lost in his own thoughts, and when he saw the others do it, he muttered, "Oh yeah" and stood up, wobbly as he struck the pose. Something then clicked and he played the set perfectly, no evidence whatsoever of his state. At the end of the night, they even led a conga line out to the street and along the road where everyone got on their knees and sang response to Peter's call. Guitarist Keith Streng was also dynamite to watch. Petite, high-heeled, and bursting with moves and kicks, he was a fantastic guitar player. He and Brian bonded pretty quickly as mutual fans.

A couple of shows in Florida were cancelled due to the death of a Fleshtones relative, so we unexpectedly had a few days with nowhere to be. As we drove, we found ourselves in a sleepy beach town we'd never heard of: Panama City. The place was empty, and the expansive beach of fine white sand was inviting. We checked into a hotel and bought some drinks to have a little vacation in the middle of our work week. Brian and our road guy Derek went for a walk on the beach, Brian in long jeans and black T-shirt, with black, chunky-framed sunglasses. He stood out enough amongst the few Florida people around that the cops stopped him. "Who are you? Poindexter of the beach?" the cop asked.

We awoke in the morning to find the town suddenly filling up with teenagers. We had accidentally plonked ourselves in the middle of the hottest new spring-break town on the first day of spring break. MTV set up on the beach. Over a few hours, the sleepy, overly lit hamlet became a seething party. We'd paid for two nights, lodging, so we stayed. I got to experience that adorable rite of passage of buying Jagermeister for underage teen boys as they shyly stopped me on the street.

That night Reid and Derek went to some dance club where, as it turned out, the National Guard were having their own party. I'd seen Reid's audaciously vivacious behaviour upset guys before, but it was a nature that many women loved. Derek described to me the next day how these uptight National Guardsmen got angry when all their girlfriends were having a blast dancing with Reid. They threatened him and told him to stay away from their dates. Some of the gals defied the men, and in a gesture of solitude, Reid picked up a giant inflatable palm tree and danced alone with his arms around it. Of course, the gals laughed and joined in. This was too much. The guys roughed him up a bit as they physically threw him out of the club.

We hightailed out of town for New Orleans the next day, leaving one party behind for another. Having another day off, we went separate ways. Those rare times apart were necessary. Derek and I went to a couple of cemeteries and tourist spots. As I walked along Bourbon Street for the first time, I took in what was happening in the bars. One advertised a live sex show that involved a donkey. Guys stood on second-floor balconies, rubbing their crotches and gesturing for me to come inside. I kept walking. Music bled out of every bar; live bands, records, or karaoke. The strains of Neil Diamond's "Cracklin' Rosie" caught my ear. Shadowy Men had once opened for ourselves as Reid Does Neil, doing a set of Diamond's songs as some kind of backwards response to Reid being called Neil all of his life, with Reid singing. That night on Bourbon Street, I looked through the windows open to the street and there was Reid onstage, mic in hand!

After the Reid Does Neil show, we briefly and irregularly played a medley of "Cracklin' Rosie" and "Sweet Caroline" when we'd get a second encore. After a night of instrumental music, a quite out-of-tune but exuberant singer went down pretty smashingly.

We were big fans of Bob Wiseman and loved his 1989 *In Her Dream* album. We'd played a couple shows with his old band, Blue Rodeo, and he was dynamic to watch. Unpredictable in his playing when he was cut loose, he'd wrench some wild sounds out of his organ and was an expressive, talented player. We invited him to tour across Canada with us, and back through the northern US. We were happy when he said yes, seeming excited by the idea.

Our first show together was shaky for him, on account of the venue soundman in Detroit unnecessarily being a prick to Bob. He wouldn't let him finish his soundcheck, despite us being okay with him taking the time he needed. It was unnerving to have such a hostile and cliché situation, one there was no need for. Johnny Winter had just played at the same venue. Staff told us they'd been instructed not to look Winter in the eyes. We too played for a packed house, making direct eye contact, and it was a great kickoff for our journey.

Being from Winnipeg, that city was a hot spot for Bob. People loved him and he was in fine form, but the further we got from home, the less people knew Bob and the less attentive they were to a solo guy on keyboard or acoustic guitar. At one show where the audience was not paying a lot of attention, he played the keyboard quieter and quieter as the din of the crowd increased in volume. Eventually he just put his forehead down on the keyboard silently. In the US, audiences were even less familiar with him, and Bob became a bit despondent and let us know what he was thinking: "I thought your audiences would be a lot smarter than they are" and "Don't you know any songs that aren't in 4/4?" But he was still game for joining us on organ for our Neil Diamond medley.

At one of our last shows together, in Kansas, the lights flickered and lightning flashed intensely through the venue's windows. We could feel and hear loud thunder throughout the second half of our set. In the light of the next day, we saw wide swaths gashed into the land where tornadoes had ripped through. We obliviously played through it, Reid cracking the mic cable like a whip, snapping it with every "Play it now. . ."

The tour obviously stung Bob, because thirty-five years later, people started messaging me: "What's up with him?" and directing me to a blog post he'd written. To make it clear who it was about, he entitled the post "Barber," my sometimes occupation. He wrote with transparent bitterness about a band who were always angry because people called them a polka band, even though all their songs were in 2/4. But the band gets a break and becomes well known only because their comedian friend asks them to make music for his TV show. It was kind of hilarious and sad, a classic case of projecting what you are yourself.

We genuinely had fun playing dumb old "Sweet Caroline" with him, and I think Bob did too, but he resented that people were really into us and not so much into him. Our audiences were dumb — but his weren't, apparently.

It was pretty rare that we were in a bad mood. We generally loved what we were getting to do, and we worked extremely hard for years, wanting to work because there were enough laughs, creative satisfactions, and other rewards along the way.

We had amazing audiences, and many bands expressed their envy about that to us. We were always grateful that we had all genders coming out to see us and that the edge of the stage was almost never solely male. As much as I love men, I get kind of creeped out when a band's audience is almost entirely male. We, on the other hand, could have been the centrefold in Lisa Simpson's copy of *Non-Threatening Boys* magazine.

When you play your own shows all the time, opening for someone else can be a lot of fun, usually a cakewalk as you have such a short time on stage. A half-hour set for us could easily be fifteen songs. Often you'd be playing on larger stages and to bigger audiences than you usually draw. But as a fan, it was like reading a long-form essay that began hours before the lights dimmed.

We were thrilled when the Garys asked if we'd like to open for Jesus and Mary Chain. We had their "Never Understand" and "You Trip Me Up" singles, and those were absolutely stellar. It was still a time when there were new places to explore in pop music. Original forms and approaches happened with some regularity. JAMC were radical in their excessive squalls of feedback, shrill high-end frequencies, and overly generous amounts of reverb. That beautiful "Be My Baby" drumbeat opening to "Just Like Honey" was as clear a marker as you'd need to hear parallels between Phil Spector's wall of sound and JAMC's '80s flurry of noise.

Between being booked for the show and the performance, *Psychocandy* was released. They were getting tons of press in the British music papers, mostly about how riotous and violent their shows were, but I didn't think that stuff would play out here. The album was as sensational as the singles, a record I still think of as a masterpiece. Really, they were never better than this first couple of years of their existence. Anticipation was high for their first show in Toronto. The venue was a cavernous barn, a place that rarely sounded good on account of its high ceilings, hard surfaces, and just too many places for sound to bounce around. It was sonically perfect for them, especially as we watched them soundcheck to an empty hall, their treble and reverb multiplied by the ugly space.

When I think of them now, they appear in my memory as huddles of teenage boys do still, sticking together and constantly looking at each other for social cues. The three guys out front had the exact same cloud of teased, cotton-candy hair on top that each of them repeatedly ran their fingers through to keep aloft. Standing out from their uniformity was their drummer, Bobby Gillespie. We thought they all looked incredibly cool, but they were comical as they shuffled about the venue huddled together like they were sharing one umbrella. All in black, they resembled an Edward Gorey drawing, spidery lines of movement making the three members appear as a six-legged creature. Shambling around their general area was Bobby, standing out with his Ramones-y flop of hair covering his eyes. He was his own creature, and we instantly fell in love with him. Shadowing them six feet behind was a giant bodyguard, as wide as the four of them put together and fifty percent taller. Why did they need a bodyguard in this empty space? We watched from a distance, giggling, as the cluster moved from one end of the venue to the other and back again, a lost centipede looking for its dressing room.

Our "dressing room" was a utility table with four folding chairs set up in a massive adjacent warehouse that was otherwise a car park for staff. The JAMC gang were assigned a small office, a little building built within the larger garage, as their dressing room. Whenever they went into the room, their bodyguard took position in front of the door, his massive presence filling the frame, stone-faced with his hands crossed. As we hung around, eventually the door opened and Bobby exited, exploring backstage as he killed time before the show. He saw us sitting at our table and, smiling, came over and said hi. His demeanour was in distinct contrast to the other three, who were as dour as we hoped they'd be. All that aloofness made them seem perfect, impenetrable, and striking. He asked who we were, what was going on. I don't even remember what we talked about. We looked like three wholesome farm boys next to him. We were fans for life. It was no surprise a year or so later when we heard he'd quit the band; he seemed like a different kind of creature than them. It took several tries for his new band, Primal Scream, to make an album as great as his look, but it did happen.

We already knew that Jesus and Mary Chain were more than hype — their first three singles alone were enough to guarantee that. Their set happened without incident. The audience almost seeming to be surprised that they were actually a band and not just a chaos magnet. They played the album in near darkness, along with a couple of extra cuts from their singles, and then were gone. Little drama, just a sensational band. We'd moved to side stage to watch the second half of the show. As they exited past us from the stage, we screamed "Bobby! Bobby!" stretching our hands out, reaching as if to touch him through a crowd of people. He giggled and smiled at us as he went by, waving with one black leather motorcycle-gloved hand.

Later, Phono-Comb played our first-ever show opening for another band we loved, Yo La Tengo. I'd discovered them around the time of their second album, when it passed through the used record shop I was working at. They were playing to maybe forty people at a popular joint, but as opener for the Waltons, a Regina folk-pop band trying to make it big in Toronto. During Yo La Tengo's set, they dedicated one of their instrumentals, "The Evil That Men Do," to us as "one of their favourite Canadian bands." Not their favourite, mind you. Earlier in their performance they'd made it clear that was Simply Saucer. After their set, I went and said hi, but Shadowy Men didn't play with them until our reconstitution with Dallas Good on bass.

The night Phono-Comb played with Yo La Tengo we were nervous and a bit shaky, but went down well. It was a bonus that the Pastels were on the bill too, who we'd befriended in Olympia at IPU. It was clearly the end of that iteration of the Pastels, as two of the members griped about what a pain some of the others were. The Pastels were sensational, at one of their peaks in their roller coaster career.

After Toronto was Ottawa, a neat two-night tour. At show's end, YLT bass player James McNew presented us each with a rare seven-inch split single they'd done with Stereolab. It was like receiving a Juno or something, a nifty prize for a job well done.

Something that drove me crazy was how deplorably Reid would treat his records. I once saw him eat a sandwich off an LP, using it as a plate! Not the jacket, but the actual vinyl. Far more uptight about my records, mine were neatly shelved in inner and outer plastic sleeves. Reid's were strewn about his floor, and if you walked on them — then, oh well. One day he bought Christian Marclay's *Record Without a Cover*, a sound piece which was designed to accumulate sound evidence of how it was treated, each scratch and crackle becoming part of its life path. That and the rest of Reid's records challenged my attempt to keep the sound pristine, as clear as possible. It made me realize that my most formative musical experiences were inseparable from the medium they were on, and that I was already loving the sound of a scratched record without being fully conscious of it.

My great-grandmother had a Victrola and a few dozen 78s. Whenever we went to visit her, I couldn't wait to play her records on it. It blew my young mind that the volume control was a pair of doors that, when open, uncovered the speaker fully, making the music louder. A favourite record she had was Vaughn Monroe doing "Ghost Riders in the Sky." The sound seemed to transmit from another astral plane, a distant place shrouded in a fog of hiss; murky and unclear. The shellac resin made more noise than the music, but in my mind, they weren't separate things, they were one sound. I was shattered when I heard a digital copy of the same version many years later; the cleanness drainin it of all mystery, it now sounded like a clean-cut Hollywood cowboy movie song.

Sitting at the edge of the stage in Ottawa, Reid thanked James for the single and continued talking with whoever it was. He immediately placed his sweating pint glass on the sleeve. James saw it happen, and I recognized that record-lover thing I also had. "Reid, that's kind of a rare record." "Oh, sorry," Reid replied to James, picking up his drink and knocking back a bit more of it. He was maybe a little tipsy at this point, and minutes later, he put his beer back on the record. James, packing up his gear behind him, saw this again. "Reid!"

I thought of this moment again years later when, after Reid died, his wife had a record party and sale. I saw that 45 in his collection, circular rings raised on the board of the sleeve. Anyone could play whatever they wanted at the gathering, with the rule being that if the record stuck, it was someone else's turn. Barely anyone got through more than a song or two before the next person holding an LP had their turn.

I often think how grateful I am for the people I've met and the places I've been because of making and playing music. A person you met on one night of a tour can become your friend forever, and you *do* meet a lot of people. There is a gratitude exchange that happens at shows. We were so appreciative of people who'd come out to see us play, and if they liked your band, they're predisposed to approaching you with positivity and camaraderie. There are bands and people with bad attitudes everywhere. But most of the time, other bands you play and connect with end up being with you forever in some way. An information exchange happens between musicians that is so often about how great some other artist is. Of course, crazy stories about other bands are catnip. In the pre-internet world, word of mouth was the fastest way for news to travel. You might get the heads-up that the Headstones are two steps ahead of you on tour, so expect the band house to be pukey, as it was in Thunder Bay.

Landscapes that others have described to me as boring have left me in awe. There is so much overwhelming beauty, and even at one hundred kilometres an hour, you have seemingly endless days to take in the vast green, treed hills and rocky waterways that make Ontario feel unfathomably large. And when you've driven the same highways multiple times, you know where that big windmill is going to be on a lawn in Sault Ste. Marie; the corner in Kenora where the highway becomes a city street and a ball diamond and bleachers stand, unchanged since probably 1900; the land rising and falling to meet your tires, carrying you through to the next gas station or vista.

To a kid raised in a big city, the Prairies are incomprehensible. I didn't understand "the big sky" until I experienced it. It can feel otherworldly to have the horizon stretch out before you, further than you're capable of seeing, with only a telephone pole or tractor to occasionally disrupt the unending blue, green and brown of sky and grain. With nothing in the way to interfere with any corner of your vision, the sky suddenly feels enveloping and closer to the ground.

It's all a big tease as you zip past, becoming a series of mental snapshots filed away in memory and luring you back to this place. Specific scenes connect me to places, like the sudden aroma of cantaloupes warming by the thousands in a farmer's field; tiny tornadoes not much bigger than an inverted Christmas tree, spinning lazily on the side of the road as we'd drive by; or a detour off the main highway to take in California's giant redwoods, the groves of trees unimaginable if you've never seen them. And the stunning moss dripping from trees in Georgia, creating an odd movie-set feel, combined with time travel back to a pre-gentrification age. I feel so fortunate to have had those brief views of places that draw me back again and again.

But gentrification and industrialization are happening all the time; it's only their speed that seems to have changed. Ever more rapidly, where there once were wild spaces there are now subdivisions.

That ball diamond is gone, sacrificed to a growing population. Some of the casual violence on the Earth can be unfathomable. Driving somewhere in the Midwest, we started to smell the distinct aroma of cow manure, an earthy smell I don't mind in small doses. As we drove for a good hour, the stench got stronger and stronger until it was nauseating, despite our rolled-up windows. We crested a foothill, and stretching out in the valley below us, as far as we could see, was a mass of thousands of cattle crowded together. The scale was nothing like the relatively small pens of the slaughterhouses near my childhood home, and the foul smell of death filled the air. That night I was awoken from a dream in which I was eating my cat. I became a vegetarian for years after that.

Similarly, a stunning drive through the breathtaking landscapes of Montana was interrupted by an open-pit mine, a horrible sore ripped open across some of the most beautiful landscape you could imagine. You don't have to look far to be reminded that human consumption will always trump beauty. If there's any comfort in the horror that humans commit upon the landscape, it's the knowledge that humans are a blip, and the Earth will be just fine once we're gone.

It was easy to underestimate the vastness of our continent. Before each tour I'd take a trip to CAA to gather up an armload of TripTiks they'd prepared for me — neat little maps spiral-bound at the top for easy flipping. As you reach the end of one page, turn to the next and your subsequent stretch of highway was laid before you. This compartmentalizing in tidy, manageable chunks gave each drive the illusion of being less than it was. How far could one line spread over four pages really be?

Near the end of one journey, we played in San Francisco, setting out the next day on a diagonal drive across the middle of the US as we made our way home. Our next show was in Milwaukee three days later. We drove through beautiful mountains and dry, scrubby landscapes, past purple cliffs and stunning canyons. We were ready for a break when we crested an ancient, rocky river edge, an immense valley before us, beyond the sign that read Nevada. In this vast beauty sat a plain, rectangular block of a building. It was featureless and functional looking from the outside, almost clandestine in its blandness. A sign pointed toward it with the word "casino" written inside the arrow. It almost felt like a Wile E. Coyote trap, so makeshift in its design, mere feet from the state border.

We stepped inside to acres upon acres of slot machines, clanging in the night that was this indoor world at midday. Before casinos were ubiquitous, this was a shocking site, a torture chamber of clashing bells and cigarette smoke. If you needed to gamble the second you crossed the border, they were ready for you.

After a long day of driving, we lounged in our hotel room and consulted our maps. Some of our calculations about how long this drive would take were off. We'd have to drive all the next day and night, and into the following day, to make this show in Milwaukee. We quickly ruled out cancelling, knowing we had to go that way to get home anyway. We departed in morning darkness for the long drive ahead. Night fell as we drove across desert plains, everything around us disappearing into the fading light as homes and towns got farther and farther apart.

Tired of our tapes by this point, we listened to the radio for some local sounds. Brian was behind the wheel, with me in the front passenger seat. The highway shrunk to two lanes, one in each direction, and jackrabbits as big as greyhounds appeared by the side of the road, their eyes fixed on our headlights as we slowed down passing them, staring at us like haunted omens. It was the middle of the night, and I remember thinking that this is what white-line fever is. I wasn't even aware of how numb I was, staying awake to keep Brian company, my eyes open but my brain barely working. Reid, who a minute before had been sound asleep, suddenly popped his head between us. "What the hell are you listening to?" In our deadened state, we'd drifted long out of the radio's range until all that was left was undulating static. I realized we'd probably been listening to it dissolve for a couple of hours.

We arrived in Milwaukee on Brian's birthday, thoughts of *Laverne and Shirley* clouding our delirium as we looked for a motel to freshen up in before going to the venue. We arrived at the club unsure if we were actually playing there. A sign outside the venue said they were closed that day. There were no posters or flyers. As we stood there trying to figure out what was going on, the door opened. We were at the right club after all. We set up and did soundcheck, then looked around, killing time until the show. The local paper also showed the club we were in as being closed, only one flyer in the hall on the way in seeming to confirm the show.

It was the owner who'd let us in, and we asked him what was going on. Despite the date having been booked months previous, he told us he wasn't usually open on Wednesdays but was trying it as an experiment! We were too tired to do anything but laugh at how stupid the whole situation was.

We were about to pack up at showtime when two people walked in. The owner had put our name in chalk on a sandwich board out front. This couple just happened to be walking by and knew who we were. "Are you guys really playing?!" they asked incredulously. We were supposed to do two sets, so we set the pair up in chairs right in front of us and played a set of songs. They bought records and stuff and helped us carry our gear out, apologizing for Milwaukee as we tried to sneak out undetected. It wasn't the city, it was the venue. The stage was in a separate room from the bar, and just as we moved the last piece of equipment out, the owner came in the room and was obviously surprised to see us exiting. "Hey!" he exclaimed. "Where are you guys going?"

Later that night, over a cold beer in our motel room, I gave Brian a white George Michael T-shirt, George banging on his acoustic guitar next to a jukebox. I wondered if this was his most depressing birthday yet.

One of the worst things about being in a mid-time band, or at least one that travelled light, was moving mountains of gear. Few people who haven't been in a group understand that a significant part of what is ahead of you is moving large, heavy things, over and over again. Unless you're playing a piccolo, being a furniture mover loses its charm very quickly. Our choices of accommodation were almost always predicated upon the ease of the load-in. Each night, we'd move our dumb boxes into the club, unpack them and set up drums, merch displays, amplifiers. Each night, or more likely in the early hours of the following day, we'd tear down and move everything out again. We'd then drive to the motel we'd usually secured before our show, moving everything into the room. Our one suite would often resemble a storage unit, the amount of gear we had creating an obstacle course to get in and out of the room. The Do Not Disturb sign always went up. I sometimes wondered what a confused cleaner would think if they opened the door and found what looked like a music shop set up in the room. I imagine if you're a cleaner in some of the places we stayed, you'd have seen everything.

Other bands would laugh, but then later come to us in tears telling us about how their exquisite Rickenbacker guitar with a built-in light organ was stolen through the smashed window of their car, or how their trailer had been unhooked and disappeared into the night. We almost never left our equipment unattended, and the moment we did, it was gone. Shadowy Men's only break-in resulted in us being relieved of an extremely heavy but rare organ, a couple of amps, and one of the van's interior overhead lights. Thankfully it was the night before the last day of a tour, so we went gear shopping in San Francisco and enjoyed a day off after returning most of the equipment the next day.

On a rare day, you'd experience a kind of magic that made your accommodations feel like something other than a human storage unit. One late afternoon, all the other guests that filled a sold-out hotel were attendees of a jump-rope competition. The parking lot was alive with hundreds of young people doing fantastic manoeuvres and spectacular jumps. In another place, the conference was for cheerleaders, the hallways buzzing with girls tumbling and jumping, the lobby ringing with a chorus of rhyming calls.

Driving across the northern US in the middle of a warm spring night, we spotted a mirage of a motel, an immaculately preserved single-storey building far from any town. Its eaves were zigzagged with green neon tubing, perfectly intact and giving the building a look of combination 1940s dude ranch and garish landing pad for a passing flying saucer. The pink neon sign invited us in. The owner generously gave us three rooms for the price of one, each suite presenting a gorgeous, matching carved-wood dresser and bed frame, everything western-themed and genuinely fifty or more years old, not corny retro reproductions. The walls were also panelled in real wood, the beds neatly tucked with forest-green handmade bedspreads, everything looking in such museum-quality condition that it felt unreal, like a time-travel film set. Lamps were hand-carved with cowboy motifs painted on their creamy shades.

None of these then-unnoticed places have escaped gentrification; all have been destroyed through "modernization" or neglect. The weirdest hotels that have been maintained are the ones designed in a theme-park way, like the nutty Madonna Inn, with caveman- and alpine-themed rooms and carpeting designed to suggest a lush meadow, if a meadow could be made out of acrylic. We stopped there once, lured by its proximity to Pismo Beach, the iconic location embedded in our brains from Bugs Bunny proclaiming that he must have made a wrong turn there. All the garbage that lives in your brain suddenly starts to have context when you realize that the scriptwriters of that show lived just down the coast in LA. This was probably where they escaped for the weekend.

In smaller cities or towns, before real estate prices went wild, venues often owned a house or apartment where they'd put bands up. As you can imagine, these would range wildly from comfy, well-outfitted spots in Saskatoon or Victoria to depressing basement dwellings, bunkbed-filled rooms like what you'd see on the news as housing for migrant workers. We too were migrant workers, peddling rock music rather than farm labour. But a few bucks saved in Sudbury could be enough to allow you an upgraded meal in Brandon, Manitoba, where Brian was ill after going for some kind of shrimp special dinner. We should have known the obvious: never order seafood on the Prairies.

We arrived the day before our couple of shows in Victoria, on beautiful Vancouver Island. What a bonus to find out that Bo Diddley was playing at the same venue on our night off, and that we'd be sharing the band house with him. We arrived to find the stairs to the second floor roped off, a handwritten sign saying Do Not Enter. We didn't want to do battle with Bo, so the three of us slept in the living room while he alone occupied three bedrooms upstairs. He wasn't interested in interacting and didn't even come down to use the kitchen.

Two of us went and watched his soundcheck and quick rehearsal with the pickup band. He asked the drummer if he knew the Bo Diddley beat. Excitedly, the drummer responded, "Yes! I do!" Bo deadpanned back in a slightly threatening way: "Never play it, only I play it." Guitarist Stevie Ray Vaughan had died the day before, so in tribute, Bo brought David Gogo, the guitarist sometimes referred to as the Canadian SRV, onstage for a night of painful blues jams. It was nice to see Bo still working, but I sure missed his old bandmates Jerome and the Duchess that night.

The farthest we travelled for the fewest amount of shows was to England. London, specifically. We were somewhat startled and chuffed to receive an invitation from John Peel to record one of his famous sessions. The sessions are a short recording of a band playing live in the studio, maybe four or five songs. We were well acquainted with Peel Sessions: they were a staple of British rock since they began in 1967, surfacing on EPs, bonus cuts on CDs, and bootlegs. We weren't the first Canadians who'd been invited to record a Peel Session — D.O.A. beat us to that in 1984 — but we were pretty close. Although our number of sessions (one) was merely a twelfth the number of times Half Man Half Biscuit were invited, it was quite an honour, and I was so grateful for Peel providing us with this opportunity and for supporting us since we began. It was because of him that we had a record deal in the UK.

We went to the British consulate to secure the proper work visas, and started making plans. With the help of the London office of Cargo Records, we had a couple of shows to bookend our time there. We'd fly in, play at the Euston Rails bar, do our session and another performance at some other pub, and then head home, all in less than a week. We arrived bleary from the red-eye to Heathrow and were immediately taken into custody by customs officers. The consulate had issued us incorrect forms and were ready to put us back on the first plane to Canada. After a couple hours trying to convince them that we really were a band, and to delicately convey that it was them that had fucked up, they decided that we could stay if someone would come to Heathrow to vouch for us. We waited a couple more hours for Cargo's office to open, and someone was dispatched to rescue us.

Because of the guitars we were carrying, we flagged down a taxi, an enormous black carriage big enough for a small family to live in, and were swept away to our tiny hotel in Finsbury Park. The most expensive cab ride I've taken in my life spat us out at our accommodations, a minuscule room with one bed barely big enough for two, and much less than enough room on the floor to allow the third person to sleep outstretched. The guitars had to be stored in the shower. But it was a major kick to be there.

Taking a walk on that first day, I wandered down the street from the hotel and there, like the Statue of Liberty in the closing scene of the original *Planet of the Apes*, was the abandoned shell of the Rainbow Theatre. I knew the famous venue from concert broadcasts of Pink Floyd, Jimi Hendrix, and Roxy Music, and its legendary status as the first stop on Bowie's Ziggy Stardust tour, its iconic sign still mounted. It was strange seeing it in disrepair, crumbling from neglect. How could such a significant historic monument be so derelict?

The name of the bar is lost to me now, but I also stumbled upon another venue famous from early punk days. John Cooper Clarke was going to be playing there that week, but it conflicted with our show. It was afternoon, but the place was open, so I went inside. Maybe three people sat around with drinks as a chunky bulldog wandered the room sniffing and exploring. I was shocked to see how tiny the space was, suddenly revealing to me that scale is about perception. Tons of bands I loved had played here, but it was no bigger than the back room of the Cameron House. Press coverage of the Adverts or the Lurkers made them appear famous while, in actuality, they were playing a place the same size as where someone like Handsome Ned would play back home. The dog squatted and took a big shit on the open floor in front of the stage — my cue to exit.

Our first London show was fantastic, playing to a full house who actually knew who we were, including the requisite couple of Canadians chuffed to see a band from their motherland showing off their good manners in Merrie Olde. Rat Scabies and Lu Edmonds from the Damned were there, and some guys from the group Gallon Drunk. Like New York City, everywhere you go in London you'll spot someone with some degree of notoriety. Gallon Drunk invited us back to play a New Year's Eve show with them and rising group, PJ Harvey, but one of the Shadowy Men didn't want to do it. We always operated on consensus — all or nothing — and sometimes that was a drag, but what are you going to do? You can't force anyone to play a show they don't want to.

We arrived at BBC's Maida Vale studio for our Peel session, a beautiful squat and ancient building in a residential neighbourhood. The style of the architecture, the fixtures in the building, the dress and hairstyle of the receptionist — everything was like the set of a 1960s British kitchen-sink drama. Exit signs, chairs, lamps, and railings all had a feeling of old significance, embedded with BBC's history and dominance of music, television and radio in the UK. Everything was old but immaculate. We were given passes and led to our studio. We knew that Dale Griffin, former drummer of Mott the Hoople, was one of two or three producers for the sessions. Being huge Mott fans, we hoped it was him working ours, but he wasn't. When we questioned our engineer for stories about him, he said we should be grateful we didn't get him, as he was a big grump. Apparently no one liked working with him.

As we set up, the engineer pulled mics from their cabinet. I gasped when he opened its doors and I saw it contained row upon row of the famous Coles 4038 ribbon mic designed and built by the BBC in the 1950s. At any studio I've been in, I still covet the one or two of these expensive workhorses they might own. This one studio had to have more than fifty of them, and they used them on practically everything.

Twice in the day, much to our delight, a middle-aged woman with a fabulous bouffant straight out of *Are You Being Served?* came around with a tea trolley. John Peel had left a note for us saying he was sorry that he couldn't be there, but that we were in good hands. By this point, he was apparently recording most of his shows from his own home. We knocked out five songs, and after a union-designated lunch break in the BBC cafeteria, we mixed what we had just laid down. The studio we'd been assigned had a plaque on the wall saying this was where that lovable old child-beater Bing Crosby had done his last recording. Everything about the place was like a museum, with us being given the deluxe insiders' tour.

Any of the bands I was in rarely played shows where you were interchangeable filler. In advance, a show with twelve other bands, three of whom you actually want to see or are friends with, could have some appeal. But sometimes, in reality, these mainstays of the working band were depressing reminders that some days you are really just in the service industry, there to lift someone's mood as they stroll past you on their way to the fudge kiosk, or to sell drinks for a short period. It was almost always preferable to play our own show to people who were excited about you being there, who were there because you were.

I think it was a case of getting more value for their dollar when Shadowy Men were booked to play at the University of Guelph, in southern Ontario. We were to play three sets in three venues on campus over the course of the day. I've totally blanked out the first one, but the second was in a large gymnasium, one of those situations where the stage is too high for you to feel like you've connected with people, and the sound bounces around the acoustically damned room in an unforgiving manner. Our night would close out playing in a cafeteria, seemingly the most promising of the three rooms. That late show was split between people dancing to a DJ spinning records and us, a live band performing our songs.

As we loaded our drums and amps through the crowd, we were met with a mix of hostility and smiles. People were getting down to Billy Idol, having fun, not a situation we really wanted to interrupt. Half the audience were there for us, while the other half told us explicitly, "We don't want no fucking band playing." Some gals there to see us laughed and called back, "Yes, we do!" We set up, did a quick soundcheck, and began to play.

In retrospect, it almost seemed scripted how exactly divided the audience were. Lining the edge of the stage facing us was an alternating set of expressions: big smiles then scowling goons. Some danced, some gave us the finger. The tension in the room was excruciating. Six or eight of the biggest guys (it's always guys) leaned forward over the edge of the stage skirt, taunting Reid and Brian. We looked to the promoter, concerned about what was happening, and he motioned for us to carry on. The biggest doofuses then concentrated their focus on our smallest guy, Reid, heckling and threatening him, telling him to get offstage. I watched tensely, trying to concentrate on playing but looking out for our safety from this mob.

Then one of the guys grabbed the mic stand in front of Reid, pushing it hard to smack Reid in the teeth. Reid fell back as I leapt from behind my kit with my two sticks in hand. The guy was now trying to climb onto the stage toward Reid. I smacked him across the face with the small bundle of wood. It was like an explosion as the entire room erupted into a brawl. Some of our supporters ran onstage to defend us, lining the perimeter of the stage.

It was a medieval invasion, us being on the mountain of a stage fighting off the goons scaling the wall of our fortress. I saw the promoter lift his foot and kick a guy in the shoulder, losing his footing and falling back as he was pulled down. Two or three guys to my left grabbed Brian and started dragging him into the crowd. I had a hardshell cymbal case that lay on the floor behind my kit. I grabbed it and swung at one of the guys pulling Brian down, cracking him in the side of the head with a swing, the impact concentrated in hard contact from the edge of the round fibreglass case. It was terrifying, but it literally felt like we were fighting for our lives. Brian was on his knees and was dragged offstage. The whole room fought for what felt like a half hour but was probably ten minutes, chaos all around us.

I don't know how things were broken up, but suddenly the police were there. They were clearly on the side of the audience aggressors, as others tried to tell them what had happened. The hostile cops told us to pack up our gear, leave town, and don't come back. We quickly gathered our stuff, trying to get out as soon as possible. The cops and our side made a human tunnel through the crowd for us to pass through, guys swinging their fists through the breaks at us.

We threw stuff into our van and sped away, wondering what the fuck had just happened. We had never, ever had violence at our shows — especially in Guelph! This was a university that specialized in agriculture and animal husbandry, a liberal oasis of hippies and punks. We loved Guelph and had played there many times, never seeing anything like what we went through. There's a reason universities used to pay better than bar gigs, and it's basically danger pay. We avoided a lot of universities, but sometimes they have the only supportive venue in town.

Brian's knee had been split open, causing serious and permanent damage. He spent weeks in a cast. The incident, which became known to us as the Guelph Riot, blew up at the university and an investigation was launched. We found out later that the line of hostile jerks along the front of the stage were the actual security hired for the night, all members of the football team who were drunk and belligerent after losing a game that day. We were told that three or four of them were expelled, not allowed to return. The school should have addressed the attack further, but without us on their back to have some more consequential resolution, that was it.

We didn't return to Guelph for years, but when we did, it felt changed. It wasn't the loving and embracing place we previously knew. I was wary and hyper-aware of everyone and everything around us that night, but we were back at the Albion Hotel, a beautiful and historic downtown bar we'd played numerous times. When a group of five white supremacists showed up and started fighting with each other, it soured us completely on wanting to play there again.

Probably twenty years later I was back in Guelph playing with King Cobb Steelie for a show with every past and present member of the band. The streets outside were rammed with police and rowdy students. Some kind of ugly culture had taken over and tainted what had been an idyllic town of friends.

A lot of this sounds terrible, but it's the worst stuff that usually becomes the thing you laugh about most. Being in a band can be incredibly rewarding, but also anarchic and life-sucking. It's rarely the audience who are crap though — it's usually the band. I certainly had some of those days — like having a sleepless night before a national radio broadcast, and then playing perhaps the worst I ever have. Those moments when your self-critic is at its judgiest usually mean nothing in the future.

Having an audience is incredibly honouring, and I was never without gratitude for people consistently coming to see bands I've been in. To have an audience there with you for the ride allows it all to happen. It's supernatural when the band and audience are in sync and have some kind of mutual energy exchange that leaves you all spent at the end of the evening. When there are twice as many people in that town the next time you go, it's humbling. It's also what allows you to carry on making music in the way you want.

Splurging on having your own bed is never ridiculous, because the most precious thing on tour is sleep. We almost never stayed with strangers, always preferring the no-obligation feature of a hotel or motel. Staying with friends here and there was always a way to have a brief extra visit with them before you split town, and often came with some beautiful breakfasts. I've slept on some lovely floors and benefitted from the affections of strange cats and dogs wondering who you are in the morning. On tour with Jad Fair, Phono-Comb had a lovely night in verdant Maryland, as we met and stayed with the people who made the kids who made Half Japanese. And another night with Jad's pal, Phil Milstein, founder of the Velvet Underground Appreciation Society, whose apartment was a pop culture museum. I could have stayed up all night checking out the artifacts on display, but instead opted for my sleeping bag on the floor under his kitchen table — one of the few spots with enough clear space to stretch out.

One night on the road with Phono-Comb, I snapped. It was our second tour after our time with Jad Fair. We were opening for labelmates and friends the Delta 72, and we weren't exactly flush with funds. Near the end of the run, someone from the audience offered to put us up, saying they had a whole house. Other details made it sound like it had good potential. We arrived to find that he'd also invited all his friends at the show over for a party. As it got late and I started to get delirious, I asked where we were sleeping. He directed me up to his attic, where I hauled my sleeping bag to lay out for the night. Dark and dirty, the room was strewn with broken glass and had no lights. Before cellphones, I definitely wasn't in the habit of carrying a flashlight with me, so getting up in the middle of the night was a tentative and treacherous obstacle course. I awoke from a very light sleep never wanting to tour again.

Of course, I have, but it's a different story now, and I know what my limits are. Every aspect of hitting the road has changed since I started doing it, little of it for the better. After Shadowy Men reconstituted with Dallas, our touring provided a very distinct comparison. We had exact past experiences to compare the present one to — and it was not good, for us or any other band. Costs had risen so dramatically, with income not having followed suit. Savvier venues recognized that bands are going to be coming through no matter what, so things they had previously covered — like sound, lights, door person, security — were all being charged back to the band. Gas prices were high and accommodation costs were through the roof. Another nasty thing that had arisen since our twenty-year hiatus was venues taking a cut of merchandise. Your record and T-shirt sales are often your flexible income and a variable top-up to your guarantee. For no reason other than they could, clubs took ten to twenty percent, a petty and nasty slice of the artists' ability to continue to tour.

We had many great and odd situations since starting up again. The less we played, the better the offers became. It was a luxury to be flown somewhere for a mini-vacation, a swank hotel room and getting to be in a big room full of happy people shaking to loud music. It can be a little utopia you make together. And then you find yourself in a taxi the next morning seated next to Tom Cochrane on your way to the airport.

I expect live music will continue to decline and 3D holograms will become more of a reality in place of touring. I know the future is not in the live-streamed performances we endured at the beginning of Covid. Those were some of the most depressing shows I "attended," although now you are less likely to hear the performer keep saying how weird this is to be pretending to be "live" when it's only them and a camera in a room.

While it means there are fewer and fewer opportunities for musicians to make a living playing live shows and releasing recordings, bands will still do that. Traditional models of performing live will be encroached upon by other experiences, and in some ways I'm excited by what possibility lies ahead, but I don't know what that is.

I'll never forget seeing the Pet Shop Boys on their first tour in 1989, directed by Derek Jarman. I wasn't much of a fan at the time, but thought they were brilliant when they executed a Magritte-like vignette, a moving painting, as they slowly crossed the stage in costume, no attempt made to pretend to be playing live. In 1978 I saw the Screamers play a concert during which they left the stage and the oscillators of their synths kept going, the song continuing to play itself despite the group's absence. That was audacious and breathtaking to me, something I'd never seen or considered. Lip-synching and miming of all kinds is standard now, but that Pet Shop Boys performance made many people upset. It was exhilarating seeing how this simple break from expectations caused their audience to rage. All around me I heard angry people saying, "They weren't even playing their own song," some people choosing to leave at intermission because of it. That alone won me over. I became a fan.

A recording engineer told me he had been polling bands he was working with as a way to inform himself about what his potential future would be. Would bands continue to go into a studio to record and release records in a crumbling economy, where so few are actually paying for the music? As with live music, he was assured by the answers he heard. No one was recouping, almost everyone creating their releases at a loss. But can that sustain forever? We'll find out.

In the meantime, I can't put all of you up, but I have enough space for two of you when you're touring, if you're well behaved.

LOUIE BEESON

THE EL MOCAMBO WAS RARELY A GREAT PLACE TO SEE BANDS. A rectangular shoebox, at one time the stage was against the wall in the middle of the longest side, making it an awkward setup for both viewing and sound. The wall opposite the stage was lined with banquettes, creating an ideal raised platform for watching the show, and of course the best sound — because it was right next to the mixing desk.

Romeo Void's second album, 1982's *Benefactor*, had recently been released, their first on a major label, preceded by an EP containing "Never Say Never," the hot track that introduced the expression "I might like you better if we slept together." My friend Jimmy was an airline steward, a "space waitress" or "air mattress" as he would say, and would describe to me a fantasy land far away where he frequently had stopovers: the 8th and Howard Baths in San Francisco. He'd bat his eyelashes dramatically, telling me about how badly he'd behaved, and he always came home from SF with a stack of records, mostly songs he'd heard the DJ play at the baths.

Even though I'd never been to a bathhouse, the idea that there was one that played independent labels and stuff like Section 25 and the Associates was pretty intriguing. Gay music scenes in Toronto were dismal, not really connected to most things I wanted to listen to. Jimmy had energy like a squirrel, a little high-strung and with rapid sudden movements as he thrilled in telling me about how he had to tell some guy to stop fucking him because he had to go to the DJ booth to find out what song they were spinning. He definitely had his priorities. The next day he'd go record-shopping before his flight back to Toronto. A fun evening of drinks and listening always followed his return.

In the new winter of 1982, we repeatedly spun the *Never Say Never* EP, which was the highlight of a recent haul. Sometime within the next year, after the just-released album caused more of a stir for the group, Romeo Void came to town. Of course we went. Our prime spot next to the sound board left us so enamoured. Romeo Void were outstanding live; the sound was perfection, drawing out the smaller sounds in the quieter spaces, every squeak of the saxophone in its right place. It can take very little of any saxophone to ruin a band. Singer Debora Iyall gyrated and reigned over the crowd with a powerhouse voice and presence, a bit of a curl on her lip to command respect.

As the show ended, I turned to the sound guy next to us and gushed about how it was the best sound I'd heard at the ElMo. He did an aw-shucks and gave me the biggest smile. We hadn't really looked at him during the show, and I was suddenly struck by what a babe this guy was. He introduced himself: "I'm Louie." We talked for maybe seven minutes, not long, probably about where the band is going next, maybe something about the sound — who knows? We said goodnight, and Jimmy and I left.

Not long after this, I happened to be in New York City and saw that Romeo Void were playing, maybe at the Ritz. I went to the show, but being there by myself, I was ready to split the second they were done. There was a tap on my shoulder as I turned to leave, and there was Louie. "Aren't you the guy from Toronto?" He asked me to wait a minute while he shut things down and then took me upstairs to the dressing room, introducing me to the band as his friend from Toronto. It was kind of a kick to be in that situation away from home. We had drinks, chatted, and laughed until it was time for them to carry on with band business and get out of there. Louie had to work but gave me a piece of paper with his address on it, saying to keep in touch. If there was anyone cute or interesting involved in music, I assumed they were straight. But knowing that the band was from SF, and that his address was also there, was the first clue to me that Louie might be gay. Now I'm almost certain that I'd think that was obvious, but then I didn't know anyone who was gay and attractive to me and also really into the music I was into. My music and gay worlds were very separate, with virtually no crossover between these realms.

I left the club, starting to heavily trip on the hit of acid I'd taken near the end of the show, and walked into the New York City night, thinking that it would have been fun if Louie could have come with me — but whatever. A little too high to navigate clearly, I walked a bit then flagged a cab to take me the rest of the way. I wasn't really sure where the Saint was, the gay dance club that had opened up in the former Fillmore East. The cabbie asked if I was sure when I told him where I wanted to go. He pulled around the corner, about a hundred steps from where I'd been picked up, and dropped me at my destination.

I know I had vague, idealizing fantasies about Louie when I wrote to him a little while later. He was quick to tell me about his boyfriend, something obviously put out there so I didn't go anywhere further in my mind. We kept corresponding and became friends. Louie was smart and funny, with that kind of charm usually attributed to boys who grew up on farms. I'd get postcards from around the world, half conversations with punchlines that would extend over several mailings, as Louie travelled doing sound for the Gun Club, Nick Cave and the Bad Seeds, Jesus and Mary Chain, and, for his first three or four albums, Chris Isaak.

Louie had been Romeo Void's sound guy for a while, since their beginning, and he came back to town maybe a year later, on tour promoting their third album, *Instincts*. He knew that I was in a new band with two friends, and we were about to play our first show. "You should play with Romeo Void when we come up there," and then suddenly, with Louie's manoeuvring, Shadowy Men on a Shadowy Planet's second and third shows were opening for them at the Copa in Toronto and at Western University in London.

Like all of our earliest shows, we would look at each other and laugh or smile when we were playing, the fact that we were doing this seeming so preposterous. I was definitely the one who felt this the most, as these were my first times on stage playing drums. I'd barely been playing for six months, so I was somewhat self-conscious about my abilities, embarrassed to play in front of drummers. It took years to not feel like I was faking, and it amused me greatly that we were getting away with it, that there was some kind of mix of chemistry and (in)ability that made it work. For maybe the first year, my face would hurt and I'd have a headache after a set from smiling; I was so entertained by us.

We thought that three people playing instrumental music would be really boring to watch, so we did things to distract audiences, mostly in the form of building sets for every show. We'd made an entire constellation of tin-foil-covered, cut-out, corrugated cardboard shapes of fish, stars, planets, rocket ships, all hung from strings. We installed the set at the London show, taking an hour to do so when we could have been visiting our friends. But being busy probably helped distract from what was about to happen — having to get in front of people and show that we didn't know how to play. Despite coming from punk rock and having such deep love for the rawest of performances, thrilling to the most amateur and out-of-tune songs like Television Personalities' "Part-Time Punks" and Half Japanese records, that feeling of being an imposter persisted for longer than it should have. Performing in front of people is never not ridiculous or embarrassing, and that self-confrontation is part of the joy of it.

Our Toronto set went fine; we made it to the other side and got to have fun watching Romeo Void. Louie hugged me after, telling me how much he loved our band.

Their fabulous singer Debora and Louie were close, and when they covered Sam and Dave's "Wrap It Up," she replaced every "baby" in the song with a "Louie."

I asked if that was about him, or did she have another Louie. "No, that's me. That song 'Louie Louie,' also about me. 'Brother Louie' too."

I was seriously crushed on Louie for those first couple of years, meeting him being a revelation. He opened a view to a possible future where there were actually men I could relate to and love at the same time. This honestly hadn't even seemed like a possibility before that. I thought if there were men like that out there, they weren't in Toronto, and it was unlikely I'd ever meet one. That Louie shared a birthday with my mother endeared and walked even more.

One of the next times he came to Toronto was to mix the Gun Club at Larry's Hideaway. The night before the show, Bauhaus were playing the same bar. I was living in a warehouse space with two others, a huge top floor on Temperance Street above a knife shop and right next door to Simpsons department store at Yonge and Queen, where I worked part-time. When I moved in, the space was so big that I rode my bicycle off the freight elevator that opened into our space and did figure eights. It was an incredible first apartment for $125 a month. Our windows faced south, looking onto office towers and a hardware store in a two-hundred-year old building. The roof of the entire building along Yonge, turning onto Temperance, was our patio. The windows were old, with no screens, and we'd have them fully open to the city night in the summer months.

My roommate Kim and I had taken acid, naturally, thinking that was the best state to see Bauhaus. Just as we started tripping, a fucking bat flew into our apartment! It was terrifying. It did aerial circles around the place, flying right toward our faces, us too paralyzed to dodge for fear we'd put ourselves into the path of the bat when it would quickly veer at the last moment. Kim screamed. We used anything we could grab to try and chase it toward the open window. After an hour or so, we couldn't see the bat any longer, so thought it had left. Off we went to get spooked by Bauhaus — and there was Louie. "We took acid before coming to see Bauhaus and a bat flew into our apartment!" We offered him some, and pretty soon he was tripping too. *The Sky's Gone Out* had just been released, and Bauhaus were tense and majestic.

We poured out of the club, wired from everything that had happened earlier. The three of us glided back to our apartment to have a late-night drink. As we sat buzzing at our kitchen table, the bat flew by, the sound of its delicate flutter amplified by our state. Louie doubled over giggling as Kim and I shrieked and put on a motorcycle helmet and a broad sunhat covered with mosquito netting. For some reason there was a fishing net in our place, so we took turns trying to catch it in the net, screaming as it hurtled toward us. After a half hour or so I somehow caught it, the bat tangled in the netting. It was inches away from me, a small scared flying mouse with bulging black eyes, working its way through the large holes, its wings like little black arms unfolding the net. I ran to the window with the net and pushed it out the window. Kim screamed one more time as the bat dropped out of the net and swooped into the night.

Louie said it was the most eventful night of the tour so far.

A few years later, Shadowy Men were travelling farther and farther from home, often to places where no one had heard of us. Our first album may have been out when we did our longest tour yet. Louie got us a show at the club where he sometimes did sound, the Paradise Lounge. I don't remember if he was working there at the time, but Slim's, the venue Louie worked in his last years, was across the road. What I mostly remember about that show was that it had two stages and an assembly line of bands filling time, a lesser thrill than being in San Francisco for the first time.

SF was gay, gay, gay, just like they said it would be — but multiplied. It was weird to see so many interesting-looking gays, and for there to actually be rock gays there. We were young enough that staying in crappy motels still had a bit of glamour to it, kind of how flying used to be. In the '80s there were still tons of immaculately maintained motels with beautiful interiors for ridiculously cheap prices. The Travelodge we stayed at in SF was not one of them. It was sketchy, but affordable for a three-night stay on tour; a notorious joint, as we found out later, that we'd hear stories about for years to come.

The transient nature of the whole West Coast made for some of the most downtrodden, cigarette-burned dumps in North America. California always seemed to be the worst. We stayed at an okay place in Humboldt County surrounded by gorgeous forests on the edge of the giant redwoods, but made a dash for it in the middle of the night when someone in the room next door started shooting off rounds. Thankfully, they didn't go through our wall, but we didn't want to stick around and find out if that was to come.

Another night we drove north after a show in Los Angeles, having to drive a lot longer than we wanted to because of no vacancies. Exhausted, we checked into a two-storey motel, the kind that looks like the set of many depressing movies, where the motel is a manifestation of the bottom falling out of your life. We lay on the two beds in our clothes, drinking a beer, wondering how so many surfaces could have so many cigarette burns, the choking stench of bug spray made worse by the chorus line of roaches dancing across the dresser. After maybe fifteen minutes at the motel, it was too unbearably depressing to sleep in. We loaded our gear back in the van and kept driving, leaving an empty motel room to sit for the night.

Louie was a perfect SF host. It was evident in the faces of so many people we'd run into that he was loved. He was very atypical, not the usual soundman personality — not the one everyone in bands has encountered, and on whom a million soundman jokes were based. He was smart, clean, well-read, and intuitively sensitive. He took us around town to record shops and restaurants, and to the famous Haight Street, then pretty much at the halfway mark between its time as the epicentre of West Coast hippie enlightenment and a gentrified tourist spot, populated by those who'd been consumed by the drugs that had once opened their minds. The stars comically aligned as we reached the famous intersection of Haight–Ashbury. Stopped at the corner we'd seen in so many photographs, who should be crossing the street toward us but fucking Marty Balin from the Jefferson Airplane! We all cracked up at the cliché unfolding in front of us, but he was no burnt-out hippie. Overly tanned and wealthy-looking, decorated with turquoise jewelry, holding hands with another absurdly sun-damaged Californian, they looked like the affluent embodiment of where the California dream had actually gone.

We returned in 1990 to play again, maybe our third time, each tour having bigger and bigger audiences, but still sleeping on floors when it afforded the opportunity to have more time with a friend, or the circumstances weren't too intrusive. Louie was living with his new partner, Steven, a sweet guy who we thought was a hippie because he had long hair, lived in SF, and wore Birkenstocks. They had a huge, beautiful apartment on Duboce Avenue, almost at Buena Vista Park. It was one of those impossibly steep streets where the grade of the hill was so extreme that his third-floor apartment was almost level with the stepped sidewalk. One whole room was filled with records and CDs, and when I turned the light switch on, the stereo came to life. The apartment was filled with the guitar riffs that opened Neil Young's then-new album, *Ragged Glory*. I still think of Louie and that moment the second I hear the distorted opening riff of "Country Home." He played a lot of k.d. lang on that visit, his "favourite Canadian singer," who had recently covered "Western Stars" by Chris Isaak, the singer who was pretty much Louie's full-time job at the time.

Reid regularly sleepwalked and sleeptalked. You weren't always aware that he wasn't awake until things got really preposterous, like the time at home when he herded his three cats into one area of his apartment, thinking he was packing gear into the van on tour, or the time we woke to find him strangling Brian. I've always wondered if he was awake for that last one.

From the streetlight shining in Louie's window, I could see Reid get up a few times and go to the window, looking out for minutes at a time, fixated on something. After maybe the third trip he called to us, "Wake up, the van door is open." We almost never left our gear in the van, slogging it all into motels and hotels, along with boxes of merch — anything that would tempt thieves. It was too many flights and too intrusive on Louie's home to drag all that crap in, and besides, the street was so steep that the van was practically right outside the living room window.

The warm night air was tense and still as we crept toward the open doors, not sure if there would still be someone inside the vehicle. The interior van light glowed dimly as we determined that the keyboard, bass and guitar amps were gone, along with our organ.

We cursed the now-missing and extremely heavy organ we were dragging around with us, having to move it almost every night. We felt as though the thief had a pox passed on to him because he would now have to be the sucker to move it every night.

One morning Louie was doing some sort of probiotic chemistry in the kitchen: feeding his kefir, something I'd never even heard of at the time and that looked rather repulsive to my uninformed mind. Another California first. I'd also never heard of a food you had to feed that didn't have eyes or leaves.

Later that day, he got the results from a recent HIV test and was devastated to find out he was positive. I remember his distressed look, both of us knowing that at that point he was unlikely to survive. We were leaving the next day, torn between helplessly wanting to be there to somehow console him or undo the hard news, and relieved to be giving him and Steve their space back. It was heartbreaking to see Louie in this state, him showing me the first signs of the disease that had led him to be tested. It seemed to be everywhere, and of course was savaging San Francisco.

Before we departed, Louie handed me a cassette, a ninety-minute compilation of his favourite Grateful Dead tracks that he had made specifically for us. None of us liked the Dead, but he felt it his duty to convert us, like a Jehovah's Witness bound by God to share the good news. "I want you to listen to this, and if you still don't like it, you have to pass this cassette along to someone else." We headed out for the days-long diagonal drive, crossing the continent from SF toward Toronto. Riding shotgun, I put it on the van stereo as we drove through the hot Nevada desert. After listening for maybe thirty minutes without anyone commenting, Brian wordlessly rolled down his driver's-side window. Casually, he ejected the tape and tossed it like a skipping stone into the scrubby landscape zipping by. What easy relief. I still picture it lying there in the sun forty years later, waiting for a true believer to come along and be enraptured by it. Sorry about the tape, Louie.

On one visit he invited us to Chris Isaak's rehearsal show before a tour. After the show, Louie came and got us, saying he was really glad we saw that show because Chris had barely talked to the audience, all concentration being on his new batch of songs. He told us that as a tour progressed, Chris would repeat the same banter, but add to it each night — so that by the end of the tour, the shows were twice as long as the beginning. He took us to the dressing room to meet Chris. He beamed his perfect teeth and flawless hair, strongly shaking my hand as I took in the sight of him in nothing but white Y-front briefs, his boxer's body in fighting form, him asking us about *our* tour.

As I read Kid Congo's autobiography, *Some New Kind of Kick*, I thought of a night I met Kid and Louie in Chinatown for dinner. They were both in the city for a Bad Seeds show. Kid described his outsider feeling in that band, largely predicated on the chasm between the straight macho demeanour of everyone else and Kid being the only gay in the ensemble, carrying the knowledge of a lifetime of unpredictability when you are around those kinds of guys. Retrospectively, I was glad Louie was there for Kid, a fellow traveller seeing parts of the world through a similar lens.

In late 1992, maybe two years after his diagnosis, Steven called to tell me Louie was dead. I'd known a lot of people who'd been taken by complications from AIDS, and it never got easier. Although our paths crossed for only brief snatches of time, knowing him changed me. He opened my eyes to the possibility of a life with love in it, with someone who was smart, challenging, a beaming ray of light, and wildly open to adventure and music. He was so supportive when I first began playing music, right to his last days. When I read Kid Congo's words about Louie on an AIDS memorial site, I laughed and cried a bit, knowing that one of those people he referred to was me:

"A handsome man with a sweet demeanour. And wry sense of humor that instantly attracted massive crushes from people of all genders. A real charisma. A thoughtful friend. Louie died in 1992, but I know our friends think of him all the time. We miss you, Louie. We love you, Louie."

REID IS A DIAMOND

THE REID DIAMOND I FIRST MET AND THE REID HE BECAME WERE almost two different people. On first impression, he could be slightly abrasive, a high-strung motormouth firing with ideas and assessments, ready to pass judgment on anyone who walked past with the wrong pants or a Sammy Hagar T-shirt. He was smart-mouthed by any definition, looking for someone's vulnerability to make a wisecrack about. I understood this more as I understood this same impulse in myself. His wittiness was both armour and a way to show off his cleverness. It endeared him to those who shared the same view, but could be a razor-sharp dagger when directed toward others.

He transformed dramatically over the years I knew him, becoming sensitive to everyone's situation, by choice or circumstance. He carried some self-consciousness and embarrassment about things he'd done or said in the past, but those things shaped him into who he is, who he was. Seeing those digs land hurtfully on someone you care about became a wake-up to both of us, that way we were being very teenage and immature. He was barely out of his teens when we first met, and I was more in the middle of mine.

His notoriety as a concert heckler began early. His friends told me about seeing Kansas supporting Queen in 1975 at the Stampede Corral in Calgary. Reid targeted Kansas's keyboard player from his position down front, mocking every aspect of the guy's appearance and ability until he burst into tears. Staff pointed Reid out to have him thrown out.

I saw this same thing happen over and over again in his first year or so in Toronto, even getting written up in a local newspaper's review of a Wayne Kramer show. Security literally grabbed us by the collars from our seats at the stage's edge and carried us out, Reid mocking the security and laughing maniacally as we were hustled toward the door. Kramer was bad, so I didn't bother protesting that I'd only giggled in agreement.

Reid and Bruce McCulloch had been best friends in Calgary, where the Diamond family lived before Reid's move to Toronto. As an RCMP officer, Reid's dad Boyd was stationed in Steinbach, Manitoba, where Reid was born, and then later Brandon, Beausejour, and eventually Calgary. Bruce and Reid hung out and worked together at Canada Dry, loading trucks. In collusion, they acted as amplifiers for each other, ratcheting up the quipping and wisecracking, each trying to one-up the other. Fortunately for me, I was rarely the target of their scathing reviews of everything — from the way you walked to how close together your eyes were.

Sometimes they were entertaining to watch as they tore their prey apart; other times I'd gasp and think, *Thank god that's not me.* They could be like two ferrets in a cage. Initially that cage was Calgary, but fortunately, they let themselves out. It didn't take too long in the big city to soften those restless daggers.

Every behaviour can be measured in degrees. Compared to the redneck and ultra-conservative attitudes in the bars and streets of Alberta in 1978, Reid was enlightened, an urban Toronto person with modern views. It was easy to feel that when you were riding the first wave of punk rock, you were part of some sort of evolutionary model in play. The music and culture scenes were artistic, wild, and creative, and the city at night was a vacated playground for those rejecting their previous lives.

The band we formed after his arrival in Toronto, Crash Kills Five, made a 45, and it was Reid who paid for everything. He seemed a lot more grown-up to me. I was in high school and still living with my mom, as was our guitarist after Brian Connelly, Mohamed. Drummer Alex was often between jobs, so Reid was the responsible adult. He had a driver's licence, had moved across the country, and had been to college, even if only for a few weeks. Luckily for us, he also had a van to haul the band and gear around.

Heather was a beautiful, tall redhead we knew from the scene. She and Reid started hanging out. Together, they looked like a Robert Crumb drawing, Reid's eyes being at the same level as her cleavage. I was a third wheel for a while as they tentatively dated, me seated on an overturned milk carton behind and between the front seats of Reid's beat-up van as we drove to Buffalo to see the banned-in-Canada film *The Tin Drum*. The van constantly had to be topped up with oil that Reid bought by the case.

We stopped at a gas station, Reid jumping out to pump gas. Remembering to put some oil in, he asked Heather to reach under the passenger seat and pass him a can. She bent over, grabbing the first rounded thing she felt, and burst into hysterical laughter as she lifted what she'd found. It was a white platform boot, brand new, half of a pair Reid had bought to be a rocker in the big city. He wore elevated shoes and satin jackets in his Calgary band, Buick McKane, up until he moved to Toronto. The fashion and genre transition from glam to punk was abrupt and humiliating in this moment. He snatched the boot from her, snarling, "Give me that." He hurried around and opened the passenger door, reaching under Heather's seat to retrieve the shoe's stacked companion. We watched through the windshield as Reid's glam period came to a sudden end in the garbage can next to the windshield squeegee bucket.

They eventually moved in together, sharing a couple of character-filled apartments downtown. Heather helped the band with photos and flyers.

Reid decided to go back to college to study theatre tech. He'd always had a strong sense of theatricality and improvised building. He and his older brother Grant would make homemade flash-pots for Buick McKane, mounting an electrical junction box on a wooden board, then hammering in two steel nails connected by a thinner wire. You'd then fill the metal casing with explosive powder, an electrical cord attached to one nail so that when you plugged the thing in, it would instantly explode, creating a crude pyrotechnic whose scale was determined by how much flash powder you used.

Reid made one for some ridiculous rock finale parody at an early Shadowy Men show. The explosion was so big that the fireball singed the carpeted ceiling of the Rivoli, stunning the audience at stage's edge, fortunately not incinerating the place. I watched as Reid hurried to the side of the stage to plug in what was basically a homemade bomb. We were all laughing, eyes fixed on the metal box on the floor as the flare and smoke blinded the room. Sightless from watching the stupid thing, we couldn't find our instruments to continue with the show after the bombastic interlude.

During and after his two-year stint at Sheridan College, starting in 1980, he became involved with local drama scenes. Newly interested in theatre and working in staging for various productions about town, he built sets for the Shakespeare plays that happened every summer in High Park. After a few years of this, he really started to hate it, mostly because of the politics and hierarchies involved. Even if you were an essential part of the creative element, actors were always condescending to the other labourers.

Bruce McCulloch had finally moved to Toronto and was beginning with *Kids in the Hall.* He'd been doing stand-up and performing loosely with another troupe before getting absorbed into the Kids. As they began doing shows, Reid was integrated, helping them execute their ever-increasingly elaborate staging ideas, building sets or props on a moment's notice. During the actual show, he'd operate the sound and music cues. The Kids were doing regular spots at a small theatre, the Poor Alex, a black shoebox space that took its name from the posher old theatre further downtown, where the biggest productions would play. Audiences were small, and there was no sign of what was to come for the Kids.

I ran into Reid on the street just before showtime one evening. He was stressed and impatient at how they were submitting their needs later and later, expecting Reid to always pull through as he did, at the last minute. He was carrying a 45 of the Doors' "Riders on the Storm" that he had just bought for the show, which was minutes away from starting. I think the Kids were Reid's final straw in wanting to get out of theatre tech.

Our second band together, Shadowy Men on a Shadowy Planet, began while Reid was at the Ontario College of Art. We naturally fit into the long lineage of art school bands. Our crafty sensibility and involvement with other arts made us good comrades with other groups who'd sprung from the OCA. Ensembles like the Cads, the Dishes, the Diodes, and Martha and the Muffins were among the first live bands I ever saw, after seeing flyers along Queen Street for concerts at the OCA auditorium, in galleries about town like A Space, and inevitably, the art school bar around the corner, the Beverly Tavern.

Much like the earliest days of punk, there was a fairly distinct difference between art school bands, with their arch cleverness, and the straight-up rock and roll outfits who traded more on being dumb. We lived on both sides of that fence, but our band's character was distinctly in the art school camp. Even the Who and Queen had their origins in art schools, as did the best of the UK punk movement. The Jam, in their song "Art School," declared a manifesto in which everyday life was the new art school. You don't need permission: do what you want, say what you want. The OCA still had a wild element to it, and we were stimulated by playing with someone like Meryn Cadell, who accompanied and harmonized with himself via a small tape recorder. Our audiences were artists, students, rockers, tradespeople, dancers, record store employees.

Reid exaggerated like crazy, not to be boastful or to manipulate something in his favour but for the fun mental play of weaving the fantastical, the truth, and some essence of history together. He'd make things up for no other reason than to provide an outlet for his constantly firing brain. After helping a friend make her first chords on guitar, he illustrated how you could make simpler chords by holding one finger down over multiple strings to form a barre chord. But then he continued with the completely made-up fact that barre chords were called that because they were invented by guitarist Martin Barre, of Jethro Tull.

He was always the best interviewee and audience communicator in any of the bands he was in, being vibrantly intelligent and clever but playful, not a jerk. In one of the earliest articles written about Shadowy Men, the interviewer was going to visit one of our homes, so we made some snacks: Rice Krispie squares. But because the publication was the *Globe and Mail*, he insisted we make them grey to match the paper's masthead colour. The finished pan of treats, fresh out of the oven, looked ashen and mouldy.

I hired him to work for a summer at the record shop where I was employed, and it was fun seeing how Reid would file or organize records. Always on the lookout for early Canadiana on the Arc label, or any of the regional artists who released a couple of country albums in 1962, he treated the shop as a gallery, kind of like I did, playing curator for a display of themed album covers.

There is a fascinating thing that happens in used record shops. You can pinpoint the exact minute when an artist or album is over, when the public have had enough of them. One day their records stop selling, and the next day scads of people are trying to unload them. Reid became obsessed with the repetitive visual of a display that was nothing but one title destined for the dollar bin. He started collecting particular records that he could buy for fifty cents, often going home with ten copies a week for the two months he was there. When he died, his wife Beccy distributed among the city's thrift stores the crates and crates filled with copies of Boston's first album that Reid had squirrelled away.

Another obsesson was Loverboy's self-titled debut, with striking cover art by Canadian artist Barbara Astman. The packaging on this record felt like it hit all of Reid's hot spots. There was a link to his own musical beginnings. He had a sort of collegial association with the band's singer, Mike Reno ("but he was Mike Rynoski then"), from his days in hot Calgary bar band Spunk. Reno and Spunk guitarist Ricky Ray would occasionally go see Reid's band, Buick McKane, and vice versa. *Loverboy* was a corny, hook-laden record, the zenith outcome of a life playing bars in the "classic rock" circuits of the country. Loverboy hit it big with this first record, and Reid would often sing "The Kid Is Hot Tonight" in a display that combined mockery with honour. The album had reached public saturation and was pouring into the shop, sellers stunned that we didn't want any more copies of this hot product. It became a dollar-bin staple, and Reid lined the shop's walls with it.

The LP and jacket also spoke to his own life as a visual artist and musician. Released in 1981, the cover features a commissioned image in which Astman, smoking and dressed in black, made a self-portrait Polaroid photo and then typed over her picture before the emulsion had set, leaving a murky, imprecise narrative behind. This text piece revealed an approach Reid also explored continually, of combining image and text to create a conversation between the two, and for them to become one.

I wonder too if Reid related in some way to the artist whose work had been corrupted or co-opted by an indifferent public, thereby causing every Barbara Astman piece done using the same method to look like a knock-off of a Loverboy album. To take this even further, many years later Reid created a series of portraits of friends dressed in black and with a slash of passionate red lipstick across their mouths, a cigarette just touching their lips. He blew these Polaroids up into a series of even more Loverboy albums, virtually identical copies of something already so ubiquitous that it had been relegated to the next step beyond clearance bins.

His art practice eventually spilled over into film. He loved the tactile nature of Super-8 and the pleasure of physically cutting a film together, determining the narrative with each splice. He shot two of Shadowy Men's music videos, one of them requiring a band trip to Tivoli Miniature World in Niagara Falls (sadly, now closed). The theme park was a wonderland of scale models. Famous landmarks like Toronto's city hall, CN Tower, and our local Pearson Airport, where a tiny plane on strings Reid had made was allowed to launch, presumably taking Shadowy Men on a journey to spectacular sights throughout the world. Hello Stonehenge, Easter Island, and the Kremlin! We flew over Rome's Colosseum en route to the titular city in "Memories of Gay Paree." Reid's discount vision of Paris included a flyby of the Arc de Triomphe, and touristy shop signs, all capitalizing on the city name — but actually shot in Paris, Ontario. All of that flying, and where do we end up? In a small Ontario town, its identity forever less than the grander European city of the same name. Reid manipulated narratives in a playful way, speaking to the place we actually lived, not the one across the sea. The French Paris was the mythological one to us, the Ontario Paris real, and boasting a Paris Fish and Chip Shop where we could go have lunch.

On a trip out to Olympia, Washington, to play at the International Pop Underground Festival, we were swept up in the small-town fair atmosphere all around us. Hearing there was going to be a pet parade, Reid got up early and went around town trying to find a used Super-8 camera to shoot the events. That footage ended up in our video accompanying the song "Rover and Rusty," on a single entitled *Music for Pets*. It's charming and sweet and, at its core, documents a community coming together to create unity and have some fun.

There was one crucial element in Reid's practice as a creator, musician and performer, exemplified when another artist he knew was doing a performance piece in which she flew about the room, attached to some kind of contraption. At the time, I was skeptical about a lot of performance art, not really understanding much of what I saw. When I asked him why she did that, he laughed and replied, "For fun!"

Fun. That hadn't even occurred to me. That two-word sentence opened my mind to other possibilities in art, and being open to not knowing what was going on. I was somehow deeply enthralled by music that I didn't understand, but had a block about some art that I didn't. His point of view made me see that they essentially came from a similar place of pure exploration. Music and art could mine hidden meanings, or just put something forward as a step toward some further understanding — or not. A visual artist flying through the air might not be so distant from Screaming Lord Sutch, in undertaker drag, moaning about wanting to play on a "Gutty Guitar." Both had elements of absurd theatre.

His sense of moral direction was strong, and he was dedicated to a fault, wanting to work with the same bands, clubs, bookers, galleries, and eat at the same restaurants in each city, sometimes beyond the point of your better judgment. If they once believed in you, he wanted to be there for them, keep the commonwealth of hopefully like-minded people growing and together, being supportive of each other.

He was generous in so many ways, stopping on the street to give money to every single person asking for it, even if he couldn't always afford it. He paid for the recording and manufacturing of a friend's record when he loved one of their songs and they couldn't swing it. His strong belief in socialism and fairness led him to donate and actively campaign for his NDP candidates. His sense of justice made him want to create the idealized world just out of reach in this one. I thought he would have gone into politics, had he lived longer.

He was diagnosed with adenoid cystic carcinoma just as Shadowy Men were beginning what was intended to be a year off in 1994 to pursue other interests. After spending thousands of hours with each other in hotels and dressing rooms, rehearsal spaces and cramped vans, we were all looking forward to a break from the other two. But he was so vulnerable and shaky through this period. For his first year of treatment, he and I continued to get together, playing music, writing songs and hanging out. He was playing guitar rather than bass, his exceptional knack for the hookiest riffs expanding with two extra strings on which to realize them. First we did an album with Jad Fair that also included Dallas Good, and then we wrote the songs that became the Phono-Comb album *Fresh Gasoline*.

At some point we had the idea of playing a show or two as an instrumental duo, under the so-dumb-it's-clever name Donna Reid. It felt liberating to be even more minimal than our years-long trio. There wasn't the same weight of history or an obligation to be fully realized. We didn't need to be perfect. It wasn't an experiment, nor did it feel like we were a new "band" as a duo. It was just us playing our new songs with the same tools we wrote them with. Eventually Dallas, then Beverly Breckenridge, joined us and we set out as a new ensemble, Phono-Comb. It was pretty clear to us by 1995 that Shadowy Men on a Shadowy Planet was done.

After Phono-Comb ended around 1998, Reid played with a few friends, including the just-about-to-emerge Peaches. Always the conceptualist, he set himself the task of covering the alphabet by doing one song by an artist representing each letter. First up, "Dog Eat Dog" by Adam and the Ants. I don't think he made it past H, and I was amused when I heard the first batch, with rhythms provided by the beat-box built into the organ he had. When I had tried to introduce sequenced sounds into Phono-Comb, he was angered by their tyrannical precision, insisting that the tempos were fluctuating. He clearly wasn't used to playing with a drummer who kept perfect time.

History, mythology, and storytelling danced together in Reid's visual art and music. I love how Reid would spotlight and amplify a moment I had been present for, with a very clear thought toward regional totems and the swirl of community that elevates those places and moments. Shadowy Men had played the Railway Club in Vancouver a few times. A long, narrow local, its name and design helped to evoke the sense of being in a bar car on a journey somewhere unknown. He made a piece in 1999 called *Transformer*, a model train set referencing the one that snaked around the upper reaches of the Railway Club, and the bar itself. In vinyl lettering, and broken up over multiple cars, his text was a kind of poem, naturally bringing an iconic Vancouver venue into the imagery. On one side, the line of trains read:

"I was — drinking — for free — At the — railway club — in vancouver — b.c. — When a — quite certain — person — Said I weren't — art bergmann — i knew — it was — time to — leave."

When you viewed the other side of the train as it made its journey through the gallery, it read, "I was — listening — to poetry — At the — railway club — in vancouver — B.C. When — an uncertain — wordman — Asked if — i were — art bergmann — I said — buy us a — round and — we'll — both see."

Reid's drive, his intense desire to connect with people and have them connect with each other, led him to a series of three purely text pieces, *Chalk Lines*. Inscribed on sidewalks in chalk, these accounts would unfold as you walked past them, telling Reid's version of a myth of his own creation, founded in reality but told as a tale you might hear sitting around a campfire. It was a very active way to create new folklore about the places he lived and passed through. Each story was written in English and a second language, referencing the narrative and the neighbourhood where it took place. A story of an arrowhead found while lawn-mowing was translated into Mohawk, and another about two men trying to find the Jewish neighbourhood was also presented in Vietnamese, which was the language of the now-dominant culture inhabiting the streets in the story.

On Cameron Street, the road that runs along the side of the Cameron House off Queen Street West, he wrote about Handsome Ned, the singer-songwriter who died in 1987 on the fifth anniversary of his weekly residency there.

Entitled "Cowboy Canter/El Canto del Cowboy," Reid wrote Ned's tale in English and Mexican Spanish:

"The critic pointed out in his review of Ned's record that, while bugs sometimes live in cement, they never inhabit asphalt. Ned's beats lived in the cement. When he walked, he'd click out a rhythm with the heels of his lizard-skinned red cowboy boots. He'd bought them down in Texas on a visit there with his brother. The shop owner tried to pump the sale while Ned sized them up in the full-length mirror. 'Ellas te hacen ver tan— guapo! (They make you look so— handsome!)' Ned had gone down south to find something. He did. He came back a cowboy singer. Ned would write his songs as he walked down the street. If it was a fast number he was composing in his head, he'd go zipping by, tipping his white cowboy hat in your direction. If it was a slower number, he'd stroll along. pretending to be window shopping. As he got more popular, he found it harder to walk down the street without people interrupting him, causing him to lose his train of song. He started taking the back lanes instead.

"One summer afternoon I asked Sheila if she'd take me to see his grave. We downed a couple of shots of mescal, and then walked north in the heat toward the cemetery. When we entered the gates, a lightning storm erupted. 'We better go back!' I yelled. 'This is dangerous!' 'No!' Sheila forged ahead. 'You always gotta do what you said you were gonna do! He's just putting on a show for us!'

"The storm was starting to pass by the time we reached the granite marker. A lyric was etched across it:

There's something sad and lonely /
about a freight train slippin' on wet steel /
rollin' back to places I've been /
old steam whistle keeps callin' /
my name again and again. /

"As we walked back up the asphalt driveway towards Yonge Street, I remembered what the critic had written. Ned's beats live in cement."

There are so many details in this piece that made up the essence of Reid's approach. It begins with a journey, then a transformation; it honours a musician Reid respected, while conjuring friendship in his pilgrimage with Sheila. His own process of songwriting is illuminated as the fable experiences and submits to the power of nature, there's some drinking, and the story ends in a place of honour for those passed. The vast frontier of the Prairies echoes in the story's gestures of respect.

His final collaborative project was Danny and Reid's Motion Machine, a drum-and-guitar duo with Danny Bowden, who brought together elements of so much of what Reid had done throughout his life: rock music, scoring for film, and visual art. Both had attended OCAD, a couple of years apart, and were on the boards of artist-run galleries: Mercer Union for Reid and YYZ for Danny. As their paths crossed more frequently, they realized they had a lot of the same ideas and vocabulary.

"We developed a creative approach or way of working on things that incorporated a visual aspect, but was a musical project," Danny told me. "We wanted to play in visual arts venues, galleries, not bars all the time."

Danny's visual art was more in video, whereas Reid avoided it. Technology that required too much time to learn, or required too much equipment, never had an interest for Reid. Super-8 film editing viewers or blocks were cheap and easily available in pawnshops and used stores. It felt more accessible. Reid was adamant that the band use Super-8 rather than video. Danny saw that was important enough to Reid that he conceded.

They shot and edited Super-8 films that acted as direction for the group's musical pieces. Playing live, the two soundtracked the projections behind them with a mix of song and sound design. Inspired by mod scooters, Danny tricked out his drum kit with rear-view mirrors, allowing him to face the audience but see the films being projected behind him!

I know from my years of working with him that the medium and what was actually on the film were significant, but so was the theatre of performance. He knew there would be a clanging analog machine that audiences couldn't avoid, with the aesthetic satisfaction of a nice-looking projector on display. Projectors were noisy, and that alone made the rhythmic clattering a distinct part of the band's sound. The simplicity of this fairly democratic medium would make it an inspirational part of the whole. And threading the film through the projector so that something as simple as a lightbulb could shine through it and make a moving picture on a wall or screen, it had a romantic quality. The physical relationship was much more tactile than pushing a VHS tape into a player. And like an old vinyl record, film accumulates the detritus of use, wondrously making its own history and treatment part of the picture we see.

Always creating new films and accompanying music, their sets began with credits and an introduction, as you'd see in most feature films. White plastic cups pushed into the squares of a chain-link fence were arranged to spell out the year, the name of the performance, who they were. As a kind of overture, the preparation for the show was shown on screen: hands thread film into a projector, the screen we were actually watching the visuals on is shown being pulled down, and at the ready, a close-up of Reid plucking a guitar string then turning a tuning peg is echoed by Reid doing the exact same motion in front of the screen.

The Motion Machine were the sensational union of art and music in equal measure. One particular suite they performed, entitled *Five Seasons*, answers the question: What is the fifth season in Canada? Why, it's more winter of course. The first Winter segment shows the Derby Tavern, a beautiful bar and hotel built in 1846, when Toronto was also home to many other Irish bars. Snow falls as if honouring the dead, the uniquely historic building about to fall to the massive gentrification transforming the Corktown neighbourhood where it sat. Open lands, a stunning tin-and-neon marquee, and a "ladies and guests" entrance show Toronto in 1999 looking not so dissimilar to how it looked, in places, in the 1920s. It's a building in character with other work by Reid, a metaphorical screen on which any number of true or imagined stories can be projected.

The next season is the most heart-wrenching for me to view. Iridescent tiny green leaves, luminous yellow forsythia, and showy star magnolia welcome Spring, the time of rebirth. Shot from a bicycle in the neighbourhood where we both lived, the moving images look up to take in the relief we feel when the leaves actually do return after months of just being dry, brown fingers clawing at the chilly grey sky. The intense spring light casts distinct shadows of new life. Although he had been being treated for his illness off and on for a few years at this point, I don't know that he knew it would be his last spring that he was capturing.

Reid's desire to have a "show," some kind of added spectacle, was not born out of pleasing an audience, although that was important to him too. He wanted to be fully present, not aloof, for an audience and for himself. On stage, his actions transcended his mood and health. Any performance should be a shared experience. So many of his art works involved transformation: turning the banal into the spectacular, making fiction somehow real, or colouring reality with just enough fiction to make it dazzling. He felt gratitude and a responsibility to give to audiences, even when he was sick.

Motion Machine were actively working toward more performances when Reid's cancer intensified, and further treatment just wasn't possible. He knew it was terminal, but he and Danny were determined to at least complete two performances they had booked.

They were to play in Reid's hometown, Calgary, at a festival presented by M:ST (Mountain Standard Time), an arts organization dedicated to performative art. Accompanying them was a film montage made specifically for the show, a sort of travelogue of Calgary's fading past. For a relatively "new" city, there is little that is truly old there, but the distinctive character of small oddball businesses, grand tin signage, and the city's torch-like tower were spotlighted. Reid recruited his photographer sister, Dallas Diamond, to film these spots, Reid using some of her archive of neon documentation as reference.

The first of the two shows was at Toronto's Power Plant gallery, at the opening of a broad overview of some of the city's artists called *Substitute City*. Danny and Reid both had work in the show. Showing at the Power Plant was significant, being one of the city's largest and most respected venues for contemporary art. There was certainly an element of validation in being invited to exhibit here, a step that often opened doors to further opportunities.

When Reid called Danny to tell him that his cancer had progressed, Danny assured him that he was there for him and they'd make this happen, in whatever way Reid was capable.

Reid died February 17, 2001, only days after his forty-third birthday. The further we get from the year of his death, the more tragic and cruel it feels. He was so young, with many different paths he'd been building laid out before him, waiting for him to explore. Once in a while I hear someone's age and am very aware that they are the age Reid would now be. I'd try and picture him at that age, but every mental picture I conjure is younger Reid, when he was overflowing with vitality. He'd be a senior now, collecting a pension, possibly scratching his cats' ears, and drinking tea in the sun with Beccy.

At Danny's invitation, Brian Connelly, the guitarist who'd played with Reid for more than twenty years since they were teens, helped conclude Danny and Reid's spectacular Motion Machine agenda. Remarkably — but also not, given my experience of Brian being quick to master the most challenging of musical tasks thrown in front of him — they learned and played two different shows a month later. Brian knew Reid's "voice" as a player, but it was incredibly moving to see and hear Brian do this. As you might imagine, both of their unique voices came through in the guitar playing, a distinct harmony between the two making the performances bittersweet.

Danny told me, "Reid was a small guy, not a particularly good hockey player or a great skater, but he had a fierceness about him that was something to behold. It was like, *Holy fuck, there is a lot of energy in that atom*. He had an intensity without any external stimulus. He wanted to do a lot of fucking stuff."

And he did.

DRUMS ARE STUPID

WHENEVER I SEE BANDS PLAY, THE TWO MEMBERS MOST COMMONLY useless and annoying are the drummer and singer. I don't think it's a coincidence that those are the two things I've done in bands.

Singers think they're the centre of the band, probably because they are. They do embarrassing things like punch the air to signify that they are so bad they are willing to beat up the thing that keeps them alive. They make dumb faces, always pointing at their heads when the word "brain" is in a song, or worst of all, they play air guitar. This is a total admission that they wish to have a more useful function in the group. The only thing worse than playing air guitar is kicking a Croc into the audience. Wait, there is something more heinous — an audience who get all excited that the Croc Kick is coming, cheering wildly.

Not all vocalists are irritating, but the irritating ones, are the pinnacle of pestilence, egos on legs making cringe faces. Singers demand too much attention for how little, proportionately, many bring to an ensemble. There's no point in naming any of them, but this town is full of them. Yours probably is too. A good thirty-three percent of groups I see would be better as instrumental bands.

I love functional singers, the ones singing because no one else will, or because they're the one who wrote the words, the ones who string words together in a curious manner that makes me scratch my head, or at least point to it. Singers who don't do *Idol*-damaged things like move their hand up and down relative to the pitch of the note they're warbling — those are the ones I prefer.

Are drummers worse or on par? Too many drummers make too much noise, always hitting their cymbals in a way that will eventually make both them and you deaf — or at least lose all the top end of your range. The ones that get on my rag the most are those whose playing sounds like they end every sentence with "Oh, and another thing . . ." When the drum part comes off like a grade twelve philosophy essay they are struggling to write, it causes me to fidget and wince. Drummers who play lead through every song, do too many fills, have little tiny rack toms, and who are relentlessly crashing cymbals for no reason really bring out hostility in me. Especially when it's those high, splashy cymbals that have a bent-up ring on their outer couple of inches, or ones with holes in them, or both. If the drummer has deliberate holes in their cymbal that are not solely intended to stop the spread of a crack, you may as well just leave the show now and go for ice cream.

As I write this, the face I picture is Stewart Copeland's. You may be right when you think it's all jealousy, because I can't play like that.

When people say "You have to be a special kind of person to be a bass player," that's pretty interchangeable with any instrument. You'd have to be a very special kind of person to have a drum kit like, say, Neil Peart's. Masochist is the first word that comes to my mind when I think about how long it would take to set that nonsense up. Drummers with too many drums in their setup just won't shut up. You can hear them noticing that they haven't hit a particular one in the past sixteen bars or so, so they hurry over to that area and filigree an irritating and superfluous roll from highest to lowest. It sounds like taking inventory on annoyance. Or maybe a kit like that is the musical instrument equivalent of a Lamborghini, or a Hummer. It says, "I have staff."

It's not just drums that are stupid. Others have noticed that drummers have something unique about them too. I winced in self-consciousness when I read a joke Lou Reed told: "What's the difference between a drummer and a pig? A pig won't stay up until five in the morning to fuck another pig."

I wasn't the singer because I could sing, I was the singer because I wanted to be in a band and couldn't play anything. But now that I think of it, I was also the drummer who couldn't play anything. Still am, more times than I wish were the case, but I still formed a band. How hard could being a drummer be? When I began, I was unaware of what kind of curse I was bringing upon myself. Unwittingly, all that tappy-tap on my lap along to records was training my brain to separate out what each of the limbs was doing, making my right foot know it was the sound of the bass drum, my left hand that of the snare.

Getting all your limbs to coordinate and interact is the real trick, and my impediment has always been my left foot. When I saw there was a movie called that, I expected it to be about a drummer's predicament. That limb is often not listening to my brain's instructions.

It may have been different if I'd grown up with jazz being much more than an inkling in my vocabulary, but it was not. My left foot was never trained to keep time — my schooling was the thud-bang of the Ramones. Actually, my schooling was one lesson in which we started with only a pencil and notation score. When I told the teacher I didn't want to learn that, I just want to learn to play, he asked incredulously, "How else can I teach you?" When I replied, "Show me," his expression was that of a person trying to get a cat to bring them a burrito on command.

I wouldn't say that I wasn't paying attention to drummers until I started along the path to being one; I was attuned to all the instruments equally. The bass player might catch my ear in the intro, the guitarist in the verse, and so on. It was pretty rare that I'd be wowed by just one instrument in any song, but once I started playing, it was pretty obvious that certain drummers and particular songs had imprinted on me in an overt way.

I didn't think I'd ever play like Ian Paice on Deep Purple's *Made in Japan*, or Buddy Rich on the variety shows I'd seen him on when I was a kid. I gave up on that before I even tried, reasoning, rightfully so, that it was unachievable.

It was only after I started drumming that I'd listen to a record anticipating what the performance would be, my focus attuned in advance. Before that, it was rare for a specific drummer to grab me. There are ones you notice because they're so famous, like Ringo Starr, who also happens to be a wonderful and inventive player. But there is so much invisible magic: turns or fills in songs, or moments where the drummer does something so pivotal that it becomes the axis on which the track rotates.

For example, the Temptations' "Ain't Too Proud to Beg" opens with one of the most elegant and expressive fills ever, a brief flash of a dynamite trick in which one instrument hands you over to the next slam, in this case the powerful emotional wrench of David Ruffin's voice. But that drummer was invisible to me. What I pictured was the drum kit, not the drummer. Greats Benny Benjamin and Uriel

Jones were not credited on most of the Temptations records, the hired hands to the main attraction, despite creating the structure on which everything else would hang. Part of their artistry was in making the songs they played on direct your body how to respond, being the golden thread weaving through a tapestry and giving it strength, direction and sparkle.

Like so many formative Black drummers, they were unseen by me. Some of that was the circumstances of growing up in a white British family in a predominantly white British city. Radio was diverse, surprisingly so in the 1960s, which meant you heard a lot of soul and funk. In the knockout break of the Jackson 5's "ABC," where the beat turns inside out, there was no drummer seen, just the J5. Drummer Gene Pello got no credit. The only Black artist that others played in our home was Harry Belafonte, my mother having such a thing for him that she sold our basement toilet to buy a ticket to see him live. I was more inclined to buy records by Herman's Hermits and Alice Cooper. As I grew up, drummers I responded to were less about gyrating hips and more about slouching, swaying, or ping-ponging about madly, or inflicting a Neanderthal thud, a reflection of the very white world I grew up in.

The first drummer I was gripped by was Sandy Nelson, or more specifically an extremely scratched, sleeveless seven-inch single of "Quite a Beat" and "Let There Be Drums." Both tracks are almost drum solos, with injections of Link Wray–styled riffs that give the whole thing a dirty basement feel, of a white dress shirt with stained collar, classy and nasty at the same time. A bass chugs along, sexily mimicking the floor tom pulse and roll. The drums rise when the instruments drop away, sounding as if in a controlled canyon, cinematic and anticipatory. They steal around after dark and smoke cigarettes. The extra percussion from an overlay of scratches on the scuffed surface injects an anxious tension of sheer ambient noise. The lacerating hiss adds to the greatness of this single and its huge impact on me. I never once thought of Nelson's performance as something I could achieve, but I'm getting closer every day.

Before music arrived at a codified genre specifically about speedy tempos (basically, hardcore), you latched onto that velocity wherever you could. It was rare, and Deep Purple's "Highway Star," from their 1972 live album *Made in Japan*, blistered. It was the sound of long hair whipping in the wind while driving recklessly fast. The churchy organ knocked down spires, oozing with bacchanalian frenzy, all shirts open. When I was eleven, Ian Paice excited me so much on this record. His rolls and fills revved me up, a music equivalent to my Hot Wheels Supercharger, a station that you'd place along your track that'd spit your car out the other side at triple the speed. As noodly-doo as the guitar leads on it are, this record anticipated the speed of punk rock.

With the forced departure of Woody Woodmansey from the Spiders from Mars, Bowie's first album without him came with a blazing spotlight on drummer Aynsley Dunbar, mixed so hot that he's practically in battle with Mick Ronson. David Bowie hadn't had such a combative sound in his instrumentation since the untethered band on *The Man Who Sold the World.* On that record, their free reign drives them to David's most fantastically excessive arrangements. *Pin Ups*, in 1973, is differently indulgent, David unleashing some of his highest drama as his anxious and opulent vocals swoop up to the most over-the-top vibrato and squeal. The group match him in vivacity, everyone tight and propulsive. Dunbar is cut loose in a way David had rarely allowed with drummers, breaking down "See Emily Play" into a dizzying stumble that is all theatre, never in danger of actually falling over. He plays the sleaziest drag for Bowie's hot cover of the Who's "I Can't Explain," a sexy slink that gave the version distinction. David's cover was all Quaalude ooze compared to the Who's original amphetamine rush. Dunbar had been in the Jeff Beck Group and was a Mother of Invention, something I'm glad I didn't know at the time because it would have coloured my listening. He was one of the most exceptional elements of *Pin Ups.* I was captivated by what he played, squirming over the thrill of so many precise and dynamic moments throughout the record. It was the first album where the drummer held my focus for the entire album, over multiple listens. Aynsley Dunbar had been in Bowie's *1980 Floor Show* band for *The Midnight Special* too, the only drummer in the world who could make "Space Oddity" supremely heavy but somehow still discreet.

There's no doubt that Woody Woodmansey is a part of me more than Dunbar though. I was so deeply into Bowie through the run of albums he played on, from *The Man Who Sold the World*'s proggy flamethrower arrangements to the fabulous cocaine anxiety of *Aladdin Sane*'s "Let's Spend the Night Together." The beautiful fade-in of his eulogistic drum beat in *Ziggy Stardust*'s opener "Five Years" reveals one of the greatest drum riffs ever invented. It was the out-of-reach beat I focused on first as I learned how to play. Fifty years on, his are records that have some of the deepest emotional resonance for me, so significant in my most crucial years when an album could be an intense and obsessive journey, a place to go and be consumed. David Bowie's records did that for me, and I found myself in an inconceivable place the day after David died.

Tony Visconti, the producer and exorbitant bass player on the brilliant *The Man Who Sold the World* album, was performing that record live on tour with its drummer, Woody Woodmansey. I was somewhat reluctant to go because of not really wanting to hear their singer do David's parts. But seeing the original players perform that LP live was just too much to consider missing, the only likely opportunity for me to ever experience that. The day before the show I was shocked awake with the news that David had died. I was to meet Visconti for dinner before the show with a friend who knew him, but the world's media needed Tony, and he wasn't available after all. The band agreed that playing was better than cancelling, and the news added a stunning, tragic poignancy to the songs, every past feeling from them fully present in my body. They were indulgently moving and great.

Tony Visconti came out and invited us into the dressing room after the show. I was in an extremely heightened emotional state from the significance of everything that had just happened. Maybe ten or twelve people surrounded Visconti. The band's ride would soon be arriving to take them to their hotels, and the other group members hovered, waiting. I noticed Woody standing by himself on the other side of the room. It was hard to know what to say about David, knowing how Bowie had dumped him so coldly. I went over and said hi, telling him how important his playing had been to me, how formative and crucial those records were to me. We talked for maybe three minutes, finally just looking into each other's eyes with our love for David reflected back at each other. I said, "I'm sorry for the loss of your old friend." We both squeezed out a couple of tears and then hugged for longer than strangers usually do. He wasn't a stranger to *me*, and in that moment his feelings were on the surface too. I could have never imagined this moment happening.

Paul Thompson has entranced me from the first day I heard him, on Roxy Music's debut album. In the more than fifty years since its release, his performances continue to reveal new nuance that my own experience attunes me to in a heightened manner. His playing is powerful in a way that is rare for such detailed players. You feel the swing and oomph of his unusually low bass drum, his precise blur of snare fills making a continuous sound that defies what can normally be made by stringing individual hits on a drum together. He drops ghost notes into his bass drum performance without ever cluttering things up. I come back to "If There Is Something" over and over as an aspirational masterwork, the great span of time since its release only enhancing its beauty. The song shifts from a cartoony cowboy filmic romp into an expanse of yearning, a driving fever that suggests an endless road ahead. His part is deceptively simple as the song breaks down, paradoxically melancholy and motoric, leaving Thompson as the only musician to keep the song moving forward. It took me more than twenty years of listening to realize the shift in character during the song's drum break was an edit, its change not even subtle as the drums precisely lift the haze into which the song's protagonist has fallen.

When you work in film or TV, you are tainted for life by the revelation that everything is faked, that a scene is rarely happening in real time. Every edit is a construction, almost every line of dialogue overdubbed or redone to enhance audibility, every passing plane or gust of wind placed there by a Foley designer. Learning music production is a similar deflator. What was once a mush of sounds, a *feeling*, is now a series of individual instruments with treatments that define the space in which they exist, or the character of their command.

Paul Thompson's drumming made me think about the character of each individual drum, how they form a conversation when played together. Much like casting in a film, each drum speaks in a different way, and his detailing of their voices to be complementary to their partners is as artful as his brilliant playing. The sound of his drum kit on *Country Life* and *Siren* indicates that producers or engineers finally recognized that every one of Roxy Music's members was a distinct voice that strengthened the whole. Thompson was never more prominent in the mix. His use of timbale as snare on one of their biggest hits, "Love Is the Drug," allows the beat to be loud and cutting without the harsh brashness of a traditional snare's buzzing wires. He sits distinguished but perfectly integrated in the musical landscape. His ghosted kick-drum patterns and rolls combine elements of jazz and Latin percussion. He remains one of the greatest players ever.

Billy Ficca, the drummer for Television, caught my ear in a different way. It took me a while to decipher what it was that made what he played so unusual. His choices were baffling, his embellished hi-hat curlicues unlike any other player. Details in fills that are always reserved for the toms or snare were different when applied to the hi-hat. It's miraculous that he did this without adding obtrusive treble to the mix, somehow controlling it and giving it a slippery quality. I can instantly tell when a drummer has been hugely influenced by Ficca: it's the hi-hat that gives away that you have learned from what he invented, or at least made his own. On Tom Verlaine's magnificent first instrumental album, *Warm and*

Cool, Ficca plays a master class in mood, falling like rain or scurrying intently like an ant colony.

Buzzcocks inverted the common formula of the guitarist or keyboard player being the virtuoso while the drummer merely kept time. Their songs would have been insanely catchy no matter what, but John Maher's wildly expressive playing made him practically the lead instrument. Steve Diggle and Pete Shelley chorded and plucked the hookiest leads, "Boredom" being a brilliant example of how two alternating notes are enough to carry a lead part. But the wild cyclone tearing through all their songs and giving them infinite propulsion is John Maher. Already great songs were made timeless classics still revered today by the perfect playing of their drummer, and the band's chemistry. When he left the group, we heard instantly that he was irreplaceable, a key component in elevating Buzzcocks' astonishing string of singles to perfection. Maher is one of the rare instances where a lead drummer enhances rather than detracts, and I suspect it's because of that magic mixture of experienced and inexperienced players making music together, creating something previously unheard or uncommon in the process.

In my own development as a drummer, it was imperative to keep the song going forward. Writing and playing songs in a band was concurrent with learning drums. There was no time to get great or even passable, because the band is happening *now*. The most important thing was to try and keep the song consistent in tempo, and not fall off the track as we raced around it together. Never stop. Tommy Ramone and the Cramps' Nick Knox were my mentors, but played with opposing approaches. Tommy cranked away beating sixteenth notes on the hi-hat, accelerating through every song in 4/4 time. It was classic pop performed at an almost mechanized, dizzying clip. He went to the part of the drum kit most obvious for the part: sixteenths on hi-hat for the verse, sixteenths on the floor tom for the bridge, and sixteenths on the ride cymbal for the chorus. Tommy's parts were almost snap-together modules interchangeable between multiple songs. He gave the songs an extra bump of speed, menace and, with practice, a goal a beginner could reach.

Nick Knox did the opposite, wringing threat by playing less, slower. Cramps songs had him hitting his drums only a quarter as much as Tommy Ramone did. The Ramones prided themselves on being dumb, while Knox was a role model for those who were simple, like me, who were better at mustering four hits every four bars than sixteen. His reductionism was thrilling, a true shining star in the formation of punk's ethos of minimalism and distilling music to its primordial essentials.

The Runaways had been a huge influence on me as a teen, but even I recognized that their drummer could sound stodgy and slightly lumpen. But I had complete love for her because *she could play*! And was playing in a fantastic band by the time she was sixteen! As a gay boy, I related to her outsider nature, existing in what was almost entirely a straight guy's world. Sandy West played at an attainable level that I could aspire to. Copying her was the second step in my progression, further out of reach than where I was when I began making records. From innumerable listens, her parts wore paths in my brain, the nuance in every song imprinted like ancient trails through a field, the way we and others before us travelled.

Almost inevitably, I had the very freaky situation of getting to *be* Sandy West. I told Will Munro — friend, party creator, and artist/activist — that I had a contact for Runaways singer Cherie Currie, and if he wanted to bring her up to Toronto for one of his Vaseline club nights, I'd put together a band for it. It happened. The members rehearsed individually at first, then were able to have only a couple of practices with all members together before Cherie arrived at our final one. I had an out-of-body experience as, once Cherie's voice was added, we suddenly became the Runaways as they sounded in 1976, the details of their recorded performances embedded deeply in our collective memory. I didn't play as myself; it was like my body played a record, or at least the drums on that record. The record was the Runaways' *Live in Japan*, me channelling Sandy.

Later, another drummer I saw myself in was Georgia Hubley of the wonderful Yo La Tengo. She plays as a melodic instrumentalist, creating parts and patterns that transcend timekeeping. Alternating between conversing with and mirroring the bass or guitar, she weaves parts that sound like language, the beats syllables. As the song moves forward, her role in the conversation shifts. Her patterning is often circular, rolling rather than subdividing a song, with emphasis pushing and pulling varying parts of the bars. Being a left-handed player, I watch her in what feels like a mirror, my reflection anticipating where on her kit she will go, what she will do. I noticed that she avoided my pitfalls, the specific patterns I have yet to play with sufficient competency.

Foremost in this is the classic disco pattern of alternating sixteenth notes as a roll on the hi-hat, with every fourth beat being on the snare, like "YMCA" or "Don't Leave Me This Way," for example. Stephen Morris of Joy Division/New Order is a master of this beat, but often plays it so fast that it becomes a distant relative of dance-floor bacchanal. He's shockingly precise and meteoric, never falling off the precision trajectory he launches and maintains over the course of a song. It's no surprise that he integrated mechanical rhythms in his setup, already being a man-machine without the extra click-track.

Hubley introduced this elusive beat into her repertoire with the song "Autumn Sweater." After its release, I waited to see her play that song, maybe revealing to me how I too might finally be able to play that part. I laughed when bass player James McNew sat at a second kit, playing the part I had attributed to Georgia. Now when I see her play, what I often notice is that that is how well I would play if I practised more.

One of the great benefits of working in a used record store was that, especially before streaming, the entire world of recorded music was available as a library for you to study in every day. I'd heard "Cissy Strut," but one day, *The Meters*, that band's 1969 debut album, rolled through the shop and lit our turntable on fire. Long before I was a player, drummer Ziggy Modeliste's phrasing grabbed me, like *What the hell is he doing in that part?* He was laid-back, deceptively so, because he constantly dropped asides into the conversation, understated details that gave the lope a little lift. His New Orleans funk playing had a stoner vibe — sexy and with a joyous grin, more loopy than the gold-standard speedier funk of Clyde Stubblefield. His parts are among the most fun ones to play and have helped me have an element of swing, or at least to know how good his drums patterns feel physically when you reach the trance-like state they put you in.

I love drum machines. I love the rigidness of them, the unforgiving, relentless nature of their exactitude that makes you so aware of your constant drift as a human timekeeper. There is an extreme satisfaction that comes (to me) when you feel that you are so locked into a sequence or tempo that you could be a machine. But then you hear what you played, and you can't escape the fact that for better or worse, you will never be as tight as the robot. But it's humanity that gives a song tension, whereas the machine is more about glide and predictability. I love that drum machines come with their own distinct mood, like the somnambulantly threatening pulse on Palace's *Arise Therefore* album, or the frenetic majesty of Plastikman's first couple of albums, comprised only of drum machine.

For years, I somehow didn't even recognize Kraftwerk's Wolfgang Flür as a drummer, despite having seen him live and on video. I thought of him as a scientist, or aesthetic object. It took reading his autobiography to realize that he was, in fact, a traditional drummer but using tools that were unknown to audiences. While Kraftwerk caricature robots, Flür elegantly invented a new way of playing, an approach that anticipated the future and ultimately put him out of work, replaced as he was by an actual machine. *And that's why I never use self-checkouts.* What Flür introduced was a softening of the attack inherent in acoustic drums, a machine-like gentler clink and rounded splash. As their masterwork "Autobahn" illustrates, a mood shift to a fast, more frenetic part can be inverted, making it skip the surface of a road or lake rather than dominating and pummelling it like any acoustic drummer would. Contrary to the common idea that mimicking machines drains humanity from a performance, I find it's often quite the opposite. Rather than being a stick hitting a rock, Flür glissades across the horizon, a sewing machine that through a series of precision incursions weaves something surprising, beautiful, and poised.

My first real drum kit taunted me by so dramatically inflicting the expectation of a heightened level of professionalism and ability. The broken-down assembly of drum parts that I used in my first year of playing was suddenly redundant when I won a new drum kit. Well, I didn't actually win it, but my pal Carson did, with help from me. My used-record-shop mental database and all that buying of collections had filled my brain with mountains of very specific, mostly useless information, like what colour RCA record labels were from what year to what year, or who was Canada's Yodelling Sweetheart.

Carson wanted to enter a contest at MuchMusic, our national music video channel. The prize was a drum kit owned by Helix, the hard-ish rock band from Kitchener, Ontario, most known for their supremely silly song in which the singer call-and-responses with the audience to spell out "R.O.C.K.," and then asks what you're going to do. Why, the title of the song, of course: "Rock You." Gimme an R! (R!) O! (O!) C! (C!) K! (K!) Whatchoo got? (ROCK!) And whatchoo gonna do? (ROCK YOU!) Lesser known was their 1981 album *White Lace & Black Leather*, but I knew it and it was essential information to enter a Helix trivia contest. Using my answers, Carson entered and won. He offered to share the kit with me if I'd teach him how to play drums. That idea was as ridiculous as the kit itself, a huge Gretsch setup the colour of grape soda, with giant double bass drums and two enormous floor toms, in addition to the rest of a complete kit. With a few additions, it could have easily made up two full kits. Total bonus was that each bass drum came with custom Helix head skins, painted with their logo aflame and flanked by angels' wings as though rising to heaven from hell. Not coincidentally, the album they were promoting at the time was called *Long Way to Heaven*. And an even longer way to set up and tear down such a monster.

Painted on the bass skin, next to sponsor Gretsch's logo, was their drummer's name, Fritz. Eventually Carson gave up, and for a nominal fee, the other half of the kit was mine. I left the Helix skin on the bass drum for a while, and over the years it would occasionally return. It really is a beautiful sounding kit, and made me sound better, made me play better.

One night after a show, a tipsy dude came up to me, angrily poking his finger into my chest in syncopation with him informing me, "I. Know. Fritz. And you. Are not. Fritz." "No, but I'm on the fritz," I replied.

Probably the most awful thing about playing drums is that, if you play in a band and go out and do things, you are certain to also become a furniture mover. With that come the pitfalls of that particular job. Two years into playing, when I was twenty-five, Shadowy Men were playing a show at Key West, a second-floor venue in London, Ontario. As we reached the end of our set, attempting to use up my remaining energy, I heard and felt a curious sproing, something I'd never known inside my body before. I remember even thinking, *Hmm, that was odd.* As I got up, I felt different. Never having had this happen before, I didn't recognize the now-familiar signs. The two curses of drumming are: a) poor posture and b) moving stupidly heavy hardware and cretinously large cases filled with boneheaded pieces of formed wood. I subjected myself to both of these, and awoke in the morning unable to stand upright.

Not knowing what was happening or how to move, I forced myself to do what had been easy and normal the day before. Struck by electric shocks and the most excruciating pain I have ever felt, I was stunned into submission with spasms in my back, butt and legs.

Despite the condition I was in, I still went on vacation a couple days later, and it was in a cheap Florida motel overlooking the Kennedy Space Center that I had my most serious back attack. Unable to sleep, I'd gone to the bathroom just to get the relief of movement. As I attempted to stand from the toilet, the intense spasm hit, worse than before. I clutched at the closest thing: the shower curtain. The famous scene from *Psycho* played out in a grotesquely comical way as I crumpled to the ground, each curtain-ring popping off in slow-motion succession as I fell.

That wouldn't have happened if only I'd played the bassoon instead. Drums are stupid.

The one side benefit from that is that I now have drumming posture that is so perfect, people regularly comment on it. I watch young drummers slouch and bounce, placing undue stress on their spinal discs, and my internal drum dad feels compelled to warn them of what's ahead if they keep it up. I did a couple of times, but their response made me realize what an old-guy thing it was to say. I'd think, *But I was only twenty-five . . .*

Fifteen years of playing and the associated back issues — combined with a desire to study piano and recording technique — caused me to put the drums aside for ten years. I didn't intend for it to be that long, but time sometimes moves faster than gravy. Eventually, the miracle that is the inability to remember what pain feels like caused my drumming desire to rise again. When I resumed, the years of annoying hand-drumming on my lap, and hours upon days of programming drum machines, had made me a better player. I imagined I'd be starting from scratch, but somehow I'd been moved a little further down the path to drummer hell.

Speaking of drummer hell, another humiliating by-product of playing is having to go to the drum department of the music shop. No matter what city you are in, there is always a guy who works there who rolls his r's. It's like a fake British accent, the person inserting a snare drag into every verbal sentence. "What arrrrre you looking for today? Oh, we have the Pearrrrrl one." And when I say guy, I mean man person. I've scanned my memory of every drum department where I have ever set foot, and I cannot recall there ever being a woman working in a single one.

It's easy to feel like it's not worth it, and that as long as I don't have someone moving my drums for me, I'm always going to be vulnerable to the disabling pain that comes with playing. But there is always some bastard who kicks my ass and makes me want to be better, makes me want to feel that exhilaration of being completely spent, or of feeling that extreme satisfaction when you execute an elegant transition exactly as you intended, or when you exceed your own abilities and levitate as the drums play themselves.

Around my town are Jonah Falco, Fucked Up's supreme basher, and Ian Romano, the secret weapon on the best records from the Niagara region, currently prominent in his band the Outfit. These two are simultaneously electrifying and humiliating, showing me how much further there is to go. They play with such speed and ease, Jonah appearing as though he's working at something equal to smashing atoms on one of those giant collider contraptions, and Ian looking as though he could ease back in a lawn chair while sipping a glass of iced tea mid-show and still not drop the intensely complex and speedy beat he's serving. Three limbs could be otherwise occupied and he'd still knock it out. What they do looks difficult to me, but is exciting and motivating.

When the band Phono-Comb began after Shadowy Men, I felt a sudden freedom of expression. It was almost a relief to cast off the body of songs I'd played for all my drumming life, including beats I played on the first day I ever played drums. They tied me to the past in a way I hadn't noticed before, and I was suddenly able to find a new level of expressiveness. Yet when Shadowy Men began playing again after a break of many years, it felt great to play those songs. I had busied things up in a way I hadn't even noticed, incrementally exercising my growing abilities. This was like going back to playing scales: loving the assertive danceability of an elemental approach.

For thirty years of playing, the beat I strived for drove the Buzzcocks song "Late for the Train." It seemed impossible, and every rehearsal I'd try it. I'd built up to maybe being able to play it for ninety seconds, but it was far too demanding, too perfectly played. I'd alternate hands, playing one-two-three with the right hand, then the left, one-two-three, back and forth. It was a hamster wheel, and I couldn't find the exit to do a drum fill or twist the part around. I was rigid and clunky in my execution.

Until one day, I saw an old video of the Buzzcocks playing that song and noticed that I had been trying to play it the hardest way possible. John Maher casually played right-left-right, left-right-left, playing the part as a roll rather than my unattainable and difficult approach. This in itself was a revelation to me about using economy, of letting momentum carry you rather than fighting gravity with movements that are contrary to the basics of ergonomics. It took me years to even discover that drums could be played lighter, quieter! So many things that are obvious can take eons for simple minds to unravel.

The other contemporary drummer who really throws me for a loop is Neil Bullock, who I know from his mind-melting performances on records by the group Broadcast. Without knowing who he was, I fell in love with the drumming on their records. It thrilled me that they used such extremes in their rhythms, from stiff corporal drum machines playing one-two, one-two into infinity, to the challenging falling-down jazz tumbles of a masterful and inventive kit player. Kind of like Sandy Nelson had done fifty years before, Neil Bullock spars playfully with organs and guitars, pushing and pulling in an ever-moving elastic spill of rhythm.

He is the first player I identified as playing with jazz technique who made me want to be able to do what he did, who excited me to play beyond my limitations in that unexplored realm. He is given the spotlight most prominently on Broadcast's *Microtronics* EPs, which really caused me to lament my left foot's inability to take direction. The band is at their freest here, proving to me that almost all improv music should be kept to under two minutes in duration per piece. He plays like gusts of wind, raising dust into spirals of varying shapes and sizes, rounded points that never show off but rather exercise an athletic machine operating at its peak. His parts are perplexing and mysterious to me, making me want to play and play.

Until I do — and am reminded once again how ridiculous drums are.

HOW TO KEEP PUTTING OUT THE SAME ALBUM

SO MANY PEOPLE I KNOW STRUGGLE WITH GETTING EVEN ONE album out. Shadowy Men on a Shadowy Planet didn't have that problem. In fact, we just put the same album out over and over again. You can pretty much say that about most bands and their records, but this *really* was the same record, with variations in cover art and track listing. Our first LP, *Savvy Show Stoppers*, is a compilation of our first five singles, and I've almost lost track of how many times it has come out.

We loved 45s, how focused and furious they could be. When you put all your best ideas into eight-minutes-max, singles are the ideal medium for short-attention-span songs. Get in, go in multiple directions, blaaaang, get out. Each one a burst of notes and feelings, every song an attempt to crack your bandmates up with the most ridiculous idea, riff or narrative, or improbable time and tempo changes.

Singles are perfect for rock music, in general. Nothing could be more enthralling than the ominously towering single-note lead of John Barry's instrumental 45 version of "Goldfinger," with its slashing violins and drums, the white-noise cymbals inseparable from the shower of worn-record hiss filling space on my copy. My bandmates and I were accidentally born for some of the best times for singles — as kids in the '60s high point of top-forty radio, and teens as punk was blowing up. These two major tides had the little 45 record at their creative core.

After the song, a bold element of singles was their graphic design. As much as the music itself, the engaging beauty of Ricky Nelson's "Teen Age Idol" on Imperial Records, with its colourful stars yearningly shining out into space, or singles on Liberty, their murky metallic torch radiating silver light, or Bobby Vinton's "Roses Are Red" on the warning-sign-yellow Epic label, with a hypnotic ring of tiny black bars that almost strobe as the record spins — they all captivated with their dazzling designs. The label of the record contained as much codified information as the music pressed in the black grooves.

Scads of records collected dust in my mother's basement before I claimed them. Thanks be to older siblings and aunts and uncles who somehow outgrew them. Only I was captivated by those Connie Francis 78s and the *To Sir, with Love* soundtrack that lived in my brother's dresser drawer. Soundtracks were ubiquitous, every home at the time had a copy of *The Sound of Music*, and I loved it all. I was record-crazy.

Of course punk rock, being hugely about tribal identification, was another glorious time for record art. A picture sleeve validated your band, stated your intention and alliances. The first ten or so Buzzcocks singles were packaged in the astoundingly tactile beauty of Malcolm Garrett's designs. Ditto the ephemeral newspaper of the first Public Image Limited single, inadvertently saying "Take in this news now — TODAY," for today's paper is tomorrow's birdcage liner.

A handful of local singles, when viewed together, stated that they were a "scene," all black and white with the occasional intrusion of colour: Viletones, the Diodes, Teenage Head, the Poles, the Cads, the Ugly. Consciously or not, these records said something profound and declared their nowness.

When Shadowy Men began, there was no agenda other than to play together. A record was the furthest thing from our minds, especially for me, who played drums for the very first time the day of our first bashing it out together. It was a couple of years on from the split of Crash Kills Five, the group Reid, Brian and I had been in together in the last few of my teenage years. Now, Brian played bass, Reid played guitar, and Ken, a friend from the Dead Bunnies, a band CK5 had shared many bills with, sang and also played guitar.

We got together in the basement where Brian worked, hiding our gear behind walls of archived tapes and films on metal shelving, hoping no one would notice that a rock band had infested the room no one went into, which was previously occupied by quiet mice. After only two or three meetings, Ken decided that the trek from Scarborough to our warehouse hiding spot near Bathurst and Queen was too much effort. Brian and Reid switched back to their native instruments, and with no one wanting to sing, we just kept going without vocals. Our best decision was an accident. No stupid PA required, we were completely portable and almost moveable in one car, and with the perfect number of band members before unwieldiness and impairment of function sets in. It was a while before we actually noticed we were an instrumental band.

It was June 1984, hot out, and by October, we'd played our first show in front of people. Is any band ever ready for their first show?

We never intended on playing but were more or less pushed out on stage. We could no longer rehearse in Brian's workplace, so some friends, the Stürm Group, offered us time in their space, only if we'd play a show with them. It was a nerve-wracking affair, Brian so jittery that he spent the afternoon of show day at a flotation tank. Although self-conscious about pretending to be a drummer, my face hurt from smiling after we played. We sounded so good loud, through a PA, and the audience was wildly positive.

I see ads all the time promising to teach you how to play the guitar, bass, or keyboards in just one week! What is never advertised as being something you can just play off the bat is drums, the instrument your cave relatives actually did bang around on. You're "playing" the first time your arms and legs interact with a kit.

In spring of 1985, Shadowy Men on a Shadowy Planet got an opening spot with Hüsker Dü. We were somehow so out of place in what was happening on the local music scene that we fit on any bill, or were so out of step that we at least made people curious. Other bands who worshipped and tried to play like Hüsker Dü were annoyed that such a new band — who didn't even have a singer and were still learning their instruments — were given such a coveted opening spot. I don't want to try and describe what we had, but it was usually the opposite of the rage and darkness that was the currency of the moment. Hüsker Dü were dripping with both of those things, and we stuck out like a sore potato. It felt like we really went over well, the loud positive reception a relief.

As soon as we moved our gear offstage, we were surrounded by people wanting to talk with us. One of them was a tall, skinny guy with Johnny Thunders hair. He asked if we were going to make a record. That seemed more advanced than our plans at the time, but we immediately liked him and said maybe. Coyote Shivers was an apprentice audio engineer at Grant Avenue Studio in Hamilton. He offered us free studio time if we put out the recording on vinyl. Once again we were pushed out into the light before we were ready, but of course, it was the best thing. We rehearsed and prepared as best we could, sloppily but with the freedom that comes with doing things for the first time, unencumbered by expectations.

Coyote Shivers took us into the studio to record what would be our first single, *Love Without Words*. Coyote and engineer David Bottrill massaged our nerves enough that we put down our three best songs in one day. David left Grant Avenue the following year, becoming one of the house engineers and producers for Peter Gabriel's Real World studio, producing albums for Gabriel, Nusrat Fateh Ali Khan, and Youssou N'dour. He went on to be most known for his production on albums by Tool, Rush, Smashing Pumpkins, and King Crimson, and his ability and demeanour made it easy to see why artists all over the world would want to work with him.

We went back the next day to mix, and I went into the Grant Avenue basement where, like the scene in *Aliens* where the cave is filled with incubating alien creature eggs, master tapes of Brian Eno's sessions there with Daniel Lanois filled the room.

I brought my drum kit with me, a ramshackle collection of parts rescued from the garbage. My floor tom had already been repurposed as a lamp and was now back to being a floor tom. My bass drum was egg-shaped, splintered in a couple of places from having been crushed at some point. My snare sounded like a tin can with a sheet of plastic over it held on by rubber bands, because that's essentially what it was. Dave kind of giggled when he saw it but was totally supportive, encouraging me to try some of the studio drums. He put me in an open room by myself and had me set up on a sheet of aluminum, making things brighter and with pointier edges. We recorded "Our Weapons Are Useless," "Bennett Cerf," and "Having an Average Weekend." There's a change in "Bennett Cerf" where we wanted to sound like a wooden roller coaster as terrified riders hit a precarious turn. We enlisted our pal Cindy Beattie to scream, her shriek like hot steel wheels on a shaky iron track. I wait for that thrilling moment every time I hear the song. "Weapons" was our slowest song, so probably the most competently played at the time. It was one of the first songs we'd written together, if not the first. For our last song, Brian played two twelve-string acoustic guitar tracks, giving the track a bright stereo shimmer, and a touch of melancholy.

We were all so excited to make an actual record that the three of us drove out of town to manufacturing plant Astro Records. Things were definitely more lax then, as we walked onto the floor of the pressing plant and saw a dozen or so machines stamping records. Bins of off-cuts from the vinyl filled the vast factory, and it was more thrilling than any amusement park for record freaks to see.

To design the single's cover sleeve, we built a little set in a box lined with black velvet, hanging a "rocket bank" that had been around my family home forever, an enticement from a local credit union to lure kids into banking. A sponge ball and ring of cardboard covered in tinfoil stood in for Saturn, and some metal jacks became satellites or something, all twinkly when light hit them right. Video equipment from Brian's job came in handy as we videotaped the box and then photographed the TV set we played it back on. The photo chosen for the cover was then black-and-white offset printed, folded, and stuffed in plastic sleeves with the record. A thousand records! We were off.

We sent them around and were pleased that it actually charted on campus and community radio across Canada.

Our second single followed not long after, *Wow Flutter Hiss '86*. We were obsessed with everything being dated, either to make it sound new or hopelessly outdated. It had to name the year it came out, like "Teenage Lament '74" or "1969." We tried that again a few times, like the hard-rock version we had to record for *Kids in the Hall*, "Having An Average Weekend '78," or our first organ-no-guitar song, "You Spin Me Round '86" — the year added to differentiate from the then-current hit song we loved with the same name. The *Wow Flutter Hiss* title fetishized measurable things that could go wrong on a record that affected the listening experience. It's all the shit that you first do to records when you begin playing them, like making that seasick sound by playing them off-centre.

We went into Wellesley Studios with Tod Cutler, who'd been a grade behind me in high school and who played guitar in Stürm Group. Four songs came out of those sessions, short enough to cram all onto a single. The schematics on the cover were printed inside a radio Reid owned, and the liner notes on the back were by our friend Scott Hyrtle. Scott was an inspirational carpenter we met at our shows, a smart guy who ended up starting his own newspaper and working the door for us once in a while. As insular as the band was, it was good to have other friends enter our ridiculous little world every once in a while. Scott even ended up writing a fake biography of the band, with the cruelly accurate title *The Songs All Sound the Same.*

A trip was made down to Union Station to use one of the last coin-stamping machines left in Toronto. At the train departures level, you could put a dollar into a machine and then basically typeset your message onto a medallion by turning an alphabet dial, like an oversized combination lock, and stamping the letters into a coin, one character at a time. It took a few tries to get it right, but at four dollars, it was significantly cheaper and sassier-looking than what typesetting cost at that time. And the centre of the medallion was a message of good luck and a horseshoe! Bonus. Black ink on a silver label made for a sharp-looking, small-holed label. Small holes were rare, pretty much only on imports, so it felt like a special little thing.

One of the four songs was "Theme from TV," which confused some people when we later actually did do a TV show theme.

As much as we rehearsed and spent days and years making new songs, we also put scads of time into building sets for live shows. Anything to distract audiences from looking at us, but probably more accurately, to distract ourselves from our own self-consciousness about being a band on a stage. Someone asked me once if I thought we were a dumb rock band or a snooty art project, and I love that ultimately we were both. Being a rock band is dumb: the whole thing is ridiculously self-important, especially when you are in your twenties and your place in local social structures has more meaning to you, even if you don't want to acknowledge it or aren't aware of that being the case.

We loved the "object," the art-making aspect of being in a band. Visual art was a major part of the allure of our individual foundational records. LP jackets were a beautiful medium for bringing together the sound and the feeling your own music gave you. We built sets to photograph, cut out and painted parts of record sleeves, and cut stencils together to make more and more elaborately layered spray-paint posters for shows. We wanted to make everything look good as well as sound good, with mixed results.

I heard more than a couple of times that Shadowy Men were real self-promoters, a term I interpreted as an attempted put-down. Mostly, I thought that sprung from envy or jealousy, like, why was our photo in the show listings in the paper? It was as simple as sending a photo along with your info about an upcoming show. We made visual art that a lot of people noticed, and rapidly received an inordinate amount of attention for a new band. Making things was part of the whole for us.

We built two seven-foot-tall masonite rockets, with a box mounted in the middle to hold seven-inch singles, as a sales display for our *Wow Flutter Hiss '86* record. It was absurdly unwieldy. Two of the biggest stores in the city laughed when we asked if we could put one in the store, a huge display dedicated to one local single! But they said yes, and consequently we sold a ton of records in those stores. The things that resulted from our continuous arts and crafts adventures inadvertently brought attention to us that other, frankly lazier bands in our scenes weren't getting.

We enacted any executable, ridiculous idea. With visions of Cliff Richard and the Shadows on *Thunderbirds Are Go*, we thought we should send a record to NASA with a letter telling them we'd like to be the first band in space, if they were looking for a band to play without atmosphere. Without really being conscious of it, it was performance art by us, for us. But when we told our friend

Richard, who played in the band the Dundrells, what we had done, he grumbled, "You fucking guys will probably get it too, you can do anything."

Him saying to us that "YOU CAN DO ANYTHING" had the subtext that his band couldn't. I loved that we could do anything! Of course every band can do anything, limited only by your imagination and willingness to do work. It was incredible to me how not having a singer made other people think that was true too. You have no singer, you'd be great to do my soundtrack! And so it happened.

SCHLAGERS! came next, another four-song little record, with an interlude in which we played the Dundrells song "Melinda," interrupted by a car's voice instructing you to fasten your seatbelt. That little piece was entirely inspired by hearing a car talk for the first time, a startling experience in that moment. *Wow! Let's record it and make a song out of it.* It was also a covert expression of our love for the Dundrells, the local band with whom we'd played the most, but they took it more that we had gazumped their song.

Another record, another studio. We didn't really know much about making records, and our "producing" came in the form of asking for something louder, crisper, or with more reverb. One engineer laughed at us when we asked if he could send the reverb track to another reverb. Reverb on reverb! A guy named Bill Aldred had built a snazzy pro studio in the basement of his Scarborough bungalow, Studio B, where other friends' bands had recorded. Our third record was slightly more evolved. We'd stripped back some of the excessive reverb of our second record, and added colour to our picture sleeve. Another level of design opened up as we learned to do overlays for multiple colours, and to cut Rubylith, a masking film that suddenly made putting a record cover together have more possibilities but also involved more work. Just to make every record even more labour-intensive and costly, we created a board game — *SCHLAGERS!* — partly based on a horse-racing LP and board game that Reid had, in which the metal surface of the game vibrated, causing your horse to race around the track — or, more accurately, to quiver and slide about randomly. It was definitely not a cheap, pirated rip-off of tiddlywinks. The *SCHLAGERS!* board game came with an instruction sheet, parts to cut out, and a little drug baggie filled with eight game pieces and a bolt. Brian drew the instruction sheet, while I created a disaster in ink for the front cover, cutting out dozens of little pieces of paper to act as shields for enhanced shading, using a manual air-brush trick I'd learned in high school art class. One end of the hollow, metal, L-shaped tube rests in the ink; you blow air in the other end, the volume of air determining how intensely the spray of ink flies from the tube.

Our pal Carson booked the Rivoli, where we'd played our first show, and for the next ten years we'd have a birthday party for ourselves (and audiences) there. He'd often patch his four-track cassette machine into the board to record sets. We loved the sound of the tape he gave us from our second birthday, so we made a live 45 from it to give away at our third. It was more accurate to say it was a 46 1/3 rpm record, as the master tape played back a touch slow, so the cover art was a rubber-stamped message stating that speed. I don't even recall that we mastered the record, and so our costs were pretty much just the manufacturing. No picture sleeve, but an intentionally disposable souvenir; a loot bag for people to take home. Throughout the two nights, we'd pick up copies off the dance floor, boot-smeared and crumpled; after the lights came up and the audience had left, we also found copies stuck down in the crevasse between the back and seat of the banquette that ran the length of the room. Not everyone wants a free record. It was super cheap to do and exciting to have another record out.

We thought this could be great, we'll just keep making singles forever. Unlike today, they were inexpensive and so was postage, so these picture-sleeveless diversions could be given away, the more elaborate cover and effort put into our *real* records. Of course, in the age of streaming, all these disposable tracks we imagined evaporating upon first listen now exist on a level playing field with our "real" songs.

Back to Studio B to record two songs for another single, *Explosion of Taste*. Our songs were all so short that squeezing two on one side was rarely an issue. Without question our dumbest packaging idea ever, we decided to package the first five hundred copies inside Jiffy Pop foil trays, the rather vile "instant" stovetop popcorn we'd all indulged in at least one late, altered night. More overlays, another three-colour affair, with one thousand full sleeves printed for the first run of records manufactured. After printing all of these, we then cut the back cover off half of them and used scissors to hand-cut the centre of the front out, replacing the cardboard lid of the original Jiffy Pop. We peeled back the tinfoil crimped onto the original round lid, an endeavour that took days and days and left us bloodied enough that fingers on guitar strings made a real mess.

The B-side contained an audio vignette of popcorn popping while Kitty Wells played softly in the background. The original back cover contained an illustration that purported to be an iron-on to make your own Shadowy Men T-shirt. It didn't really, and we were tickled every once in a while when someone told us they'd ruined their record cover trying to make use of the fake heat-transfer.

Somewhere around our fourth single, we were approached by Randy Boyd, a guy we knew from a booking agency he was briefly involved with. The new label he was partnered with, Cargo Records, wanted to put out a compilation LP of the singles we'd released so far. We thought it was a ridiculous idea; after all, we'd sold one thousand copies each of some of our singles. Everybody who'd ever want one, we reasoned, already had it. But we did think it was a good idea for overseas, as we weren't about to get into trying to distribute a few copies at a time over there. We could barely manage the tasks we'd already taken on for ourselves.

When *Explosion of Taste* was released, I sent it to John Peel and mentioned that we were going to be trying to find a label to compile the singles as an LP. When he played the record, he repeated this on the air, and suddenly we had a bunch of offers from labels in England and Scotland. It was so novel, a new record — an LP — and with songs we'd already recorded! It seemed like a scam, our intrinsic imperative to give value to audiences being challenged, but we were ready to participate.

We ultimately settled on a London-based label, Glass Records. We swooned when we saw that they'd released records by the Pastels, that alone practically being enough to sway us in their direction. Nikki Sudden, Spacemen 3, and the Jazz Butcher in their catalogue clinched the deal. We were smitten. Label owner Dave Barker was going to be in New York at the same time we were, both of us going for one of those pointless music festivals. The federal government even gave us a $125 grant to do our part in spotlighting Canadian culture abroad. It would allow us to meet and sign the contract we'd bandied back and forth a bit.

Times Square in 1988 was a very different place than it is now. It had squalor and magic, porno and elegance, some of the grandest and most stunning theatres and restaurants already having fallen into disrepair or in the final days of their 1950s and '60s luxurious charms, just before turning tawdry. Overlooking Times Square on its north end was Hawaii Kai, a tiki bar/restaurant over the Winter Garden Theater. The sophistication of the place was a little dusty, dioramas of Diamond Head and traditional dances lining the room. Drinks were served in ceramic skulls and tiki heads, and booths were made to look like thatched huts. It was no surprise that the bar closed down the following year, not enough distance having happened from the heyday craze of Hawaiian tourist style to save it. Perhaps it was an omen of what was to come, but at this moment, it was a grand place to sign our first record contract.

An album gave us greater expanse for cover art. An album in England and another birthday show coming were the perfect opportunity to make another sidebar record. If we made one thousand, we could give five hundred away over two nights at our shows and then ship the other five hundred overseas as a bonus in first copies of our album. These weren't tracks we thought people should be paying for.

We recorded a medley of a couple of Neil Diamond's hits, which we were about to perform live in our "Reid does Neil" shtick. The other side was filled up with our take on "Batman," recorded for Ron Mann's film *Comic Book Confidential*. The world definitely does not need another version of that song, and it should only be acquired on record for free, but we spruced it up with some overdubbed observations by Quentin Crisp.

The remaining cut was our entry in a write-a-song-for-Calgary contest. Reid and Brian had spent too many good years of their youth in Calgary at one of its worst times. Recorded live to cassette, our post-multiple-cocktails, *Bonanza*-theme rip-off song, "Friendly Town," didn't win, but was played on national radio when CBC profiled a few of the entries. That and having an actual vinyl record of our paean were more than enough of a win. I don't remember the victor, but I do remember our song, audiences in Calgary actually calling out for it years later.

We were footing the bill for all of this, wanting to have some extra neat thing for our first album, and it gave us an excuse to use the Glass logo, as it was presented as a co-release between our label Jetpac and them.

Artwork was assembled, a luxurious 12.5-inch x 25-inch space for lurid graphics. Brian X-Acto'd out the band name and title — *Savvy Show Stoppers* — and the three Shadowy characters that became a stand-in for having to show our faces. I found the retouched and oversaturated old postcard of Toronto's "new" city hall in the Reference Library archives, the Viljo Revell spaceship and semi-circular towers simultaneously gaudy and beautiful, a distinct statement that we were a Toronto band. There were so few examples at that time of bands drawing attention to this city, and we were well aware that most of the examples were cornball, silly, or overly earnest. From our vantage point, our city hall record cover was all three, while also expressing our love for Toronto. We loved Martha and the Muffins for how they showed the city on their record covers, and it was a real kick as a kid to hear Murray McLauchlan sing that he had gone "Down to the Henry Moore," referring to the sculpture that lived on the square in front of city hall. His was a real thing in a song about a real place you knew, a kind of displaced mythologizing at odds with the usual Toronto character at that time of feeling lesser-than.

There was an early punk-ish band here called the Existers that issued a single with a song on it called "Spadina," a Springsteen-ish, overwrought homage to the street that intersected with the hottest part of Queen Street at the time, where most of the live music clubs were. As ridiculous as we thought the song was, we loved the street being honoured in song. Spadina was where Reid worked his worst job for a half day, before going for lunch and never returning. Cars angle-parked on Spadina, one of its neatest features along with great delis and the city's Chinatown. Every time we drove on or passed that street, Reid would sing "Spadina! Spadina! Everybody knows, everybody finally — gooooeeeessss." I have always known Reid's version more than the Existers'.

For the album artwork we built a constellation of planets and rockets made from tin foil, cardboard, and a cheap inflatable ball, and hung them from Brian's workplace ceiling with wires. Not actually from the ceiling, but from the sprinkler system, adding a few actual amps, a bass drum and floor tom, along with a bass and guitar. None of us knew what a bad idea that was, but we got pictures of it and managed to get everything down without bursting the pipes.

Any part of making art or music that we could do, we did. Our graphic skills were improving: the album, in full lurid colour, looked like it was designed by a seven-year-old rather than the five-year-old of some of our earlier records. We put it all together, laying the layers out on fancy board and packaging it up for transport to England. Our first album! In England, even!

We waited and waited for word from Dave about the release date, thinking we might go over there to play. It seemed like he spoke quieter and quieter on the phone, as if he were fading away. One day he just stopped answering when we called. We wrote him letters, asking what was happening. Jilted, we sat by the mailbox awaiting reply. How could everything just disappear? Glass Records and Dave Barker went away, the label basically folding the day our album came out.

We didn't hear from Barker again until a few years later. We told anyone who'd listen to our preposterous but oh-so-familiar story, so our friend Calvin Johnson knew the whole scoop when he happened to meet Dave one day in England. Calvin asked him, "Hey, why did you do that to Shadowy Men? Why didn't you even send them any copies?" We'd heard that a small number of copies had dribbled out, but we'd never seen one. Dave mumbled something like, "Yeah, I shouldn't have done that." Sometime after that, a box appeared in the mail with seven or eight copies of the album, each with our bonus 45 inside, and an apology note saying he's not really very good at running a business.

It's sadly hilarious in retrospect that the only record of ours to successfully come out on Glass Records was not really a Glass record and was put out by us, our free bonus seven-inch. It was indicative of the whole fiasco.

We'd put so much effort into putting *Savvy Show Stoppers* together, and it had such a super snazzy cover, that we decided to accept Randy Boyd's offer to put the album out on Cargo. We had run out or were about to run out of most of the singles, so that justified them being an LP. Besides, they all sounded so great together, like a real album.

Cargo was a label and distribution company, a good combo in a country like Canada, where getting your records around can be costly and incredibly time-consuming, a few at a time. Their distribution in the US made them the perfect choice, and we really liked a lot of the people working for the label, usually indicating a positive organic experience. Once again, *Savvy Show Stoppers* was released.

But then they wanted more. A thirty-five-minute album should have more music when it comes out on CD and tape. Cargo wanted both of those, so the third and fourth editions of *SSS* were fleshed out with our sumptuous covers of Johnny Mathis's "Misty" and Frank Sinatra's "Summer Wind." The third add-on was "Big Baby," lifted from our score for Ron Mann's documentary *Comic Book Confidential* and featuring graphic artist Charles Burns reading panels from his *Big Baby* serial.

We now had four versions of *Savvy Show Stoppers*. And then the Cargo Montreal label started falling apart. We had a few nice years with them, doing our second album a couple of years later.

We were handed over to Cargo's Chicago office, which also had an exquisite staff. We made lots of friends there who we'd encounter in different ways over subsequent years. Our third album came out while we were working with the Chicago office, and they really helped us do some things we wanted to do.

Our publicist's name was Stacey, and after she left Cargo, she went to Capitol Records. I met up with her in New York City, and she gave me her business card for her new situation. That night I happened to go to the Tunnel to see Marc Almond, who was then signed to Capitol. When I arrived, I discovered the show was sold out. I showed them her business card as if it were mine, telling them I'm Marc's US publicist. They let me in. Sorry and thank you, Stacey!

And then Chicago Cargo folded.

We were then handed over to the last remaining Cargo office in North America, the one in La Jolla, California. When we met them, they felt like relatives we were forced to visit because they were family. It was functional, but the two main guys we dealt with there were oddballs who always seemed like they were in the wrong business. The owner, Eric Goodis, was more like a character from a David Mamet play, a businessman who'd accidentally stumbled into music, but it could have been anything. He was somewhat communicative when we were selling a lot of records, but there were hints things were not so sweet. Every other band we knew on the label asked us if we were getting paid. We were, but things were active and records were moving, so it was apparent we were getting better treatment.

When the band split in 1995, so did Cargo's attention toward us. They stopped paying us and we later learned the company had been sold to someone else. Owing us for at least twelve thousand records — a huge amount for a band at our level — we had to cut our losses. There was no legal way to make them pay that wouldn't cost us more than we were owed. We got a letter from Eric promising to pay us, but it didn't happen.

We owned the master tapes, so we cancelled our licensing to Cargo and the records went unavailable for the next fifteen years or so.

Around 2011 we got some messages from a label in Lethbridge, Alberta, asking us about reissuing our albums. We'd poked around for someone to reissue at one point, but none of our options were appealing. It was hard to even know if you were reaching someone at a label, and we just gave up. It was a stupid business and it was easier to just not be part of it. We checked out this new Alberta label, Mammoth Cave Recording Company, and watched them for a while. They were very proactive and they did things in the way that we had, working with friends and with a close community.

I dealt with many labels in subsequent things I did after Shadowy Men. I'd been screwed and supported by independent and major labels equally, so that part didn't seem to make a difference. We had been staunchly independent and worked with people — booking agents, promoters, other bands, labels — that we connected with personally more than we did from a purely business strategy. Mostly that worked out for us.

I met with the two guys who ran Mammoth Cave, and was moved by their enthusiasm. They were both so handsome too, as good a criterion as any in an unpredictable business. We knew we were taking a chance on a small label. Their bands were occupying similar spaces to what we and our friends' groups had twenty years earlier. Deluxe reissues of each our albums were to happen with Mammoth Cave.

When they announced they wanted to space out the releases, we knew it was likely a cash-flow issue for them. One of the label cohorts was working with Calgary's Sled Island music festival and asked if Shadowy Men would consider playing at the fest, coinciding with the new release of *Savvy Show Stoppers*.

Shadowy Men had ended in 1995. Reid Diamond died in 2001. There was no band. With Reid went the band. I never once thought of playing again with Shadowy Men; how could we without Reid?

On the day I was asked about Sled Island, I was working with my friend Dallas Good, who had played in Phono-Comb with Reid and me. I told Dallas I had a very strange offer: one show, in Calgary, where Reid and Brian had begun playing in bands, and where I had met them to hear Buick McKane rehearse. I asked Dallas if he'd consider playing bass for one show. Without a second's thought, Dallas said, "Absolutely."

I called Brian and told him of the idea and offer. He couldn't believe I was serious and asked, "Who would even play bass?" When I said Dallas, he laughed, saying he'd never do that. I told Brian that Dallas had already said yes. I recall Brian saying "Huh, huh, hmm" a lot during this conversation.

Even though Shadowy Men had been extremely self-contained during its time, I was less and less attached to the idea of a band being a precious thing. It should be able to be whatever you want it to be, only defined by self-imposed guides, not external restrictions. I thought of the Sex Pistols' first reunion, which I thought was a terrible idea. It was music and a band I did not want to hear in an arena setting. My idea of them was so fixed at a specific moment that I couldn't accept they'd have any interest to me in that setting in 1996.

Despite my scoffing, I still rode my bike down to the outdoor lakeside venue where they were playing. Ticket flippers were unloading seats, but I still opted not to go in for one dollar! When the sinister intro to "Bodies" blasted over the fence, I was struck by full-body goosebumps and thought, *I'm an idiot.* I should have been inside.

In 2010 the Stooges played a free outdoor show, in the most discrepant situation — Toronto's public square, in daylight, across from downtown's biggest mall. Not a place you'd want to see them, but there they were. Original guitarist Ron Asheton had died the year before, and in his place was James Williamson, another brilliant player who'd helped lead the last few years of the Stooges. Iggy Pop came out leaping, full of fire, and shouted, "We're the remains of the fucking Stooges and we're going to play some songs before we're all dead." It was delivered with so much urgency, alarm almost, like this could be the last days for *all* of us.

I thought of this when trying to decide if our own show was a good idea or not. This made me realize: it was just a band, it didn't matter. Dallas was Reid's friend, he was our family. There were no good reasons to not do it. Do it *now.*

As we got closer and closer to the date, there was no sign of Mammoth Cave's deluxe *Savvy Show Stoppers* album. They assured us things were under way, that they were waiting on this or that. I knew they hadn't even submitted the album for manufacturing when two weeks before the show, one of the label guys called me in a panic, saying there was something wrong with the album artwork. I was shocked, because what he described indicated he didn't understand the elements that had been delivered, and that he just didn't know how to open them correctly. It was obviously the first time they'd opened the files.

We'd added a second show in Toronto, our first in almost eighteen years. We had rehearsed for seven months for the Calgary performance, too much to not play our home.

Of course there were no albums for the big release shows, a witheringly common situation generally. But with communications being evasive and then eventually going silent, it was a sad and frustrating echo of the Glass Records fiasco. The label owners' personal issues had caused the whole thing to fall apart. *Savvy Show Stoppers* came out for the fifth time months too late, and it was only satisfying in that it had a beautiful package, the awful colour reproductions of previous versions made vivid and exquisite. The label imploded. Needless to say, the next two album reissues were not going to happen with Mammoth Cave, so we just gave up for a while.

Most bands in Canada feel that it's imperative to sign with a Canadian label, as it's pretty much a prerequisite to access grant money. As a defunct band, that wasn't an issue for us, so when the Sadies and other friends told us about their good experience with North Carolina label Yep Roc, we approached them. It was a relief that they said yes. Most aspects of the music business are so repulsive that I've learned if things are not flowing easily, they will probably always remain in turmoil. Yep Roc proposed a box set first, including our three albums plus a new compilation of the stray tracks we'd put out: compilation cuts, singles, soundtrack bits, home tapes and such. Once again, *Savvy Show Stoppers* was released. Like a Liz Taylor marriage, maybe the sixth time would be the one that stuck!

Technically it was the same run of records manufactured, but the seventh time it was released was as a standalone months later. In many ways, this last version was the most satisfying. There were no problems, and the people we were dealing with were all meticulous, on the ball, and delightful. After so many editions of the same album, there was some kind of sense of accomplishment with this one. We'd finally got the album right.

That people were still interested in this record was quite astounding, particularly when, more than thirty years later, new audiences were the same age we were when we made the records. As with everything that has happened regarding the band after our breakup, the regrettable missing element is Reid Diamond. But our dumb surf band and/or snooty art project still somehow had resonance.

Reid's death becomes more profound with each passing year, as his age at passing seems to get younger and younger, the gap between where we are now and where we were then wider and wider.

The current one is probably the last reissue we have left in us, the rewards both creatively and financially diminishing. If I ever think another reissue of *Savvy Show Stoppers* is a good idea, I'll line up all the released versions and reread this catalogue of buffoonery.

WENDY COBURN

WENDY COBURN SAT BY THE WATER'S EDGE AT A MUTUAL FRIEND'S wedding. The ceremony was over and people chatted and mingled over drinks, taking in the beautiful view of the city skyline from Toronto Island. The rolling contours of vertical towers made the city look pretty, a panorama made to be seen from this vantage point. I spotted Wendy sitting by herself, a wine glass in her hand, her back to the guests circulating around the lawn next to the clubhouse. She gazed solitarily at the opposite shore.

I went down and asked if I could take her photo. She sort of half-smiled and shrugged, "Okay." I wanted a few pics, one of her as I first spotted her and maybe another with her head turned so that you could see her face. After a couple shots of the first scene, she said, "No, no, let me take your picture." She stood up and directed me to sit on the folding chair she had been on, and to pose for her. I only ended up with two frames of her, almost identical to each other.

In the images captured, I was struck by not only how unreal the city looked, everything bathed in the softest blue-grey light with just enough cloud to add drama without threat, but by how rarely I look at our skyline and think it's actually beautiful.

It was 2014, in the midst of a middle-aged growth spurt, the city becoming uglier and blander with each bad new architectural choice, all replacing something that was distinctly more beautiful. The Royal York Hotel, once the tallest building downtown, now partially peeked out from behind the growth around it. The singular intrusion on the skyline in a photo I shot in 1967 from the same vantage point shows one of the new TD Tower buildings, the Mies van der Rohe–designed towers that must have been stunning for people to take in when they were new, the only towers downtown at the time. Black monoliths stretching into the sky, they are shockingly futuristic compared to the Georgian and Victorian architecture that made up most of Toronto, and must have jarred many when they first viewed them.

At the bottom of the photo, the lake wall is capped by an iron band, giving the whole scene the appearance of being a pull-down screen, like one of those maps of Canada once found in every classroom. It's a seemingly serene moment.

I didn't know Wendy that well, but she was clever, witty and sharp, with an air of melancholia. As well as being an instructor at what was then the Ontario College of Art and Design, she was a dynamic visual artist. A few months after the wedding, she had her first major solo exhibition at University of Toronto's Barnicke Gallery, a stunning collection of new work, the centrepiece being a video entitled *Slut Walk: Anatomy of a Protest.* In the video, she documented the first two Slut Walks in Toronto. The first was in response to the words of a Toronto police officer at a public safety forum following a series of sexual assaults at York University's campus. The cop advised the attendees that "women should avoid dressing like sluts in order not to be victimized." This prompted outrage and sparked the peaceful protest as a way of owning, defusing, and bringing attention to the victim-blaming inherent in the inflammatory comment.

Over two Slut Walks a year apart, Coburn's video shows a crowd with creative but angry messages. But in amongst the throng were people who drew attention to themselves by being camera hogs for the media, wearing silly outfits and costumes that helped conceal their identity, and carrying nonsensical signs. She turned her camera on them, sensing something was off. Eventually she realized that at least some of these people were cops, agent provocateurs who were riling people up and trying to incite the crowd to violent action. A familiar tactic already, this same strategy was known to Torontonians from police action during the G20 protests in 2010.

Wendy eventually asked some of the individuals if they were cops. Smirking and responding with intimidating body language, the ones she confronted disappeared into the crowd, but reappeared other places in new outfits. Their behaviour and footwear gave away that they were indeed the same people.

Her 2014 video exposing police techniques for infiltrating and undermining social justice protests resulted in unwelcome attention, with a system of surveillance allegedly put in place on her street, at her workplace, and on her phone. I say "allegedly" based on what Wendy reported to others, but her evidence was pretty compelling.

In my photograph of her, she has her back to the camera, a stance that limits interaction, keeps herself at a remove.

The following year, she made the choice to end her life. It's hard not to speculate that what she experienced was a significant factor in this decision. Was her feeling of safety and security compromised in a way she felt she couldn't recover from? Could she not bear the scrutiny from authorities? The veil was lifted: the idea that police are there to protect you was corrupted. Did Wendy just know too much, too clearly, about the reality of the illusions we must carry inside us to be okay with just moving about the world, interacting with and trusting others?

In taking photographs for more than fifty years, I am frequently struck by the changing meaning and feeling contained within a photograph. Over time, what you see evolves, even if the fixed image itself does not. Pictures that once held the fire of wild youth, people high on their own primal energy, or friends just doing things that indicate that the time we have is infinite — they all change.

Photos I took of Reid Diamond pretending to off himself in a gas oven were once silly gestures that mocked death and any idea that we would actually choose it. Those photos have a completely different feeling now that Reid is gone, dead from horrific bouts of cancer, and many of our closest friends have made the choice to end their lives. Our youthful naivety is revealed in the fact that it's not even a gas oven! The idea we would actually gas ourselves was so foreign that we missed that detail.

The notion that death could be played for laughs is something you can only really fully get into when you haven't experienced the reality and pain of it.

I have a photograph of Frankie Venom and Gord Lewis on the wall of my studio, in a place where, when I look up from my work station or out the window, I see it. This picture of Teenage Head live at the Horseshoe Tavern in 1978 exudes untamed potency, and the reckless abandon with which Frankie threw himself about the stage, an adrenalized contortionist utterly focused on being in the moment. Gord is behind him, effortlessly cool in a sweater and sunglasses equally in place on a high-fashion granny in 1960s Paris as they are on him, his Les Paul poised for full sonic assault. Like more and more people in my photographs, they are no longer here. The image now takes on the melancholy of memorial. Frankie died in 2008 while dealing with throat cancer. Gord was murdered by his own son in 2022.

It's the beauty and the curse of holding any moment as a still image. It will all crumble eventually; nothing will remain the same or be seen the same way twice. I think of these photographs and people often when I take the streetcar across the Queen Street East bridge over the Don River, and read the text of Eldon Garnet's art on it. "This river I step in is not the river I stand in." The passage of time reminds me how truly and deeply constant those words are.

THE MENACING THREAT OF SELF-DETERMINATION

PHOTO BY LISA KANNAKKO

IN 2013, ARTISTS ALLYSON MITCHELL AND DEIRDRE LOGUE CREATED a fantastical installation called *Killjoy's Kastle*. With a large support cast, the physical environment was built in a large warehouse, based on evangelical Hell Houses but devoted solely to the "horrors" of lesbian culture. The space was perfect for the Kastle, a labyrinth of rooms with creepy nooks and crannies, and staircases leading to tiny crawlspaces. I was thrilled when they asked if I'd do the sound design for the project. A series of vignettes would each depict some aspect of queer feminist history, with a bonkers haunted-house twist.

Undead women decked out in coathanger couture haunted the alleyway, moaning to those waiting in line, "My body, my choice, aaaarrrggh" as they stumbled slowly, back and forth, looking for solace, comradeship, and relief from their existence. I made sound environments for maybe fifteen installations, and the audience was escorted through them; narration about what they were seeing provided by "demented women's studies professors." One stop had a giant clam looming above, its gaping wet maw threatening to swallow passersby, accompanied by slurpy sounds and a horrifying musical soundtrack. In an icy room of mirrors, ghosts whose sheets ended at their waist laid back and shone flashlights into their vaginas, craning hand mirrors to get a better view in a distorted reflection of Annie Sprinkle's well-known performance piece.

Two of the inner dioramas in this funhouse featured manipulated soundtrack collages of existing music, layered with horror sounds and messed up in ways to make them off-kilter, inducing queasy unease. I played DJ to accompany a "Riot Ghoul Dance Party." Ghastly goblins in outfits signifying the early-'90s revolution danced around a cauldron to nauseous takes on the greatest hits of the riot grrrl movement, confronting and intimidating guests.

Another beguiling display featured a few elderly lesbian grannies nestled in rocking chairs and knitting contentedly in their yarn-cobwebbed den, soothed by a mixed-up soundtrack of lesbian oldies. These sisters were retirees from the Michigan Womyn's Music Festival, nostalgically reflecting on their youthful hedonism.

Researching artists whose songs I would use as raw material to petrify was a treat. I was aware of some musicians in what was defined as the "women's music" movement of the '70s from examining and listening to their LPs at the used record store I'd worked at, or from encountering their names over many years of paying attention to, and investigating, queer music histories. There was a time when every older gay man I met had a Jane Olivor album in their home, but the burgeoning women's music scene was more overt, and became increasingly empowered as the artists creating it found more and more sympathetic women to support each other.

I approached my research with a forty-year-old bias, a judgment that blanketed a wide variety of recordings with the ignorant viewpoint of youth. I lumped together many of the tracks I heard as one thing: overly earnest folk songs that were the musical equivalent of herbal tea. Too light, amateurish in their cover designs, and wildly variable in musicianship. The voices were remarkably similar: trained vocalists skilled at vibrato and with a soft white touch, accompanied by too many percussionists and usually a pianist who was accomplished but sounded more at home in a Sunday school class than on an insurrectionist's stage. They sounded old and laughably outdated, even though many records I'd heard had only been made in the last five to ten years.

My favourite records by lesbian singers were older than these, and if they were coded, it was too subtle for me to see then. Long after their hit-making eras, Dusty Springfield singing about the only man who could ever please her, or Lesley Gore testifying that she knows her boyfriend is cheating — but, sigh, what can she do? — upended perceptions about themselves when they acknowledged their queerness. Even Joan Jett was singing about checking out a guy at the record machine, years after the folkies in the women's movement were delivering unambiguous messages of same-sex love and tenderness.

Starting around 1969, women in various parts of North America started forming collectives to share their experiences. Many of the artists had roots in folk protest songs, union activism, and the civil rights movement. One of the most well-known singers to arise from this scene was Ronnie Gilbert, previously of chart-topping group the Weavers. Formed in 1948, her band, which also included Pete Seeger, was eventually blacklisted from concert bills, tracked by the FBI, and vilified as communists. A strikingly similar eye was cast on Canadian folk troupe the Travellers, who had a big hit with their Canadianized version of Woody Guthrie's "This Land Is Your Land." Pete Seeger had worked with the Travellers too. These folkies posed a menacing threat to authorities, booking agents, and record labels. Canada and US customs agents ensured they would prevent them from contaminating each other's countries with messages of unity, fairness and co-operation.

For weeks leading up to *Killjoy's Kastle*, I listened to all the defining albums that had previously passed through my hands: Meg Christian's *I Know You Know*, Cris Williamson's *The Changer and the Changed*, Alix Dobkin's *Lavender Jane Loves Women*, and more. Those three had clear connections to their folkie predecessors, with acoustic guitars gently delivering their news. While the music was in a vein I rarely listened to, I began to find unexpected connecting points.

Meg Christian's live recording of "Ode to a Gym Teacher" had the audience roaring with laughter, her sly delivery amplifying the embarrassing teenage love, its deliberate over-earnestness now revealed to me as its strength. She catalogued her pubescent feelings and expressions of desire for the teacher: "Well, in gym class, while the others talked of boys they loved, I'd be thinking of new aches and pains the teacher had to rub," and ending with "So, you just go to any gym class, and you'll be sure to see, one girl who sticks to teacher like a leaf sticks to a tree, one girl who runs the errands and who chases all the balls, one girl who may grow up to be the gayest of all." Me and the women on the recording cracked up over this, with me reeling from the boldness of this being on an album from 1974.

A song that really captivated me was by Alix Dobkin, called "View from Gay Head." A rousing sing along, it was led by a jaunty flute and a chorus of singers whose pitch varies wildly. And the lyrics! They sing in the choruses that "any woman can be a lesbian," presenting the wild idea that when you've had enough of male society, there is a welcoming place for you. It's true, any woman can be a lesbian. "So those sexes do battle, they batter about, but the men's are the sexes I will live without, I'll return to the bosom when my journey ends, where there's no penis between us friends"!

The overtly sincere and powerful message of unity was simultaneously comical and breathtakingly convincing in its ownership of separatist ideals. Rationally, I was against separatism, believing all are stronger united in community and inclusivity, but this song was like a slap, and more in line with my always increasing awareness that so many of the awful things in the world are committed by men. It's men on TV behind most wars, behind control of women's reproductive rights, who are perpetrators of gender-based violence. Men are fucked — who can blame any woman for wanting to be a separatist?

As I dug deeper, I heard "Angry Atthis," a song written in 1969 by Maxine Feldman — a month before the Stonewall uprising and apparently the first song to use the word "lesbian." She doesn't just say it, she wails it, proclaiming that she's "no longer afraid of being a les-beeee-annnnne"! She rerecorded the 1972 single release for her 1979 album, *Closet Sale*. Things were clearly blowing up in 1973, as the all-female label Olivia Records was formed by a group of women, including singer Meg Christian, and Redwood Records was founded by Holly Near. These labels, and the artists who released records on them, were primarily lesbian, causing conflict between the earlier women's movement and lesbians; older feminists felt they were co-opted, or that lesbians would be a deterrent for general audiences. The women's music scene was already rife with dykes, but now that they were singing about their sexuality, some felt it was a threat to the integrity of their original messages of equality and organization.

These women were committing radical acts of community, and I was blown away that this independent label scene predated what I usually thought of as the heyday of independent labels: the explosion of punk rock in 1976. While there have always been self-run and independent labels, this was a scene that I thought was criminally underrepresented in the entirely male-dominated record industry. Music I had previously heard as slightly embarrassing and square sounded fresh and unchained. I thought of how sisters hearing these songs for the first time, when they were new, must have freaked out that these words were spoken or sung aloud! I was now hearing some of the amateur sound on records from these two labels as inspiring music of invention and self-determination. So many women played congas or other drums, self-taught or taught by peers because of lack of access to music instruction. Music teachers were more often than not male, particularly with drums.

I was struck by the fact that these drummers started the same way I had, not knowing how to play and entering into a group situation with a democratic instrument. In fact, the whole scene had all the same elements as punk rock! There was an urgency in not waiting until you were traditionally competent before going into the studio to put your tracks down. This new feeling made me hear records I had previously been dismissive of in their true light — as actually being radical and groundbreaking. The amateurism contained on those songs was something to be celebrated.

I thought about what gay men were doing from 1969 to 1978, and it was completely different. Sure, there were anarchist collectives that sprung up, and fringe movements like the Radical Faeries, but for the most part, men were focused on getting laid, not working together. All genders had outliers who fought for equal rights, but it wasn't until the AIDS crisis started in the early 1980s that men unified as a strong group of activists. While women were organizing and supporting each other, men were getting down in cruise bars and discos, indulging in the sexual freedoms recently achieved, more keen on satisfying themselves.

Alix Dobkin's 1973 album *Lavender Jane Loves Women* was released on her own label, entirely produced and performed by lesbians. Recorded on four-track, the record's engineer had never recorded music before! And Cris Williamson's *The Changer and the Changed*, released by Olivia Records in 1975, went on to sell more than half a million copies. How is it she's not known and revered by independent music historians everywhere? The actual music can be a barrier, but so many circumstances around these releases add to my love and respect for these artists and what they created. It's exciting, to me, to see a timeline unfold within a community that is creating its own infrastructure. By 1975, an all-female sound production company, Woman Sound, had formed, and that same year, two distribution companies for getting the scene's music around sprung into existence, Goldenrod and Ladyslipper.

D.I.Y. is usually put into a contemporary perspective, with people participating often feeling that they are the first to do what they are doing — and often they are, because there are always unrepresented groups who are compelled to get their message out. There is always new ground to cover. What is usually called Do It Yourself is actually D.I.T.: Do It Together. Women empowering each other by example created something substantial and amazing in the early '70s.

The punk explosion wasn't created in a vacuum, and it's time these radical, visionary predecessors received more due for their revolutionary actions. They were selling their 45s through the mail, and one at a time at concerts, long before Rough Trade or Quintessence Records. The early women's music milieu was part of paving the way for the next revolution. When punk began, women were in bands in numbers never seen previously.

Somehow, technical roles have not caught up though. Sound, lighting, and stage production are still woefully and overly male. Organizations like Girls Rock Camp are incredibly valuable resources in adjusting that balance.

I wrote something down that I heard in an interview years ago, forgetting now where it came from. It neatly and beautifully summarized the scenes I was now swooning over as "not a sound, not a type of music. It's a consciousness, a sense of ourselves, who we are."

THAT TIME I WAS A GAY HAIRSTYLIST

FOR YEARS I'D MADE A LIVING BY MOSTLY FOLLOWING MY URGES. Before the musical economy really collapsed, that was okay. I'd recorded and mixed lots of records, composed music for a couple of TV series, scored lots of short films and a few feature films, did a few themes for shows, and really explored the photographs I'd shot in the past but hadn't printed or scanned. I played in a couple of bands, had two books published, and generally loved the way I was able to work.

After a long period of scoring music in isolation, I was feeling the ennui that sets in when you don't have enough social contact. I'd been self-employed since I left my record store job in 1988, and was fortunate enough to have not had a straight job since. Around 2013, that feeling of freedom that comes from a self-directed life started to change. Productions were paying less and less, and the principle I'd always worked from was evaporating. I loved being able to work with friends or young bands for free or cheap, as long as I could balance that out with the occasional good payday.

That equilibrium shifted, with sudden catastrophic drops in income resulting from broadcasting moving to digital streaming, followed by music streaming becoming a thing, paying next to nothing compared to a single terrestrial radio play. Anyone who's been creating things that support them financially knows that all those little bits of work from the past supplement current income to something livable, if you're lucky. Most of those bits eroded into non-existence.

I was always appalled by the hustle, found the act of pursuing friendships for social advancement not to my taste. I'd experienced so many colleagues becoming competitive and aggressive in their hunt for attention or money, in a repulsive way. I know that idea seems quaint now, when social media is all about the personal hustle — but with the payoff being some kind of attention or validation, rather than actual money. The personal became the product, an echo chamber of Likes.

It was a surprise to get to a place where I wanted a regular job, something I'd go to and then leave behind. I wouldn't be consumed by writing music in my head while sleeping, or distractedly going over something I was writing in my mind when I was watching a movie. I craved social interaction after years of loving only occasionally working with others.

A few friends who were barbers seemed to be living an ideal life. They made good money, had lots of interesting conversations every day, and had the flexibility to play music too. The guest spots they did in other cities appealed to my urge to travel. Working and travelling was pretty much what my life had been for twenty years, and I missed that part.

Forgoing the other musician cliché of becoming a tattoo artist, I decided to train to be a barber, but that wasn't as simple as it should have been. The province of Ontario's laws were in flux; I just happened to enter the fray at the same time as new licensing was imposed on barbers. Trying to find training was hard — hardly anyone was offering it, and there was no certification for barbers. "Cosmetologists," meaning hairstylists and pedicurists who worked in salons, were required to do training and exams, and pay annual fees to maintain their licence. "Barbers" only had to buy a pair of clippers. The two were now being rolled into one category, under the title "hairstylist."

Trying to navigate licensing was a ridiculous house of mirrors, with few of the people in charge really knowing what was going on, what was required, and what the reality of the business was. The College of Trades, who issued the new licence, told me I had to get a certificate from a recognized program, but first I should do an apprenticeship. That made no sense. Who would take on an apprentice who'd had zero training? I set out to find an apprenticeship, but instead heard stories of how fucked the system was. I received as many sets of advice as places I approached.

A barbershop I'd been to multiple times was run by an old guy who was often asleep in his chair as I passed by, sports blaring on the TV. I gave Vito my résumé and asked if I could apprentice there. In less than a second he said, "No, the other chair is for my son" — a son I'd never seen once in my fifteen years as a customer. He looked at my résumé and said what I'd been thinking: "Why would I hire you? You have no experience." He told me the College had recently been on his back to get licensed, something I was hearing a lot. "What are they gonna teach me at seventy-eight? They're crazy." Licensing meant that every old guy in a barbershop would be required to do new training and exams.

One of the beautiful pleasures of touring in a band was getting my hair cut in other places, or getting a shave when I suddenly caught myself reflected in a window and saw how haggard I looked from days of not sleeping enough, being out too late every night, eating crappy food, and expending all my energy. I loved beautiful, old, or unique shops, classic barber shops like Astor Place in New York, a subterranean village of barber stalls, each customized like a little home reflecting the personality of the barber. Some would be covered in Kiss memorabilia, cheesecake pinups, or barber kitsch like old razors and signage. That spot was like some kind of outsider art gallery where you could also get your hair cut, a freshening-up to make you feel lighter on your journey. Or the more than century-old Geo. F. Trumper shop in London, its custom-built wooden stations and gorgeously maintained ancient fixtures creating an environment where I wanted to linger and come out smelling like one of their house-made colognes, the only time I ever wanted to be scented in that way.

And the haircuts! It was no coincidence that the movie *West Side Story* came out the same week I did, its rival gangs sporting immaculate pompadours, bald-fade flattops, all the styles that signified some kind of place in social hierarchies or occupation. Men's hairstyles of the '50s and '60s always caught my eye, especially on faded display photos that had been soaking up the atmosphere for a half-century in some antiquated shop. You'd just point at the picture to say what you wanted. I loved greasers' and military cuts.

The erotically intimate nature of haircutting appealed to me too. I'd never shaved another man's neck before, but many men's necks turned my head, the fine taper of an immaculate fade emphasizing the contours of their head. A barbershop was one of the few areas of overt masculinity where I felt comfortable, an aesthete's alternative to sports or cigar clubs.

Acquiring a hairstylist's licence meant having to go to some verified school. Learning how to do French curls, perms and roller sets, colour theory, and elaborate sectioning — all were the furthest thing from any goal I had. But I rationalized, thinking it might be fun. Visions of Cindy and Kate in the B-52's were my inspiration. Wouldn't it be cool if I could do that? Plus, I was playing in the band Long Branch with three women. I imagined myself blow-drying and putting a curl in their hair in some mid-price hotel room as we toured about.

Barbering was part of the program, so I thought get in, learn it, get out. But this was no quickie course. The fastest of the ones I could find was nine months long. I had just begun scoring a TV series that would mean working full-time and going to school full-time. And playing in two bands. But it had to be done.

Every school had horrible reviews. Almost no one seemed to have fondness for the school they attended. I chose the most preposterous one, located in the food court of a nearby trashy mall. The idea of going to this loathsome place every weekday for that long sounded like torture, but there was a slight appeal to my sense of black humour. There was a pretzel kiosk in that mall. And a record store, a forgotten branch of a once popular but now extinct chain. I'd grown up with this mall, from before 1973 when it was only a plaza. I bought my first cassette deck at the Consumers Distributing in the plaza, and my first two pre-recorded cassettes the same day at Sam the Record Man: Todd Rundgren's *Runt* and the Velvet Underground's third album.

I went for a tour of the hair school and saw a side of its director that I would never see again. She laughed and was friendly, encouraging. That all changed the day after I handed over a series of postdated cheques to pay for nine months of training.

School was to be fifty percent theory, fifty percent practical. "Practical" was the most impractical situation — working in their salon staffed by students with varying degrees of ability. Day one was in a classroom that would serve as our home base for the first month. Most months of the year, the school would have an intake of new students, so the attendees ranged from newbies like us to those beginning their ninth month, the bitterest of all students. I'd find out why.

My cohort was a United Nations of personality types, one of each archetype: the party girl always nibbling on a bagel she'd bought in the mall cuz she'd slept in; the bleached-blonde, brassy gal from the new condo developments, looking for a fun career that she'd eventually abandon to become a mortgage specialist; the Hello-Kitty-obsessed young woman, tall and lanky with a sweet personality but always a bit confused by what was going on; a young person who dropped out early in the program, who cried every day from social anxiety and their chest binding being too tight; the studious, sheltered mama's girl who didn't know how to use the subway; and a mature student — the other male in the class — there on the government's dime networking for his burgeoning tattoo business. A veritable Breakfast Club of misfit odd lots.

Our teacher was half an hour late for our first class — a regular occurrence, we were to find out. Nearing the end of a pregnancy, she'd giggle before every late arrival and early departure and say, "Baby brain!" We lost an hour of class time each day as she flustered through lessons and came and went on a schedule that would have resulted in expulsion for any of the students.

On day one we unpacked our new kits: a blow-dryer, curling iron, hair colour bowl and brush, bobby pins, a rubberized apron, and an 18-inch stack of large study books. Each of us was given a name tag we were to wear at all times. When I saw that mine said Donald, I laughed inside. The only person to ever call me Donald was my mother, when I misbehaved as a child. I felt like I was in some existential theatre piece, and Donald was my stage name. I took on the role of playing the hairdresser, which felt correct because this wasn't anything I'd have otherwise chosen for myself. I would sometimes look behind me when someone called me Donald, not knowing for a second who they were talking to.

"Just for fun," the instructor gave us all salon mannequins, those dead-eyed heads with a full head of hair sourced from some person with fantasies of growing their hair to sell for a fortune, only to find out it pays three dollars. First we had to take the head to the washing stations to shampoo and condition the hair, learning how to massage the customer's scalp in a pleasant way. Of course, with the head detached, it was a little more like cleaning paint trays after you've spruced up your living room. We then towel-wrapped the damp hair to keep the client dry while leading them back to our station. Our results looked like an impromptu first-aid course. Back in the classroom, the heads were fitted onto a clamped device that allowed for swivelling. I wondered if Vlad the Impaler ever did anything like this with his head collection. Day one we were cutting — and by that, I mean our fingers.

Each morning, school began with all the students in the main salon for attendance and lecture, instructors berating students for having a grey tassel on their shoe or purple piping on their blouse — piffling infractions of the school dress code, which was all black. I was definitely the oldest student there, and my presence amused the twenty-year-old women who'd left their babies for the day to start a new career. I related to them, because I was doing the same with my cat at home.

Either the director or one of the instructors would lead the opening. Many days it was just a tirade of shouting at the top of their voices about the stupidest things. Me and one other mature student were the only ones who didn't have patience for being treated like a child, but she was more direct and would talk back to them, eventually resulting in her expulsion. Pettiness was at the top of the agenda for every interaction instructors had with students.

The days dragged as we learned the pH balance of hair, and what the various parts of a hair strand and scalp are called. Our first instructor was giggly and flighty, sometimes stern but mostly sweet. At least she didn't yell. Our classroom time was generally in month-long blocks with one instructor. After three weeks of introduction, our teacher took maternity leave, so rather than have someone new finish the remainder of the basics class, we were sent onto the floor to cut people's hair. For most of us it was our first time ever.

I pushed for clients that wanted barber cuts, but it was first come, first served. My hands trembled as I sectioned someone's hair and tried to do what had been only partly explained to us. It was an ordeal designed to fail. Customers were already mostly hostile because they thought the student often didn't know what they were doing; students were nervous because, well, they almost *always* didn't know what they were doing.

My very first customer, a man, said, "You seem nervous, do you know how to do this?" When I told him he was my first-ever customer, he asked to see someone else. Next day, the instructor yelled at us to never say you aren't experienced. "Even if you've only ever cut one person's hair, you are experienced."

Our four weeks on the floor turned into five because of our lost basics week. We were given a quick tutorial on hair colouring before any of us knew the full extent of what was involved with that, and how things can suddenly turn bad. Probably seventy-five percent of the clients came to the school for regular root touch-ups to their dye job. I was scolded: "Never call it dye, it's hair colouring." It was really the only service that was of good value, as all the others didn't include the cost to go somewhere competent to have your bad hair treatment fixed. I quickly realized that recolouring people's roots, in an ongoing attempt to extend their previous colouring job, was the cash cow of the school. Students had paid a lot of money to churn out touch-ups over and over again, always at the expense of actually learning how to do most services.

Who would go to the food court of a mall to get their hair done? Lots of people, it turns out. It was a weird mix, and when we arrived in the morning I was often reminded of *Dawn of the Dead* as creepy crowds desperate to hide their grey pushed against the accordion gates, anxious to be first in.

While all the instructors were competent, a petty culture of punitive punishment permeated the place. Even the "nice" teachers would follow the example of the other instructors, permission granted to scream at students as loudly as they could over the smallest of inconsequential grievances. The matriarch of the school was an elderly Japanese woman who everyone only knew by her first name. Close to eighty, she constantly moaned about hating the students and the school, complaining that the curriculum had been corrupted so many times over the years that the education was fairly useless. It seemed that she either felt the school couldn't function without her, or more likely, her identity was so tied up in it that she couldn't imagine what else she'd do with her time.

School was a daily spectacle of rights violations that would shut down most businesses. The matriarch would often complain to students that they were too fat, too slow, too stupid. It was an archaic system of "motivation," meant to inspire students to somehow magically know how to do the absurd braids or sectioning we skimmed over, like every other subject. One day while two students were attempting to create an up-do on a mannequin head, the matriarch asked them where they were from. When they both replied Iran, she scrunched her nose and made a face, saying, "I don't like Iranians." Paradoxically, she was the instructor most respected by the students, partly because of her age and skill, and partly because these cruelties could be delivered in the sweetest tone. She was not warm, but exuded something that made you want to please her, to do good work and receive her approval.

Each service had to be inspected and signed off by an instructor before you'd allow the client out of their cape, free to roam the mall. Instructors would always say that you need to have a vision before you begin, know where you are going. I had never once in my life looked at any woman's hairstyle and imagined how to achieve it. They harped on us to connect the hair, a term that had some kind of vague meaning that I only understood after a significant amount of experience. No one explained it.

I had a woman client one day for a haircut and blow-dry. The client seemed quite happy with her new cut at the end of the service, giving me a great sense of relief because she had mostly been hostile since arriving. The matriarch came to inspect the cut, combing out and extending the hair to see if it was all the same length. As she did, she kept turning and making a disgusted look at me. "What are you thinking?" The hair was uneven in places, no surprise given my inexperience. Usually that was no big deal, because the instructors would always do some touch-up fixes and the cut became acceptable.

In this case, the teacher started cutting. And cutting. There were times we could clearly tell that her vision was not good and, oh boy, this was one of them. After another inch was cut off, the customer asked her to stop, saying that she was quite happy with it before it was "fixed." The teacher kept going, repairing the unevenness that she was now creating. I was smiling inside as the crabby customer got more and more irate until it was her yelling at the instructor, who yelled at us. Raging, the woman left and, like most customers before her, there was no tip. The rare clients in this shitty salon thoughtful enough to tip would leave between twenty-five cents and two dollars, a deflating insult after how hard you'd worked on them.

An hour later when school let out, I walked with a fellow student who'd sometimes give me a lift home. There was the irate customer waiting for the elevator to the parking garage. She saw me and gave me the most deliberate fire-breathing glare, which had the inverse effect and caused me to burst out laughing at her terrible haircut and miserable face. These small pleasures and subversions were what got us all through.

Our lunch break was only thirty minutes, barely enough to get your food and eat it, but they'd always tell us this is standard practice when you work in a real salon and *never* get a lunch break. The terrible stores in the mall were small consolation, and the tiniest pleasures helped me survive another day. At least there was the record store, a typical mainstream dump for crappy headphones and Kiss toys, but it was something. A grounding force on an otherwise bleak day. But even that crumbled. One day it closed, its ghost sitting empty for a couple of months until suddenly, the saddest of businesses opened in its place: a whole store dedicated to nothing but fidget spinners. I'd overhear kids from the local schools, who wasted as much time in the food court as the clusters of seniors who were there every day, excitedly telling each other about the deal they got on one of these landfill toys.

A stereo shop a couple doors over was also of interest, as I was in the market for a new TV set. After a few months of eyeballing what was available, I bought one. The shop then immediately closed down, almost as though he were holding out for me to make that last purchase before he could lock the place up.

The mall had way too many hair salons, for some reason. Months into the program, it became obvious that another function of the school was to provide a steady stream of exploitable and naive workers looking for their first salon job. The best students would be recruited from the current cohorts, all lasting no more than two months — until they realized they were not only making no money, but were again being taken advantage of. I wasn't surprised to discover that the plethora of salons were owned by the school.

The default was to talk down to all the students, treat them like children, which did not sit well with me at fifty-five years old and having little patience for this immature professional modelling. Many of the teachers avoided talking to me in that way, most of them being younger than me; my age provided some kind of shield for their worst behaviours. When another instructor left, a snippety pinched-face marm about ten years my senior came to teach. He had dyed hair, a lifted face, and a permanent bad-smell expression. Unlike the other instructors, who we called by first name, he could only be addressed as Mister. For the first few days, I thought of him as possibly a peer, another old queen who might relate to me on some level more than a teenaged woman. This was not to be. He established hierarchies immediately and let me know that I was a mere student. Like the others, he screeched at the students about how stupid and disobedient we were.

We were doing more colouring than just root touch-ups by this point, doing full dye jobs and more labour-intensive — and sometimes fun — colour bleeds, balayages, highlights. You had to look for little things to enjoy. Most of the time it was the camaraderie of my fellow students that made it tolerable.

Regulars had their preferred hair colouring notation on file, and teachers always approved your materials and goal colour before you mixed it. One time, the student who had previously recorded my client's hair colouring had drastically missed the mark, writing something on their record that was way off from the desired shade — but I didn't know that, and neither did the instructor who approved my colour concoction. When the customer freaked out, it was obvious there was a mistake, but it was too late. Her honey-gold brunette was now a witchy shade of night and dirt.

Two instructors yelled at me, even though it was obvious, even to them, that it was their fault. I had a signed card from the first one who shrieked at me that had given me the go-ahead with the colour. I was getting angry that I was being made the scapegoat, them passing the blame to the inexperienced student. Then Mister had a go. He yelled and called me an idiot for choosing that colour. I was enraged and told him two instructors had already yelled at me for this. It was their fault, and this low-rent school's poor management and instructors were the cause of this. I suspect he was not used to students talking back, because from that day, he inflicted spiteful vengeance on me.

Despite having only one jar of Barbicide for every ten students, hygiene was constantly harped on. Disinfectant spray was something I'd learn about when I started working in a barbershop, not at the school where we should have been using it. We were constantly nagged to never use a comb that had not been sanitized: always use a new one if you drop it. As I was standing nearby, Mister came up to my station and picked up one of my combs, looking at himself in my mirror. He made eye contact with me as he drew the teeth through his hair, fluffing and coaxing his coif into neatness. He then placed my now-unsanitary comb back where it had been to use on another customer, an act that would have made him melt down at any student.

My next punishment client was an older lady wanting a perm. Mister brought her to me, his glee uncontainable at what he was about to inflict. While the process itself was horrible, and my inexperience caused it to drag on for twice as long as it should have, we chatted as I sectioned, curled, and pinned the grid of future curls on her head. So few customers were friendly that those who were really helped the situation not feel so dispiriting. Something she said made me ask where she'd grown up. In London, she replied, where she'd been a teen, crazy about music as the mod explosion was happening. She'd seen the Who and the Small Faces, and was sent to reform school when she started "dating" someone in the Yardbirds!

I could converse easily with elderly clients and started being given more of those, despite my protestations that barber clients were what I needed. I pulled my big equipment case over to the space-helmet hairdryer she was under, turning my kit on its side so I could sit with her through the drying and hear more about her adventures. I could totally picture her as a sassy eighteen-year-old, something the nineteen-year-old students at this school didn't yet have the vision for.

Those clients were a rarity.

Another was an eccentric local singer-songwriter getting her colouring done. This was the longest I'd ever spoken to her, our chat being about local music and the state of being a musician. I had a lot of respect for her inventive style and motivation, even if I found her music hard to listen to. She was sweet and kind and asked for me on future visits. One day I saw my picture on Facebook, shot with a janky camera-phone zoom. The photog was someone I knew of but didn't really know from the music scene, a friend of friends: "I think I just saw Don Pyle working at the salon I went to." It was a curveball to everyone else as much as it was to me.

The pettiness of the school and our mistreatment put me in a juvenile state of mind. I exacted revenge in the brattiest of ways. In the hallway to our locker room hung a gallery of perfectly styled hair photos. Some were ads for the school, others just random salon garbage. I would nudge a few of them every day so they were crooked, wanting to illustrate the disorder forced on us. Our minuscule salon stations didn't have nearly enough room to work without banging elbows with the clients and students next to us. The mirrors were too narrow to be very useful. I was offended when, one day, the administrator went around and taped up an ad on each one for some hair colouring product they were pushing. This left only a tiny sliver of mirror on each side. These ads the clients and I were forced to look at every day were offensive enough that I had to take action.

There were more of them stuck up around the rest of the salon, four variations for each of black, red, brunette, and blonde. I peeled one off the wall when no one was looking and snuck it home. After scanning, I cropped out their model and replaced it with someone I'd enjoy looking at, a face who'd make me smile and have a laugh inside, even if no one else noticed. It was to save my own sanity.

The first model was replaced with the Velvet Underground's golden-tressed Nico, her head slightly turned, with perfect hair and a professional's poise. This coolly glamorous picture made the ad look completely real. The next day, giddy with petulance, I sneakily peeled the ad on my station off and taped up Nico, her icy gaze and neutral expression almost making her appear complicit. I felt better about the annoying ad situation for a couple of days, but knew I had to keep going. That weekend I made three more variations.

The brunette was replaced with a rare glam shot of Patti Smith from the photo session for her album *Easter*. It's rare to see Patti in blue eyeshadow and black mascara, so at first glance, she was convincing as a model. On closer examination her hair was just a little too dishevelled, a manicured chaos that looked intentional, but far from the wholesome whitebread model she had replaced. Her tank top was a taupe dinge, her full breasts clearly visible through the top, and a peek of armpit hair that eventually caused at least one customer to comment that that model looked "a little rough."

For the black-hair-colouring ad, Siouxsie Sioux seemed quite appropriate. She was also convincing as a real model, but her excessive makeup was veering into drag in the conventions of mainstream advertising. I laughed at my own cleverness when it occurred to me that a drag queen should be next. I found a fantastic photo of Lady Bunny in which her face appeared as a tiny peekaboo inside an immaculately coiffed window of giant hair, a chilly platinum candy-floss confection styled out of what had to have been ten wigs.

These four became my team, and I stealthily set about replacing the real ads. One by one they came down and my adrenaline increased each day, anticipating being busted. Incredibly, almost no one noticed. Over a couple of months, only two of my customers recognized someone on the ad. "Is that Patti Smith? How did she get on an ad like that?" One day a classmate saw me switching an ad. She had no clue who the people on my version of the ads were, but she was amused by it. I swore her to secrecy — so she immediately told my classmates. This definitely turned the heat up, because all that giggling raised suspicion.

After two months, our hair-colouring instructor was speaking with the one gal I'd told. They were just chatting in a friendly way, but as the instructor lingered, her eyes set upon Lady Bunny's flawless visage. All you had to do was look to tell she was a drag queen. The teacher burst out laughing and, perplexed, asked "Who did this?" Without a second of hesitation, the student blurted out "Donald." I'd saved all the original ads so I wouldn't have some disproportionate punishment foisted on me for destroying school property. The teacher came over to me, and as she did, she started noticing all the other wonky ads. She laughed almost uncontrollably as she tried to wrap her head around what was going on. After she stopped laughing for a moment, she said, "I love this, it's so good, I can't believe you did this. But you have to fix it. Now." She was afraid of the school getting in trouble with the hair-colouring company, or worse, the evil school administrator, the one who was only nice until she got my payment.

As we neared the end of our nine-month cycle, the hairstyling became more challenging. We did messy up-do's for weddings, grids of pin curls, nine-strand braids, back-combing and volumizing, oblong roller sets, and the closest thing to my B-52's fantasies: French finger waves. It was only the finger waves that gave me any sense of satisfaction, everything else seeming like randomly invented methods of torture for both client and student. French waves were like a challenging sculpture, and it took days before I could create an acceptable finished product. When they told us early on to envision the end result before we began, this was one of the few times I could, the wet-look switchback of tight-to-the-head, rock-hard hair being familiar from 1940s glam looks and contemporary high fashion. It was labour-intensive and methodical, but looked great in the end.

For the exam at the conclusion of each learning module, we'd have to find a model to come in and have a service performed on them. This wasn't always easy, as many people weren't available at 1 p.m. on a Tuesday or whatever. I put the word out whenever I needed a model, and was tickled when Mickey Skin responded to my plea for my final exam. I had come to know and become Mickey's friend over time, starting from first seeing her as the lead singer of the Curse, the fantastic and inspiring 1977 group who may have been the first all-female punk band in North America. I loved her band and had seen them play many times, starting from about age fifteen. The Curse were heavy, confrontational, and fun. Back then Mickey had a medium-length haircut that would have been described as tomboyish. For this exam I had to wash, colour, cut and style the model's hair — a bit of almost everything we'd learned so far. I suggested a dark burgundy colour to Mickey, not so far off from her long, gorgeous natural brown. It was subtle but bold. I thought she'd look great in it.

As I washed her hair, I was struck by how weird this situation was. Not only was I now a gay hairdresser, I was doing fucking Mickey Skin's hair! The bonus of working with someone you really like is that the process can be a great social experience, and guards are down when you're doing something so intimate. A couple of hours later, after colouring and cutting her hair, I set up for the final phase: blow-drying and giving the beautiful hair she had tumbling down past her shoulders a wave, set in with a round brush and some product. I started laughing as I dried her hair and prepped for the finish. I told her, "Mickey, if sixteen-year-old me could see this happening now!" I could have never imagined *ever* in my life that one day I'd be doing a full hair service on Mickey Skin, of all people! Of course she laughed too, saying, "Me neither." She looked fantastic and I got top marks for the exam.

It was not uncommon to see students having breakdowns in the food court, another student rubbing their back as they sat at a table dirty with cold McDonald's fries. Other students would cry over a cigarette in the back lane behind the mall. And others would get high every day, smoking pot while hiding within the wall of weeds that covered the mall's perimeter wall. No one loved school. If it was preparing you for a future working in a salon, it came with the message that a salon was an awful, soul-destroying place to be. Not even half the students I knew went on to pursue doing hair, all of them either discouraged by the demeaning way their apprenticeships treated them, or the lousy wages you'd have to accept until you got faster and better.

The week we were to do barber training was cut short on both ends, so the entirety of it was three and a half days. When the students complained, the school got an instructor to bring one of his regular clients in after hours to watch him cut the guy's hair. All of this just to get the stupid licence I needed.

When I completed the program, I was hired by the best barbershop in town, in large part because I had just had training. Being a punk helped too. I watched and learned from real barbers, unsurprised to find that almost nothing in the education I'd paid for was of practical use. A couple of years later, the misguided hairstylist licence scheme was abandoned, barbers once again free to roam with no training or licensing. The thought of the wasted money and time I'd put into a bogus hairstylist's equivalent of a puppy mill was angering, but maybe it was the path I needed to take to end up where I wanted to be.

A couple of times I've deliberately strolled past the school, slowing as I passed to see if any of the instructors I had were still slinging it. Inevitably, some terrorized student's eyes would lock with mine, their expression unmistakably saying, "Please save me."

STEVE ALBINI

ONE OF THE BEAUTIFUL THINGS ABOUT BEING IN A BAND IS THAT it creates a reason for you to go to those places that exist in mythology, the towns on maps that you might only know from a Stompin' Tom song, Buck Owens albums, or because there was a massive explosion at a gas storage facility there.

Everyone in Toronto knows Windsor. It's the place you pass through to go somewhere better, or where your friends who've been rejected by every other university they applied to end up.

Shadowy Men on a Shadowy Planet went there to perform, as bands once did. It's wildly unpredictable how many people will turn out when you book shows in certain towns, but it's great to be surprised. Those oddballs ended up being some of my favourite concerts.

Our show was in a tavern on the Detroit River, that waterway most famous for catching fire now and again. Due to some geographical anomaly, this Canadian town was south of Detroit, and the view to the other shore was of the twinkling lights of hard industry, flames lighting up the night sky in the same way that Hamilton's did: toxic and romantic at the same time. We played this place twice; I don't remember if it was the first or second time, probably 1987, and maybe fifty people showed up. It was early enough in Shadowy Men's life that we didn't have albums out yet, just singles, and we always sold a bunch. We chatted with a guy who bought vinyl, a sleepy-eyed dude in sweatpants and glasses. I can't remember why I had his name and phone number on a piece of paper and how that connected us to him later, but we'd cross paths with Dave again.

We suddenly received a flurry of messages from friends and acquaintances. "Oh my god, have you seen the new *Forced Exposure*?" The US-based magazine had published an interview with Steve Albini, asking him what he charges for recording, how he determines his price. As part of his reply, he said he'd charge Depeche Mode a million dollars but that he'd do Shadowy Men "for beans." I was kind of startled that, of all bands, he'd named us. We didn't know him, had never met him. Given that his current band, the confrontational Rapeman, was as aggressive and abrasive as his previous band, Big Black, I'd wrongly assumed that he'd think of us as cloying and annoying.

Then a postcard appeared in the mail. It was a promo card for Goya guitars and was from Steve. He clearly stated that he liked our band. We somehow had a cluster of interest from Chicago. From Steve's postcard, we learned that the guy at that Windsor show,

Dave Viecelli, was now living in Chicago with Albini as his roommate. Those singles had spread through a bit of the music scene there and people knew who we were.

Another letter arrived, this time from Rebecca (Beck) Dudley, someone else we didn't know at the time. She asked if we'd come to Chicago to play at a "special party" she was having. As all musicians are made pliable by flattery, we replied that, well, since it's a *special* party, yes, we'd come. A follow-up clarified that it was to be the reception for her marriage to John Mohr, just in case that was a deterrent. We'd played a couple of weddings and had a slew of songs that wouldn't drown out the clinking of forks on wine glasses, so plans were made to go to Chicago. We got in even deeper when she asked if we'd consider recording some *special* songs for a seven-inch to be given to wedding guests. We polished up a bunch of potential wedding favourites, including themes from *The Odd Couple* and *Love Story* — and of course, the staple of every horrid wedding we'd been to, "The Bird Dance." Recorded in our garage on a Portastudio, we sent the tape off and suggested they have custom napkins made as a picture sleeve.

The wedding was months away, so in the meantime, I became friends with Beck via increasingly lengthy letters to each other. She revealed that she was the drummer in a band called M.O.T.O. and her husband-to-be was in Tar. When we heard them, we immediately asked M.O.T.O. to come to Toronto and play some shows with us.

We'd been looking for someone to book us in the States and had been directed to a guy named Boche. We'd heard that Dave Viecelli had also started booking bands, so I called them both to find out what was possible. "Hi, is Boche there?" "This is Dave." "Oh hi, do you guys know each other?" Like some kind of James Bond episode, the covert agent revealed his double identity: "I'm Boche." His Billions Corporation agency would go on to big success, booking Nick Cave, the Jesus Lizard, and Pavement, among hundreds of others.

We arrived at Lounge Ax, the wedding reception venue that was instantly one of our favourite clubs. The party was packed with the warmest, most welcoming humans, a sweet reflection of the lovely people Beck and John are. We made so many friends that night, people with whom we are still close. Among the guests we were introduced to was Steve Albini. As far as you could imagine from the caustic persona he sometimes cultivated, Steve was hilarious and animated. The show came with a bit of pressure because of the number of musicians there, ones we knew from records or magazines. But we were prepared, and it thankfully wasn't one of those nights when lack of sleep or nerves catch up with you and you play like shit.

In our set around this time was "Autobahn," the immaculate Kraftwerk song. I'd one day realized that "Autobahn," when played with guitars and drums, was basically Link Wray's "Fat Back." It felt corny not long after we started performing the song and we soon dropped it, but that night, Steve Albini danced to us playing it, with a huge grin.

Aesthetically, we loved the sound he'd achieved on other bands' records he'd engineered, very much in line with what we'd mostly unsuccessfully tried to capture: a live band in a live space. We not only had a room full of new friends in Chicago, we had a booking agent and a recording engineer who seemed well matched to us.

We booked some time at Steve's studio, then located in his home. It was US Thanksgiving, and we were fairly oblivious to Thanksgiving being such a big deal in the States. To us it was like Easter or Mother's Day, a day when you'd get together with local family and friends for a good meal, but definitely not a day that comes with the same baggage as Christmas. We arrived to find that Steve had cooked us a spectacular turkey dinner with all the sides. We set up our gear in the basement's live room while Steve and his then-girlfriend ran up and down the stairs, tending to the gravy and the microphones. The kitchen and dining room were alive with one of the best feasts we'd had in ages. I can't recall what he was making in it, but he had an industrial blender on his counter with two settings: "fingers" and "rocks."

From things he said to us, or that I've heard or read over the years since, we were an ideal band for Steve. We were a trio, his favourite format, and were extremely well rehearsed and efficient. No overdubs necessary, just straight to tape. We didn't use drugs either. Although he expressed being open to accommodating whatever a band brought to him, he had clear judgments about drug users and time wasters, or more specifically, drug users who waste time. He told us that he drank for a brief period of his life, but didn't like who he was when he did, so he stopped. He smoked cigars and played billiards and was confident and bitingly witty, verging on macho compared to how we carried ourselves. When we met other Chicago people in his company, you'd see how others would shape themselves into an acerbic reflection of who they perceived him to be, to appear cool. He was liberal and smart, and we had a great time recording. Our first session was brief, maybe five songs, which we used for a single and a couple of compilations.

He wasn't a full-time engineer yet, and one of his regular jobs was as a photo retoucher. He showed us some of the things he worked on, skillfully and meticulously altering pictures of people, landscapes, and products with a two-haired brush. When I asked about other things he'd worked on, he described retouching Belinda Carlisle's thighs on her debut album cover. Belinda had lost weight for her solo act, appearing on the cover in black tights. When I see that album around, I always picture Steve and his paint brush creating Belinda's stick-thin thighs.

Steve owned an old punch clock, rubber stamps, and a barista's coffee maker, all indicating his appreciation for archaic, overly elaborate and singularly functional equipment. We connected over our mutual love for stationery stores before chains took over, when they were all old, and good for finding a self-inking Shred rubber stamp. Chatting during a pause, he said, "You know what I'd really like to get for this place?" I replied without pause: "A pneumatic tube system?" He lit up, jumping from his chair with a laugh. "Bing!" he rang, like a bell.

His living room had a display case of oddities, ancient medical equipment, and sticks of dynamite. We'd used our Shadowy Men on a Shadowy Planet Worldwide Inc. Visa card to pay for something, and he thought it was hilarious that we had a band credit card with that name on it. I'd received an updated card just before we left for Chicago, so I gave him the expired one. He opened the cabinet and placed it in a prime point of display, under a light like a precious jewel. He then gave us a bag, kind of like my mother would before we left on tour, but instead of date squares, there were small sticks of dynamite in it: quarter sticks. He explained that these were perfect for when a venue refuses to pay what they owe you, or you need to exact some kind of covert revenge. Once lit, water wouldn't extinguish them, so he advised flushing them down a toilet, where they'd do the maximum amount of difficult-to-fix damage. I was sort of afraid to even touch them. I'd had firecrackers go off in my hand when I was a kid, and that hurt like hell. This looked big enough to blow my whole hand off. As he was finishing explaining their best use, his then-girlfriend walked in the room. Steve sort of discreetly covered the bag, which caught her attention. "What are you doing? What is that?" Steve replied in a sheepish, silly voice, the kind you'd use on your mom when she caught you red-handed doing something explicitly forbidden. "It's dynamite, honey!" She kind of scowled and said, "Who even are you?" before saying goodbye to us and walking away.

Years later when Phono-Comb worked with Touch and Go to release our records, it was on their subsidiary label, Quarterstick. Bing!

One time, Steve had recently acquired a guitar, an aluminum-neck Travis Bean. He was surprisingly adept at playing conventional rock, knocking out AC/DC riffs and following that with bits of "Swan Lake," as interpreted by P.I.L.'s Keith Levene. The guitar had allegedly been Keith's and sold for drug money, and he was excited by pics I had shot of the Viletones showing Freddy Pompeii playing a similar model, both of them having a single ruby embedded in the headstock. Whether it was then or six years later while recording with Phono-Comb, he told me he was playing a lot of "conversational" guitar these days. Of course, I had to ask what that was. He described it as having phrasing like talking, or more specifically, how the adults on Charlie Brown's *Peanuts* talk, followed by a quick conversation between his guitar and me — *plink ba bink wah blam.* To this day, Charlie Brown's teacher or parents blabbing conjures an image of Steve mimicking the scattershot, bird-pecking sound of their vocalizing.

Recording music was an intimidating process to me for a long time. Not so much the playing, but how to get sound onto tape and dealing with the number of interactive variables in the process, including the mysteries of electricity. Brian had always been the one in Shadowy Men to operate the cassette Portastudio he owned, mic'ing, recording and mixing any demos we'd put down. I bought a half-inch eight-track recorder, knowing it would be the best way to capture ideas for songs, and looking to properly record us in the future. I asked Steve a bunch of questions about some of the basics, and he spent hours on the phone animatedly answering them, encouraging me. He told me to call any time to ask questions. Unprompted, I received a letter-sized envelope in the mail. In it were pages of notes and diagrams he'd written out for me. *Tape Op* magazine hadn't been founded yet, so this document, these ten pages, were an invaluable resource. I referred to them constantly and was actively guided by Steve's info and insight in my first ten or so years of recording.

I loved that he shared knowledge, rather than hoarding it. Protecting what you know is so common in the recording biz that proprietary info equated with power, work, and therefore, money. I got to share those same docs with a few other people in the position I once was. Most people, guys particularly, can be condescending about the recording process. Steve was an absolute socialist in that regard, implementing collectivist principles. He never talked down to me, no matter how basic some of my questions must have been.

A year or two later we returned to Chicago to record with Steve again. His home studio was either shut down or limited because of noise issues. We were going to record what would be our third album, titled *Sport Fishin': The Lure of the Bait, the Luck of the Hook.* It was the first and only time we didn't do an album in bits, accumulating tracks until we had enough for an album. We'd record about twenty-six songs, everything we needed for the album and a few extras.

He recommended we work at Chicago Recording Company, a downtown studio then owned by Jimmy Jam and Terry Lewis. We loaded our equipment in, passing platinum discs of Janet Jackson's *Rhythm Nation 1814*, and set up in a line across three glass-walled rooms, with Steve in the mothership looking into our enclosures. Shadowy Men occupied the main studio for maybe five days. Brian's guitar amps were set up in the room where the grand piano resided, and Steve mic'd the strings inside it as well as the amps. I'd never heard of this being done, piano strings vibrating in resonant response to what Brian played, creating a ghostly stereo reverb effect. Reid was in another room, me and my drum kit occupying the largest one. Arrays of microphones were placed at intervals further and further from the kit to take advantage of the natural reverb of the space.

Albini was renowned for the drum sounds he captured, many of them having a distinct quality that people often identified as the "Albini sound." When we listened to playbacks, I asked if there was delay on the drums. No, it was the spread of mics capturing the sound as it arrived at mics in varying intervals from the kit. We soloed each of them, then listened in combinations, hearing the delay in action. Later when soloing some drum, I asked again if there was delay added to the drum. "No, there isn't." I was convinced it was more than the straight sound of the mic. He lowered his voice and asked, "Can you hear that? The delay?" He affirmed that he had extremely short delays on some mics, particularly the snare, which I came to believe was one of his secret ingredients.

Steve's not-so-secret ingredient was his superb skill. He had as much love for the visual beauty of a microphone as he did for its sonic properties. He lit up with delight when he later described to me the unique side-address of the Josephson e22S mic he'd designed. Even the "e" on the model number was expressed using the "e" logo of Electrical Audio!

We worked from morning until long after dark, making the most of each day and then going for great meals afterward. The tracks sounded fantastic to us, the long tour we had completed just before going into the studio helping to tighten us up and giving us the ability to knock out one song after another, moving on with relatively few overdubs. We had an old organ that made a great dying wheeze when you shut it off, so we took advantage of it for the end of our song "Memories of Gay Paree." As the sound descended in pitch and volume, Steve smartly lunged for the input faders, riding them up to capture the last breaths of the organ.

We knew the last song on the record was likely going to a sort of sleepy lullaby called "Babywetsitself™." There's a phrase that precedes a stop in the song, punctuated with a single note on a xylophone. Steve made a point of never playing on records he was recording for other people, but he suggested that he run into the side isolation booth after hitting record to play that one note, thereby eliminating an overdub. When we asked if this was the first record he played on, he replied that he didn't *really* play anything.

While he was crucial to the sound of that record, we were mostly on our own to evaluate our performances. He'd just bought a car, and our album was his designated research time to find the ideal stereo for it. His nose was often buried in a stack of magazines dedicated to car stereos. When we finished one take we were uncertain about, we asked how it sounded. "If you mean the Pioneer XT blahblah car stereo with blahblahblah subwoofer blahblah, it sounds pretty promising" was his reply.

He was in negotiation to buy the building that would become Electrical Audio. We shared some chatter about design and aesthetics, particularly logos and graphic identities, how that could be half of your reason for loving some band. It was before Shellac, but he was already an excited kid showing me the Lomo microphone logo that would show up on their records. And when he described the future Electrical, he was delighted that it was next to train tracks, the challenge of their noise almost being a selling feature. Like a scientist presenting a hypothesis, he drew out a diagram of how he'd build interior floating rooms out of adobe to absorb sound and isolate them.

After we'd finished tracking, we went to a scene bar, north from downtown near where we were staying. There and at restaurants, it was like being out with a mafia don. Some guys from Urge Overkill came by to pay their respects, and the chef came out to ask how the food was. It was after the Pixies' *Surfer Rosa* album but before the PJ Harvey and Nirvana albums mentioned ad nauseam in every piece written about Steve, the ones that brought him to mainstream attention. He was clearly admired by almost everyone we encountered who knew who he was.

Having so much attention paid to him put him in a rarefied position. He had his choice of clients and could do whatever he wanted with his bands, but then so could anyone. Steve had an audience though, so if he wanted to put out a record sheathed in rusted metal, or a three-inch vinyl cover of a Mary Jane Girls song, he could execute it. In some ways, I saw a sympathetic collaborator in that regard. Shadowy Men had little concern for profitability, and much more of an interest in producing things that indulged our sense of absurdity and aesthetic urges. We packed our singles in Jiffy Pop containers, turned records into board games, spent hours and days making stencils and sets and anything else we thought of to appease our creative impulses. Some things made money, some lost money, but after a certain point, we managed to always be able to earn some kind of allowance from the band to keep us afloat. Steve and his bands were similar.

He respected that we weren't beholden to any record company, had no management, travelled without entourage, and that we had made our records independently and paid for everything ourselves. We licensed the finished thing to whomever we wanted to, maintaining ownership of everything we did. It meant something to me to have his respect. Ultimately, we were all following the ideals and possibilities laid out before us in the birth of punk rock and the explosion of independent labels. We and Steve knew that the best musical experiences are often going to be with people you have great social experiences with.

When people hear that Steve said he'd record Shadowy Men for free, they always assume that we took advantage of that. Absolutely not, we were always about fairness and paid him a fee in line with his going rate at the time. He told me that Depeche Mode had indeed approached him about working with them. They were trying to go "hard" and thought Steve was the guy to do it. True to his past interview, he asked them for a million dollars, thinking this would dissuade them and he wouldn't have to say no. They responded with a plane ticket to England to come see them play. Steve said he didn't know them at all, knew none of their songs. He invited his friend John Loder, the English audio engineer who'd recorded half of Big Black's *Songs About Fucking* and most of the Crass Records releases, to go to the venue with him. Loder definitely would have known who Depeche Mode were.

They arrived at the arena after the group had already taken the stage, and made their way to their seats down front. Steve said they started through the aisle, excusing themselves as they passed those already seated, toward their reserved spots. Mid-aisle, an intro started up: *dun dun, dun ta dun da-da*. It was their massive hit "Just Can't Get Enough." Steve thought, *This is that fucking song from university* and promptly stopped, turning around and exiting before even reaching his seat. Needless to say, that collaboration never happened.

From 1994 to 1997, I was also in the Guelph-based band King Cobb Steelie. A six-piece ensemble, over time the group moved further and further away from rock music into something inspired more by dance music, dub, and African highlife. I operated the sampler and sequencer in the band, and we had a percussionist, Michael Armstrong, who was increasingly more prominent as our sound and rhythms caused eruptions of fantastic dance parties. I knew that Steve was disdainful of some of these elements, but I also knew him to be open-minded and utilitarian, wanting to achieve the best sonic results. I'd had such great experiences recording with Steve that I recommended him to the band. We had a fantastic live sound, and if that could be captured, we might have something good.

I was naive to recognizing that other ethical elements in place might not be to Steve's taste, like dealing with management or a major label — in this case, EMI. I too had an uneasy relationship with the band being on EMI, and refused to sign those contracts. Under the terms issued, they would own all other music I was making, including Shadowy Men, and that was just not going to happen. I was now in the awkward position of being a contracted player, an appendage to the "real" band.

I met him at the airport with a couple of other King Cobb Steelie members, his work papers issued to my name. His plane had apparently landed, but after a long wait, there was no sign of Steve. The airport was packed, and since it was pre-cellphone, the only way to find someone was to page them. The PA was drowned out by the cacophony of the crowd, and it wasn't until I went to the quiet bathroom that I heard the announcement. Sitting on the toilet, the message echoed through the room: "Don Pyle, please come to the customs office for Steve Albini." I pulled my pants up and quickly got out of there, smiling to myself at the ridiculous situation.

We recorded at Metalworks, the suburban studio complex founded by Canadian hard rock band Triumph. The studio we were in had limited isolation for instruments, with the advantage being that it was adjacent to the bands' storage warehouse and loading dock. That latter space had great sound reflection and height to theoretically capture a big drum sound.

Things turned sour pretty quickly and the band became unnerved when Steve made digs, both subtle and not-so. As we readied ourselves to do another take of a song, instead of saying "rolling," Steve would intone through the talkback, "Continue to blow." When he had to mention the band name, King Cobb Steelie, he called us Pablo Doobie Santana. It really shook people's confidence. I felt bad for being the one who sold the band on an engineer who'd brought bummer feelings into our recording.

We did have some fun though. Steve found an open cabinet filled with Triumph materials, like stationery and envelopes with the Triumph logo as letterhead. A glossy presentation folder to prospective sponsors became our reading material in the studio. In the crassest terms, the proposal laid out the business plan with investments and returns, the corporate strategy they hoped to achieve with a partner. It was cloaked in the colourful logos, designs, and photography of a rock band making rock, rather than a business making business, that was the reality of the proposal. The real jackpot in the cabinet was the reproductions of line-drawing portraits of each band member, executed by their guitarist Rik Emmett, and printed on "fancy" textured paper. It was hard to imagine what these could be used for other than pre-made courtroom sketches if one of them ever ended up being accused of some salacious crime. We departed with handfuls of each portrait.

For years after, Steve and I exchanged letters and notes on this stationery, signing off under various band members' names. I'd receive a letter, ostensibly from the drummer of Triumph, telling me that he was going to be in town soon, and could I recommend a good wig cleaner? Whatever bad feeling was laid down on the tapes from the session was enough that they were scrapped. King Cobb Steelie started again with another producer/engineer.

Phono-Comb were ready to make a new album by 1995 and asked Steve to come over to Toronto to record it. Lots of local friends had worked at the Gas Station studio, where we wanted to record, including band members Beverly Breckenridge and Dallas Good in their previous groups. The studio consisted of a small control room next to an undivided and cavernous warehouse space. We thought Steve could make any space sound great, and he did. Upon arrival, the studio owner Dale Morningstar catalogued all the things that didn't work, including several bits of gear Steve needed. Some of the channels on the mixer were dead too. Steve spent our whole first day repairing equipment, a fantastic deal for the studio at the rate we were paying. Dale later told us that the studio had never worked better than it did after Steve left.

Steve was so low-maintenance, making do with whatever was going. He insisted that we not put him up in a hotel, so for a week he slept on a futon under my mix console in my apartment studio. Once again, great meals and lots of laughs made the album a joy to record. Unlike the KCS debacle, we were so at ease working with a friend. He was also tickled to be recording so many Garnet and Traynor amps. Both Canadian brands were still relatively obscure in the US, and their amps weren't yet going for collector prices. Generally they were pretty cheap, the insecure logic being that if they were Canadian, they couldn't be that great. Steve knew better. He, Dallas and Reid weinered out over amp talk and gossiping about Randy Bachman.

He told us how some woman had contacted him, knowing that he was into those amps, and said she had some he might be interested in. After going through the inventory and describing to us the long process of dealing with the person for amps, he paused and said, "And that girl was Buffy Sainte-Marie."

Years later, Steve and Dallas invited me to be Steve's assistant, as he was hired by the Sadies to record their double live album.

They'd done their 1998 debut, *Precious Moments*, and 2001 record, *Tremendous Efforts*, with him. Hearing from both sides, the first album sounded not entirely satisfying for Steve or the Sadies. On a tight budget, they were banging things out too quickly. But by 2006, they were a tight machine, made precise and sharp by incessant touring.

Dallas wanted an analog recording, a hi-fi capture of the parade of guests and past collaborators performing at the two-night event. I was amused when Steve got dressed for work, slipping out of his street clothes into his work uniform: a pair of navy blue coveralls with his Electrical studio's logo printed on the back. He and his studio's staff had been wearing these since Electrical opened, a utilitarian statement of a proletariat aesthetic, workers there to accomplish their mandated assignment. It was both practical and cute. He wears them in almost every video clip or photo I've seen of him at work in the studio, or out in the field, like he was with this Sadies album.

We enjoyed being at a remove from the backstage party scene happening during the show. While everyone else was getting drunk and high on one side of the stage, we watched tapes spin and meters bounce in the dark stairwell off stage right, listening to the band on the other side of the wall, only a small glimpse available for view. After all the meticulous setup and level checks, Steve scowled as the band cranked the volume on their amps relative to the amount of beer they were consuming. Soon everything was overdriven, but Steve was casual about it. Their record, their choice.

I heard a Vish Khanna interview with Steve, from 2022, in which it's mentioned that he had sent a note to the band Dry Cleaning. As it was described, it sounded very similar to the one we'd received from him many years before. I loved hearing that, knowing that Steve was still a fan, was excited by new things he heard, new ways of making and presenting music. No matter who it's from, it's a nice ego thing to receive a message saying your work is appreciated. Even though Steve had become some kind of celeb, he was still thoughtful and supportive. His bar of standards was pretty high. If he saluted what you were doing, it really had weight.

Every obit piece mentions three particular bands (Nirvana, PJ Harvey, the Pixies) Albini recorded, but the vast discography of released records is filled with gems. From the beginning, Big Black were magnificent in their metallic treble fury, deliberately grating but not painful on the ears. Heavy records from the Wedding Present, the Breeders, Volcano Suns, and Electrelane brought out the best in each, all having an attack that never overwhelmed space, sonic magic being revealed in quieter passages that were almost like coming upon an open field in a dense forest. There was room to breathe.

Nowhere was that more apparent, to me, than on the Palace records he made, or Dirty Three's *Ocean Songs*, a masterpiece of multi-faceted mood, the band's dynamic not squished by the common overuse of compression but presenting a truer sound picture of the performance. If you want to hear the quieter parts louder, just turn the volume up. I think of his two albums with Low, *Secret Name* and *Things We Lost in the Fire*, as being transitional records for Steve. So many had overlooked that Steve's quest for clarity and accuracy was perfect for a very quiet band. Dimensional planes are created by placing the drums in a more distant space, through the use of minimal reverb and natural room sound. Guitars and vocals are shockingly present, the voices of Low's Mimi Parker and Alan Sparhawk being forefront and unburied. Steve's range was incredible, as one hopes their craft becomes after years of practising it. I suspect he would be a master at orchestral recording, and I'm surprised more ensembles didn't hire him for that.

The last time I worked with him as a musician, rather than engineer, was for the recording of Fred Schneider's second solo album in 1996. The future of the B-52's was precarious at this point, it being uncertain whether the band would even continue. Fred knew he had to make his own statement, make the record he wanted. Loud and heavy was Fred's imperative, so he recruited Steve, this time acting as true producer, not just engineer.

Fred needed help. He and a writing partner had written a bunch of songs, but he didn't have a band and wanted Steve to put the ensemble together. Steve's idea was to do it with three different groups, each of them bringing some particular quality to a portion of the songs. When he called me to ask if Shadowy Men would be interested, he told me that he wanted us and Six Finger Satellite. The third band hadn't come to him yet and he asked if I had any ideas. Immediately I thought of Yo La Tengo. I loved them, they had a good history of collaboration, and they were inventive and dynamic. Plus, they were in Fred's neighbourhood, not so far from where the album was going to be recorded. I suggested them, but Steve hemmed and then replied, "I like the idea of Yo La Tengo more than I like Yo La Tengo." I laughed and had to ask what the "idea" of Yo La Tengo was. "You know, really smart people playing rock music."

I was grateful to Steve for creating this kooky situation for us.

Fred would come up to Toronto to rehearse the songs already written, and we'd see what fit. We had a little garage across from my home that we'd rehearsed in for years, so Fred came out to Parkdale to whip things into shape. We had a fun time putting the songs together and thought they sounded pretty good. Reid and I took Fred out a couple of nights, one of which was to see the disco cover band Chunk o' Funk, a fourteen-piece outfit that was a full-on revue with horn section, percussion, singers and players. They were fantastic, and Fred loved them. People freaked when they recognized him, and he spoke kindly to every person that approached him, being funny and gracious.

Days later I saw the Fred effect happen when we were in a record store. He is a deep digger, with a love for soul music, so the thousands of singles in this shop were heaven. We'd separate and come back together to talk about records we were finding. I saw the look on people's faces as they heard The Voice, slowly turning their heads to see why it was so familiar. The look of puzzled analysis, the knowledge that they *knew* the voice but were dreading what relative it was who they hadn't quite placed, was instantly replaced with the hugest grins, the joy Fred had brought them evident in their sudden beaming expressions.

Unlike the other bands on the record, we wrote a couple songs with Fred: one before Fred arrived, the other coming out of a conversation about the hot news topic of the moment, biker gang wars in Montreal. "Oh, please," Fred said, after hearing they'd fire-bombed and shot each other, with uninvolved people caught in the crossfire. More than one hundred and fifty were dead, so Fred imagined a gentler war where retaliation would be exacted by putting sugar into a rival's gas tank. Spontaneously, we started playing a sinister riff adapted from every Link Wray and Cramps song, Fred making up words. "You put sugar in my hooooggggg!" Fred belted with blood-curdling intensity. It was weird for a while, being in the presence of that voice that is so satisfying to imitate. He was fantastic to be with and work with.

Years later when talking about the album that became *Just Fred*, and Yo La Tengo's non-involvement, they told me about being at a birthday party for Yoko Ono where Fred was also in attendance. For years after and on any occasion, they'd say in Fred voice, as he had, "Yoko's here!"

Shadowy Men were on tough footing at this time, and it would be the last thing we recorded together. After we finished the album, we came back home, played two songs at a benefit concert, and that was it. The band was done.

Recording with Fred and Steve was fun and easy. It was kind of like being an opening band. We showed up, did our parts, and then left for our Manhattan hotel after we were done. We shared a couple rides and meals in Manhattan, and it was mostly efficient work. Fred did the majority of the vocals live, so we and Steve were smiling a lot at just how entertaining the whole thing was. It was sweet seeing Steve in the role of producer, being a caring midwife to Fred, supporting him when he needed it. After we moved out, Six Finger Satellite took our place. We arrived back at the studio the next day to move our gear out, just as 6FS were recording the blistering cut "Bad Dreams," the best track on the record.

Production paused for a bit as we hugged and said goodbye to Steve, Fred, and recording assistant Tom Zaluckyj — who was also the bass player in Deadly Cupcake, the third band Steve had assembled for the project. I had my camera so I handed it to Tom, asking him to take a picture of Shadowy Men, Fred, and Steve. After a couple shots, Tom handed the camera back. Steve lit up with his bratty prankster expression and said, "Let me show you something, get the camera ready." He placed one hand above the other on the signpost next to us, lifted his legs off the ground horizontally, and blew away.

Rest in phase, Steve Albini.

SHIRL

MY MOTHER WAS A COMPLICATED WOMAN, BUT WHO DOESN'T SAY that about their mother? She'd come from a big family, the oldest of six kids "that your father inflicted on me," my grandmother used to say. Harry, her dad, had been a custodian at a high school, working in a time when a sole-earner labourer could feed that many mouths and also have a lovely house for a family to grow up in. Sensitive and relaxed, he was soft-spoken and had a love of gardening and nature that was instilled in my mother, and subsequently me. Of course, I only knew him after his kids had all grown up, with families of their own, but even in old photos of him as a young man, almost the entire backyard was planted with orderly vegetables, roses, giant dahlias, and an explosion of colour that lasted until first frost.

The bottom of my grandparents' yard was a gloomy spot, shaded by a giant oak tree from which a swing dangled, an ancient stone wall separating the south end from a graveyard on the other side. In the last light of day, it felt spooky and shadowed; you were on high alert for the sound of the unknown coming from the cemetery side of the wall. My mother told me that before that area had been planted with people, locals had Victory Gardens there, public plots of land used to grow food during the Second World War. She and her father would work the garden and hike the ravines nearby in search of berries, other edible things, and beauty — all abundant in the 1930s and '40s.

Quite opposite to Harry was Molly, my grandmother, a cranky lady whose sour expression was fixed for most of the time that I knew her. She didn't have an outside job, didn't like cooking or cleaning, and definitely didn't like being a mother. Or maybe she did, but just told whoever'd listen otherwise. She would have to have been caretaker for the first few children, but as each became old enough, responsibilities were handed to them to care for each other. As soon as some kids were gone from the family home, she moved into her own room away from my grandfather's needs, a smaller bedroom at the back of the house, where we were forbidden.

As the firstborn, my mother became the surrogate mother to her siblings, caring for them and having to be responsible for their well-being as she carted five small children across town on public transit to her own grandparents' home.

For years I never really understood how much of a part these details had in forming my mother. For better and worse, these were the models she grew up with.

In my earliest visions of her, Shirl is always wearing an apron and doing some kind of work: cooking, cleaning, and washing the mountains of laundry that a household of our size produced, using an old wringer washer and hanging everything on the clothesline that spanned the length of our deep yard.

Until just before kindergarten, I had two parents, but the only real memory I have of that is standing beside my kneeling father as he went through the cedar chest in their bedroom. He was removing his coin collection. Feeling something wasn't right, I asked, "What are you doing?" I don't remember what he said, but he moved out of our house to a one-bedroom apartment in a deco low-rise in the west end of the city, where he had webbed lawn chairs for furniture and an ornate rosewood and glass lit cabinet to display his favourite antiques. The fridge held only a jar of lemon curd and his "medicine," which we later learned was white rum.

He had a small record player too, a beautiful, portable green machine with a chrome grate that could be operated by batteries so you could take it to the beach, which we never did. He only had a couple of records, so I played his 45s of "These Boots Are Made for Walking" and Napoleon XIV's "They're Coming to Take Me Away" over and over, the B-side of which was the same song backwards. This was something he'd never have listened to when he lived with us. I still don't know how these odd records fit in with his new life, other than the fact that he was only in his mid-thirties, and these were chart singles. Before that, it was mostly me and my sisters who played records, things the whole family liked: the *South Pacific* soundtrack, and the Huckleberry Hound album with the Kellogg's cereal logo on the front.

When Roy departed, he told Shirl she could have the five kids, the mortgage and the dog, and he'd move out — or he'd stay and keep those things. Knowing what I did of him later, this was just a power play to make her feel like she had a choice, and in a way she did — but her choice would have always been obvious. The house had been her grandparents' home. She had practically grown up there, my parents buying it from my great-grandmother after her husband died. Great Granny Smith remained living with them for a long time, and I'm not sure why she eventually moved out — maybe too many kids, but she was very loving with us too, our favourite granny if we had to choose.

My older brother and sister moved out not long after my dad, but for a time there were eleven of us living in a small, three-bedroom house, with only one bathroom we had to line up for to use. So it was me and my two sisters who went off to babysitters while my mother began working, her first time having a job outside the home since she married at age seventeen.

She was hired at a large department store downtown, Simpsons, as a secretary in the general supply department, the office that bought anything in the store that wasn't merchandise: bags, racks, shelving, cash register paper, all of that stuff. I loved going to her office, hidden as it was on an odd half-floor behind the women's wear department. It felt like a secret place back in its warren of hallways. She had her own desk. The office air was blue from everyone smoking while working. She started her new job just before I started kindergarten, taking the morning off to walk us to school for the first couple of days. On my fifth birthday, a month and a half after kindergarten began, she told me to go to Foodland, the corner store across the street, and pick up my birthday cake. Something about that felt strange — we were used to others doing everything for our birthday, but many new experiences happened after old Roy Boy left. Roy Boy and Shirl Girl, no longer a pair but linked for life.

With my two older siblings and my father gone, the dynamic at home shifted immediately, and at first it was okay. My mother took in boarders. The first two were my older brother's friends, the third a slow-moving, sleepy-eyed guy named Ted, who had perfect, brilliantined black hair and a soft, lilting Irish accent. He drove a big yellow convertible, always wore neat dress pants and shirt, and was kind and caring to us kids. For a while I thought of him not as our father, but as a welcome presence. He went camping with us and took us out for ice cream, and we all really cared for him.

Years later my mother told me that he had fallen in love with her and wanted to be with her, but she wasn't interested because he drank. I had never noticed that as being an issue because every adult seemed to drink, and the Legion Hall was where my mother, Ted, aunts and uncles, and other friends all socialized. At the time, I didn't have a context to know what drinking to the point of it being a problem even was. If Ted drank, it never seemed to affect us negatively. He'd laugh and sing along to Dean Martin crooning "Little Ole Wine Drinker Me." We wanted my mother to be with Ted, wanted him to stick around. At the same time, we also plotted how we could get a message to Johnny Cash so he could meet our mother and become our father.

We still did things as a family, going to visit relatives and having people over for BBQs. Christmas and other holidays in our home were lively and fun. I never had a sense of my mother being unhappy. We were too young and oblivious to know the effect of having so much responsibility put on her, but things seemed alright.

The reins on us were pretty loose, my mother having too many demands on her already. As it was at the time, she trusted in the neighbourhood community to all watch out for each other. It seemed expected that my next older sister was put in the role that my mother had had put on her, to be the mother when she was absent. Shirl would leave detailed instructions for her to start preparing dinner, which my mother would finish when she arrived home at 6 p.m. The other two of us would run to the bus stop to meet her and walk home together while my eight-year-old sister cooked, all of us happy to see her after a long day's absence.

I'm still astonished at how lenient she was with our pet situation. Three kids were enough to take care of, but into the mix were added two dogs, a multitude of rabbits, guinea pigs, hamsters, birds, gerbils, a snake — and even an alligator for a while. My brother had brought it home from the pet section of a nearby department store.

It lived in our basement laundry tubs. My mother would have to cycle the alligator from tub to tub, moving it into the second tub as clothes squeezed through the wringer washer's rollers into tub one, then moving the gator into the washing machine as the clothes went for a second rinse in tub two. The alligator kept growing, and we played with it like any of our other pets. One day I had it in the backyard, me laying on the warm ground between rows of tomato plants in the garden and stroking its head, when it suddenly bit me. I leapt up screaming and shaking the alligator, still attached to my finger, sending it flying through the vegetable patch. Besides that, it was getting too big for its basement home, so it had to go.

Astonishingly, it was two white mice, named after my brother and his wife, that were her limit. She took them outside and freed them in the field behind our yard.

She didn't go out a lot socially, but every once in a while some friends would come back to our place after the Legion. Truckers and army buddies of my dad's, or aunts and uncles. A few guys had designs on her, but she was never interested. I think it was all too much for her, too much work. I was too young to know anything about heartbreak, but I'm sure she was burdened by that, and the worry of being a single mother with so many responsibilities.

One night she came home with one man, something that hadn't happened before. Knowing later who he was, I feel certain that he forced his way in, wouldn't take no for an answer. As soon as I met him I had a bad feeling about him, disliked him immediately, and was wary. From then on, he started coming around for dinner uninvited, with a two-four of beer to just hang out. Watching him trying to be nice was like seeing a snake smile — you instinctively knew not to trust the forced expression. He would drink all the beer and then stay overnight, at first sleeping on the couch, but soon going to her bedroom. We know he was uninvited because she would quietly try and ask him to leave; two of us kids in bunk beds in the bedroom we shared with my mother would pretend to sleep, but be on high alert. It always felt like something bad was going to happen. He was nothing like anyone who had lived in our home before. He was loud, opinionated, pompous and macho, all of which were amplified the more he drank. He drank continuously.

One day he just didn't leave. My mother had strength in her ability to forge forward in taking care of her home and children, but in other ways she was meek. If someone was aggressive or demanding, she'd give in to their wants. I can't imagine that she ever saw something good in him, but she let him move in. Everything changed.

He didn't work; we later learned he had a disability scam going. His rotting teeth made him appear as ugly as his personality was. My older sister and I withdrew when he was around, which was now pretty much always. My younger sister became a betrayer, being nice to him when we had previously been allied about everyone else who came through our door. She was too young to recognize the evil in him so obvious to us, and so the first of many wedges came between family members. We were sad that our boarder Ted was forced to move out. It was hard to understand why she chose this awful person over Ted, but they weren't our decisions to make.

My mother changed, no longer in control of her own life. It didn't happen right away, but incrementally as he dominated more and more. He hadn't been hanging around for too long when I was in a serious car accident. Not knowing how precarious my life was at that point, relatives came to visit as I'd come into and out of awareness in the first couple of weeks. He came, not with my mother, but maybe she was there and only one visitor at a time was allowed. I thought, even then: "Why is he here? He doesn't care." It felt manipulative, pretending to be concerned in a performance intended for my mother.

For years, he'd get out of bed long after my mother had gone to work and immediately open a beer, sitting in front of the television set all day in his housecoat. Not having the extra income from a boarder, and now having a freeloader to support too, my mother took a second job working as a server at a banquet hall on weekends. She was often gone seven days a week. We resented it, not having a full understanding of why. It meant that we were forced to be at home with him alone far more often. She eventually bought a cottage, a small rundown place that was pretty much his. He'd spend a lot of his time there, and for a few years of summer holidays, I was forced to as well. My sisters and I would go out and spend as many hours away from the place as we could, going from beach to mini-golf to beach, avoiding him. Some of that was fun, but it was also oppressive, the tiny space providing nowhere to get away from him at night.

He'd drink to oblivion almost every day, and on his way there we'd witness the rage that lived in him, the bully who took pleasure from slapping kids around and punching my mother, taunting her with his physical power over her. "What're you going to do, cry-baby?" Even as a child, I knew he was simple, a lout who everyone hated, even his children from previous relationships. My mother withdrew more and more; keeping track of us became less of a priority. We asked more and more frequently, "Why are you with him? Why is he here?"

In cartoons, a halo of stars would appear circling over a character's head when they were bonked on the noggin. I experienced that for real twice: once when he punched me in the head when I was eleven, another time when he smashed my head against my younger sister's, who was eight. It was only when I read about concussion symptoms as an adult did I realize what had happened to me.

We stopped referring to him by his name, and to my mother and among us siblings, he became known only as the Creep. Relatives stopped coming to visit, backyard gatherings ended, no guests came over — any laughter or fun that I remember my mother having ceased. He would be belligerent and pick fights with my uncles, one of whom was a gentle missionary, a religious guy married to my mother's youngest sister. My two oldest siblings came around for visits and for holidays, and they began taking us three smaller kids out and away more frequently.

Whenever I would tell anyone about some of the things that happened in our home growing up, people would be horrified. It's shocking to me how much of that became normalized. It was our everyday lives, and we coped by avoiding. My closeness with my mother gradually fell away. I isolated more and more, staying only in my bedroom and escaping into books and music when at home. Otherwise, I was out as much as possible, taking the dog for hours-long walks, exploring distant trails on my bike, or hanging out at the record shop and library.

I developed tics that I later knew were a reaction to the anxiety I was experiencing. My head began to snap to one side, violently shaking until my brain hurt. No one recognized this as a manifestation of what was happening at home, only as something stupid that I was doing. I couldn't control it. Other kids and my oldest sister mocked me, making fun of the faces I'd make as I twitched. Then I started biting the inside of my mouth so continuously that it bled and was raw for years. I still touch the scars from it with my tongue, grateful that it stopped. The only way I dealt with my head-snapping was from within. After a couple of years, I consciously had to decide to stop doing it, monitoring myself continuously and actively fighting the impulse to do it. There were times when that was all I could do, the concentration required so great that I couldn't do other things.

I had some close friends, all of whom avoided coming over, knowing instinctively that the atmosphere was tense and unwelcoming. Their parents even knew, some of them telling me I could come over or stay any time. My favourite teacher in grades five and six started asking me if I wanted to stay late and play badminton with him in the gym. That could never happen now, and I'm so grateful that it did then, his care and attention being what I needed. He would ask how things were at home, somehow knowing things weren't right.

The Creep was aggressively handsy with almost any female, not caring who saw. He boasted about being able to have what he wanted, any time he wanted. In one forced Christmas picture when my oldest sister was nineteen, the Creep is pressed up against her back, leaning over her shoulder and making a grotesque leering face for the camera's benefit, so there's no mistaking that he's staring at her breasts with lust. My mother stood beside him, blank-faced.

My two sisters at home and I plotted how to kill him, wondering which ways were guaranteed effective. Pushing him down the stairs was too risky. Any method that caused bleeding was too scary. Getting someone else to do it was a good idea, but where would we find them? And how would we pay them? We agreed that poisoning was our best option, and we considered which of us would do it, measuring the consequences by what we imagined the punishment at our various ages would be. We believed that twelve was the age where you would be tried as an adult, so more and more, the task was upon my youngest sister. We procrastinated, thinking he'd probably die from drinking soon anyway.

Our family was, in many ways, two families. Two children were born and raised with both parents, followed by a gap of seven years, and then three more offspring raised by a single mother. An eighteen-year span separates the first and last kid. When I was old enough to guess what had happened, I asked my mother if she had us three younger kids to keep the marriage together. She burst into tears, telling me, "But I'm so glad I had you all, I wouldn't ever want to change that." It was rare for her to talk with me frankly about feelings — hers or others'. She went on to say that my father wanted her to have a third, fourth and fifth child, something so blatantly about control over her body and destiny, to put her at a relative disadvantage to him. He was already seeing another woman when he split, my mother still recovering from the birth of the last of her children.

I sought freedoms wherever and whenever I could. High school at fourteen came with the beginning of punk rock and my elevated focus on photography. I began going to see bands, connecting with the local underground music scene that detonated after the Ramones' 1976 performances in Toronto. My cheap camera and snapshots documenting pets and sisters gave way to a good Canon 35mm camera, bought with earnings from delivering flyers and stocking shelves at a local pharmacy. Up to that point my mother had indulged my interest in photography, paying for photo processing and bringing me a new roll of film after development of the previous roll. It was standard at the time that photo processing places would give you a fresh roll for free, similar to what you had just processed. It kept me hooked, until one day she implored me to slow down, it was costing too much. I knew money was tight. We'd go grocery shopping at the discount store, where dented cans and label-less food sold for lower prices. It's hard for any kid to really appreciate what every dollar means. Hers had to be stretched far. Although photo processing was only a few dollars, it all mattered. My mother's generosity and support is something I grew more grateful for with each passing year.

Joining the school's camera club and shooting bands gave me the final excuse I needed to never go to the cottage again. I borrowed enlargers from school and printed at home on weekends while the rest of the family was away. I pushed the limits of what was okay, and my mother went along with it. While her other kids had acted out in more delinquent and confrontational ways, I was open with her, telling her I wouldn't be coming home until late, or maybe not at all. She trusted me. But as much as my forthrightness about what I was doing gave me a lot of leeway, I always thought that she knew we all were engaging in some form of escape from home life. I would stay with friends after a night out seeing bands, preferring their floor to our home. I only wasn't honest about the reason I was staying out all night when it was because I was in the home of some man I had just met.

She didn't really have a context to understand being in a band, so when three friends and I started playing together, she was hands-off, not really asking about where we practised, what we were doing, or even how we made a record when we eventually did. She did come and see Crash Kills Five play once, and her one question was to ask if I was on drugs. I wasn't.

I interpreted her lack of curiosity or interest in what I was doing as not caring, not loving me. When you're looking for evidence of that, it's easy to find, especially for a young mind that doesn't know how complex a simple expression of love can become. She never said she loved me, never said it to my siblings. The absence of those words, and the choices she made, led me to believe that she didn't care about me, didn't care about us.

When that first band ended, I stepped back from the music scene that had consumed me. In the situations around the punk bands and clubs I was engaged with most, I didn't see any place for a gay kid. When I started making my first homo friends, my attention shifted to my first boyfriend, going to gay bars, and — quite surprisingly to me — joining a gay baseball league. I had zero sports ambitions or interests, but I had new friends who played in the league, and the level of ability ranged from where I was to players who could be pro. Everyone was welcome, and it was a lot of fun for a couple of years. My best team friend would pick me up in his car for games. He was twice my age, and with his impassive demeanour and moustache, he came across macho in a way that I thought was a dead giveaway to my mother.

I wasn't out; being out at home was too dangerous. At eighteen, I was barely out in the rest of the world. Part of me thought that my association with others would do half the work for me, letting her figure out that I was homosexual. She didn't, somehow. She asked questions about so little, mostly because I think it was just too much for her to know some things. Her capacity for dealing with *more* was probably used up.

The Creep's presence motivated my siblings and me to get out as soon as we could. Each of us sought security, care, and love, in ways we weren't receiving at home. There's no doubt some kind of father complex was going on: each of us moved in with much older men, my youngest sister doing it on her sixteenth birthday, the very first day she could without permission, and me after a couple of years of roommates. I at least had some period to be free, at first sharing a huge warehouse space as downtown as you could be, with two women. One was a school friend I barely knew. But as the last of my family to move out, I was motivated by an affordable situation and the unease I had at being sole witness to the beatings and beratings regularly forced upon my mother. It was horrible seeing her spent, with unslept, baggy red eyes from crying all night, then getting ready to go to work.

She came to my new place a few times, bringing things I'd need for bachelor living. Pots and pans, and a brand new copy of *The Joy of Cooking*, so I wouldn't go hungry. I made more and more space between myself and her, and the rest of my family.

Maybe five years after moving out, my youngest sister was to be married. Knowing the havoc the Creep had inflicted on every Christmas, birthday, gathering, or day of the week of any kind, my sister specifically articulated to my mother that she was invited, but he wasn't welcome.

Anyone trying to tell him what he could and couldn't do infuriated him. I spotted him in the parking lot of the reception, sitting alone in his car, drinking. He arrived drunk at the party in progress and was aggressive with guests, taunting people to hit him and making passes at women, including my then-partner Kirby's mother, who was there with her husband. My mother gently tried to get him to leave, and led him outside.

When we later went out to the parking lot to decorate the newlyweds' car, I saw them in the dark behind the community centre. He was holding her by the throat against the wall, slapping her face. It was the first time I'd seen it since moving out. I reacted with all the pent-up anger from years of this treatment. I sprinted toward him, an unfamiliar voice coming out of me like a war cry. Both arms were up as I plowed into him at full speed, sending him flying to the ground. He started swinging fists from where he lay, stumbling to get up and fight. Kirby joined me as we pushed him back down, telling him to leave. When he tried to punch me, I kicked him, wanting him to either stay down or leave. We pulled his shoes off, throwing them onto the street for him to have to retrieve, trying to disable him from further attack. Suddenly the whole wedding party flooded out to the parking lot, led by my crying sister in her wedding dress.

I hate recounting this story, the visceral anger rising in me as I do, along with an awful helpless feeling for my mother. I was trying to help her, but I'd just made her life worse. Once again, we all asked, "Why are you with him?" We encouraged her that now was the time. I only recount this because it was my breaking point. He pressed assault charges against my partner and me, my passive mother undecided about which side she was going to defend for two and a half years until it came to trial. I cut myself off from my mother, angry with her for what her choices had done to all of us. I didn't want to be a part of my toxic family. Although I never thought that I didn't love her, this was necessary. I couldn't stand seeing her being treated the way she was, but there was nothing I could do about it. She refused all offers of help from anyone, telling them it was fine, she was fine.

We seldom saw each other. I lived my own new life, away from home. All of my siblings moved to other cities, also needing distance from the festering disease who lived in the home we grew up in.

My mother's way of dealing with so many critical things was avoidance. She remained in this mode until the court date finally arrived. I went out to the courthouse, dressed in a suit on the long bus ride into industrial suburbia. I still didn't know whose side she was going to take, inner dialogues of imagined conversations about this keeping me awake at night. I couldn't find the courtroom; no information about our case was posted. When I asked at a desk, I was told I should have been notified that the case was thrown out. He hadn't dropped the charges, but the courts were so backlogged that a slew of cases deemed of lesser importance had been dropped. I just didn't know how my mother could defend him and his actions, and I don't remember ever thinking of the reality of me having a criminal record as a result of defending my mother. My own sense of justice and naivety about the justice system caused me to believe I would win. Once again, my mother didn't have to take a stand, further reinforcing my belief that she cared more for him than she did for her kids. She did the same when he also charged my youngest sister and her husband with assault, also from defending her during a beating.

After a few years of not being involved, I began seeing a therapist. Much like every psychotherapy punchline, my relationship with my mother was at the centre of my issues. I had to figure out if I wanted a relationship with her, and if so, how do I navigate it? How can it even happen? Do I want a life without my mother? Ultimately I didn't.

I was in a relationship, and my mother was welcoming to not only my partner but to his parents as well, our mothers developing a sisterly bond. I tentatively reconnected with her, in a more arms-length way. I wouldn't go to her home if the Creep was there. She never spoke of him; I didn't ask. Some time after my relationship was over, she invited me to Christmas dinner. Of course I asked if the Creep would be there, and she said no.

I thought of one childhood Christmas where he was drunk and beating up on the family. He chased me through the house, and I ran out the front door in only socks, T-shirt, and pyjama bottoms. I was probably twelve. It being Christmas day, nothing was open. There was nowhere to go. The only place I could think of was my sister's boyfriend's apartment, almost five kilometres away. I ran in the snow, crying as I went, my startled sister coming to the door to let me in when she heard my voice on the intercom.

This time, after she promised he wouldn't be there for Christmas dinner, I arrived at her house to find him there. I put my coat back on to leave immediately, but my mother begged me to stay, saying he'd promised to behave. Annoyed that she had not told me the truth, I relented and remained, uncomfortable and quiet the whole time, wanting it to be over with. I was grown-up and strong, confident I could disable him if necessary. He probably knew the same, so we avoided each other, never being in the same room until it was time to sit at the dinner table. We sat at opposite ends, not interacting, and as soon as I finished eating, I got up and said my goodbyes. I arrived home sad, depressed and alone.

The twenty-four-hour video store across the road from me was open, so I went to get a movie to spend the rest of Christmas with. My eyes set upon a documentary I had read about: *Silverlake Life*, a 1993 film documenting a male couple's relationship as they navigate one of them dying from HIV/AIDS-related complications. I held the box in my hand, thinking it was probably the wrong day to watch this video, but I'd never seen it for rent before — it felt like this might be my only opportunity. Against my better judgment, I took it home. I'd experienced so many friends dying, including my best friend, so I wasn't unfamiliar with what would happen. The film was more brutal and stark than I was prepared for, one partner filming the other's death as he now faced a similar fate. I watched to the end and cried for the men in the film, my friends, my mother, and myself. It's going to be hard to top that one as the worst Christmas ever.

Over time, my mother and I developed more friendship, more care. My first boyfriend, at some point, said "I love you" to me. I froze. No one that I could remember had ever said that to me before. My mother hadn't; we didn't say it to each other. I became extremely uncomfortable, not knowing how to respond. To me, love was a word you might only use with one person in your life, and somehow you'll know who that is and just feel and know it. I cared for him, but I didn't really know what to label "love." I loved my dogs, I loved my records. I said something stupid back to him, deflecting with a joke. I was quick-witted, and for years I used that to evade real feelings. I didn't know how to talk about emotional states.

I couldn't bring myself to say "I love you" back, I didn't even know if I felt it. Over the years, I know that I did feel it, as we became best friends instead of boyfriends. I did love him, but the modelling I'd experienced growing up made that too scary to say.

My third, and then-longest, relationship changed me. He said "I love you" all the time. It got easier and easier to say and feel. I recognized that I loved so many people — friends and family — but not knowing how to say that had built a wall, an obstacle so monumental that it prevented me from seeing and feeling it from others. When I finally said "I love you" to my mother, I could see it took her off guard. She didn't know how to respond, her eyes darting as if looking for escape. She said it back to me, kind of laughing as if she were delivering a comedy bit. Over time, saying it more manifested it, made it happen. By this time, my mother was retired and I was self-employed, earning my living making music, and with flexible time to go grocery shopping with her or have lunch together.

For the next twenty years, we grew closer. I was forthright with her, told her uncomfortable things, and asked her more about herself — and sometimes she was able to answer. A question that all us kids inevitably came back to was: "Why are you with him?" One day during a dispute that somehow involved the Creep, my sister angrily asked that question. For the first time, she answered it: "Because I have a right to not be alone."

I'm still saddened by the implications of that. My mother *was* alone because she was with *him*, but she couldn't see that. By then I'd had so many incredible experiences in my life, given and received so much love and care from people, and it broke my heart that the same hadn't happened for her in all the time I'd known her.

Bit by bit she distanced herself from him, but always remained connected. He'd go away for long periods, but would show up in the middle of the night and let himself in. She'd tell me she was breaking up with him, had broken up with him, had told him she didn't want to be with him. I never knew what was true because his heavy shadow was always there in the background.

She was making a break in whatever way she knew how, but got sucked right back in as full-time nurse and maid when he had a stroke. On the couple of occasions that I saw him, I felt not pleased but struck by the cosmic justice of seeing this monstrous person weakened and helpless, the physical power he had used to terrorize us now gone. I could have easily kicked him in his wheelchair and not felt regret. There was no reconciling of feelings — those will always remain ambiguous and unknowable. Why was he that way? Why was she that way?

He was simple, stupid really, a bigoted cruel idiot who couldn't do single-digit math, could barely read, and had no curiosity or care for the people or world around him. His bullying was physical compensation for his mental weaknesses, his macho arrogance his power. With that drained, he was empty, nothing. Alcohol amplified his inner anger. Many people fall prey to enacting the role of their oppressor, becoming alcoholic or substance-dependent in the same way. Thankfully, my mother, myself and my siblings did not.

A feeling of repulsion at some alcoholic behaviour has lingered in me. In the bullshit mythologies of bands, so many people have laughed about certain bands, giggling as they say, "They were so wasted." "The Replacements were so drunk they could barely play." "Mark E. Smith couldn't even walk, he was so pissed." My feeling is often: *just fuck right off.* I don't find that cute or endearing, and over time, acting out as a result of alcohol abuse diminishes my respect for an artist.

I love the Fall, but I saw that same inner, seething rage multiply over many years in interviews with Mark E. Smith, watched him belligerently control his band by fucking with their amps. I had heightened awareness of the rock-star corniness of the Replacements. Don't get me wrong, I enjoy drinking when I feel like it, but it's the hateful interior monster seeping out that makes me turn away. It's there on the surface when we see certain artists, or even friends, over a long period. My family had enough of our life experience taken away by a selfish alcoholic.

Why my mother was that way is a harder question to answer. She almost never drank, only enjoying peach schnapps once a year, from a bottle she had to hide behind the dining room curtain. For a time, from my perspective anyway, she had a lot going for her. She was only in her thirties when she became a single mother, still beautiful and with friends and family that could help carry her to the time when she would really blossom — but that was all derailed. She'd worked her way up in her department at Simpsons, becoming the head buyer of the general supply department for all their stores in Canada. She'd done incredibly well for a single mom with only a high school education and few practical occupational skills. What she was really great at was finding a bargain, a necessity to keep her family and home afloat. This was the skill that made her so good at her job, that allowed her to rise to management when few women did.

Shirl was so bargain-conscious that in 1991, she prepaid her cremation and related expenses in order to beat the Goods and Services Tax that was about to be introduced.

Her insecurity and low self-esteem were so apparent to me later in my life, when I understood those things more. By example, over and over I saw with friends and family how the models that we live with affect us for all our days. I developed empathy for my mother when I looked at how her mother had treated her. She was forced into the role of mother from a young age, and that echoed through the generations. I sometimes wonder if that is a modern construction, because before the world became industrialized, children were a commodity — another hand to help on the farm, an insurance policy that you would be taken care of in your old age. That can be done with love, or it can be done with cruelty: each approach will directly affect the type of relationship one generation has with the next. My mother was born into the incongruity of a loving father and a mean mother.

I saw that my mother didn't have the skills to navigate the situation she put herself in, didn't know how to say no to someone using her because she was always afraid of rocking the boat, always wishy-washy when it came to *her* care. Because her self-care was so minimally evident and her last priority, that way of being was passed on to her kids. She was always in the role of caring for others. In so doing, she lost herself.

I'd witnessed her own mother be rejected by her family. I feel empathy and more understanding for my grandmother now than I did at the end of her life. Even though she was nasty, her selfish and erratic behaviour near the end caused everyone to refer to her as Granny Flipwitch. I later understood that she was exhibiting signs of dementia or cognitive impairment, just as her daughter would later. She was in control of some of her behaviour, but more and more often not as she approached the end of her long life.

The Creep eventually died. Only my mother, one of his sons, and a cottage neighbour attended the funeral. Everyone else said good riddance. I had to bite my tongue from saying that to my mother, trying to understand that in some way, she cared for him. Did she see him as a lost dog in need of help, like so many of the pets that we took in? His death was freeing for her, his unpredictable fury no longer ready to spring out unexpectedly.

She began travelling and living more of the life I hoped she'd have, especially after retiring. She'd go with her brother and his wife to Mexico to see monarch butterflies wintering, and took a trip to Alaska on the back of my brother's motorcycle. She said "I love you" and talked guardedly but increasingly more openly with me about her feelings. When I told her at twenty-one that I was gay, she said she cried and blamed herself, something my sister had already told me. But I knew she meant it when one day, at a time when all my other siblings were going through divorce, in-fighting, or hard times, she said to me, "I sometimes wish all my kids were gay."

As an adult, I recognized that our lives had been really fucked up, disrupted by the worst demon you could ever invite into your home. I also saw that, even though she wasn't able to say it, my mother did love us, did love me, and she showed it the way she knew how — by working so hard, for so many hours, every day of the week, to house and feed us. Continually showing up with bags of groceries, long after I depended on her, illustrated how much she connected being fed to a display of caring, of love. Her worth was tied up so deeply in how she could help, what she could do to be of service to us. She made clothes for my sisters and their kids, shared her garden, gave us twenty dollars now and then to go out to dinner. She cared for me when my back was so bad that I couldn't walk, trying to carry me. She climbed through a tiny opening in a closet ceiling in the first home I bought, helping me insulate it when she was in her seventies.

We rarely ever mentioned the Creep.

As she got into her older ages, our roles reversed and I became more of her caretaker, the one who took her to appointments and helped with her home. I was the only one of her kids living in the same city, so the demands were intense at times, but I'm grateful that I was able to reflect back to her the aspects of good care that she had shown me. We somehow were able to redirect those ingrained imperatives and make things better, just in time.

When she died, I had no regrets, had nothing unsaid to her, no subject unbroached. She wasn't always capable of answering the questions I asked, sometimes willfully but other times because she lacked self-reflection. She hadn't asked herself some of the questions I asked her, something that astonished me to her last days. I saw that some of the things I needed from her were things she wasn't capable of giving, not things that she had intentionally withheld. She had a guarded melancholy that co-existed with a delight in simple pleasures, like seeing beautiful flowers or sunsets, or sitting on her porch and having all the neighbourhood families smile and wave at her when they went by. There had been many years when that wasn't possible. I finally saw her at peace.

Each of her children, and all the relatives with whom she was once close, live with some degree of damage. It shaped us in negative and positive ways. Revelations about how the husband of author

Alice Munro abused her children reignited internal debates in me, but there is no absolute reconciling. There are no more answers other than the ones I imagine, or that come out of what will surely be a lifelong process with my siblings. Judgment about Munro has been absolute, but I imagine few who make those assessments have lived through a similar situation and see Munro in very defined terms. I can't speak for my siblings, but we all had relationships with my mother at the end of her life, were all in her life actively. She wasn't a monster. On the contrary, she was mostly kind and generous. I can't fully account for her choices, but only try and understand.

As her cognitive abilities started to slip, so did some of the gentle and warmhearted aspects of her personality, many of the traits she exhibited consistent with cognitive impairment. Some of her grand-kids knew her more as a crabby old lady, and I wondered if this was a way of being that was always there but so shielded that it could never be let out. Was this her own anger and resentment about her own decisions, her internal feelings that she'd repressed, now manifest?

I can never fully know who she was, only that I said everything I needed to while she was still here. I got the answers she was capable of giving. And I know that I'm left with a feeling of deep love for her. Her love was uncomplicated, like the bag of on-sale apples she'd show up at my door with — that was her way of showing it.

I took the apples and made something for us both to share.

KIDS WHO ARE MEN

THERE'S A NEIGHBOURHOOD IN THE SOUTHWEST OF CALGARY called Braeside. After Reid Diamond and his family moved there in 1973 from Steinbach, Manitoba, Reid met up with another neighbourhood kid, Bruce McCulloch. Both were short smart alecks, witty and mouthy, and shared a love for the same music, like the Who and Montrose. I didn't know them then, but would later regularly hear stories from those who did: how they'd taunt and confuse dim-witted bullies and Calgary yokels with vicious insults and clever parables, sometimes resulting in the two of them running away, laughing mockingly at some lumbering doofus who couldn't catch these scrawny brats. During and after high school, they worked together at Canada Dry, best friends loading and washing trucks, and stealing bottles they'd sell back to other depots.

I'd hear how Bruce, despite cultivating an oddball persona by wearing pyjamas as street clothes, was still a bit of a jock, carrying around dumbbells in the trunk of his car. These did double-duty by giving him rear traction in brutal Calgary winters, and also allowed the opportunity to do curls and flys when he was waiting around somewhere. He was fairly jacked when I first met him.

Buick McKane — the band that Reid, Brian Connelly, and Alex Koch were in — got out of Calgary after having had enough of racist bar fights, and being called faggots on the street for wearing badges or straight-leg jeans. It didn't take much then. Reid wrote letters to Bruce back in Calgary, telling him about his new life and all the amazing bands he was seeing in Toronto, and imploring him to come out and join them. Bruce was in his early days of doing comedy, being part of Calgary's Loose Moose Theatre Company, and a troupe called the Audience with another future Kid, Mark McKinney.

Bruce came to feel out Toronto a couple of times, once with two pals from Calgary and Edmonton. They were like untamed animals escaped from their cages, drinking as much as their bodies would allow on the roof of Alex and Reid's boarding house, and going out to see bands every night.

It was 1979 and the Cramps were at the creepy peak of their first wave, before they had an album out and when the ultra-sinister-looking Bryan Gregory was strangling shreds of buzzsaw guitar from his polka-dotted Flying V. They happened to be in town playing the Edge, so the group of us went to the show, becoming copiously lubricated before doing so. It ended up being a debauched evening with one of Bruce's pals, Terry, passing out with his head resting on his folded arms on the table at the Edge. During the song "Human Fly," singer Lux Interior climbed along the back of the bench seat until he reached our slumped pal. Lux's pants had come down at some point, as they often did in early Cramps shows, and he squatted on our friend's head, his balls splayed across Terry's forehead and his long dick rubbing across the rest of his upper face, wiping our friend's brow. He waved the shaft around as though his cock head was the pesky fly he was channelling in the song — *bzzzz.* Terry later became a cop.

Another of the western visitors was too drunk or impatient to use the bathroom and decided the clear, accordion-doored phone booth across the road was a good place to pee. Not being a local, they weren't so aware how that part of the street had an active sex trade and was crawling with cops. He was busted and charged with indecent exposure, forcing him to return to Toronto later for an unscheduled visit.

It was inevitable that Bruce would move out here. Like Brian, Reid, and Steve Koch before him, his first few nights in the city were spent in the basement of my mother's home. I was living there, still in high school, and didn't know the extent of Bruce's sense of humour. He came down from the shower and said straight-faced to me, "I left some pubic hair on the soap for your mother." I could never have imagined at that moment the history we would have together.

Like my bandmates at the time in Crash Kills Five, Bruce was clever and bitingly quick with a comeback or comment. It was pretty clear that we had all been steeped in the same comedy marinade, a dirty cocktail of *Mad* magazine, Bugs Bunny and Daffy Duck, *Get Smart*, *Laugh-In*, Woody Allen, Bob Newhart, *SCTV*, and to a lesser degree, *Monty Python*. Our sensibilities were as reactive *against* shitty Canadian comedy, like *King of Kensington* and *The Trouble with Tracy*, as they were *for* the good stuff coming to us from other places.

Bruce and Reid obviously had a connective force between them from long before I knew either, finishing each other's lines and being flippant about the same dumb things around us. I recall making a reference to the Pink Floyd song "Any Colour You Like," but before I could finish the sentence, Bruce interrupted: "How about brown?"

For a while in 1982–83, Bruce and Reid had a duo, Orion's Belt, where Reid played guitar and Bruce was the bass player, accompanied by a rudimentary drum machine. Reid was pretty raw as a guitarist, and Bruce was barely functional, with Reid mostly writing the music and showing him what frets to press on what string for what song. I always thought the name Orion's Belt was in the same lexicon as the Canadian-ness of bands like Brave Belt and Scrubbaloe Caine, all connected to the Guess Who somehow. One of Orion's Belt's songs, "Happiness Pie," even ended up being recorded by Bruce and The Odds for the soundtrack of the KITH movie *Brain Candy*, and was almost the title of the film.

There were about four years in between Crash Kills Five and the beginning of Shadowy Men on a Shadowy Planet in 1984, the same year that Bruce and Mark joined the already rolling *Kids in the Hall*. We were all absorbing and reflecting the atmosphere of what was happening in Toronto. We were disdainful of everything, as young brats are wont to be, but it was a heavy, sometimes overly serious but ridiculous time. From the nauseatingly colourful positivity of Parachute Club's "Rise Up" to the post-goth junkie scene that dominated local live-music circles, we each came into being in a time of extremes, with so much richness to react against. We were entwined from day one, and as a few have pointed out, musicians who wanted to be comedians and comedians who wanted to be musicians. Not quite accurate, but close enough for a rough description.

Reid was enrolled in a theatre tech program at Humber College, learning stagecraft that ran the gamut from sound to lights. He'd played in bands for years, so he had a good idea about how things should be run, and now he had the carpentry skills to build sets and could run the mix of a stage show. Immediately, Brian, Reid and, by extension, Shadowy Men were recruited to provide the occasional piece of music to soundtrack a sketch the Kids were working out. As their live sound tech, Reid would also set up and run their lights, playing back tapes and records as musical cues for sketches. He was effectively producing their live shows.

The Kids had a residency at Poor Alex Theatre, where they performed a mix of dismal experiments and brilliant, unorthodox, conceptual and intellectual comedy. Plus lots of dumb stuff. I didn't see them enough nights on that run to know if there was any build happening, but one night I attended had maybe ten or twelve audience members scattered in clusters. On this night, someone in the audience discovered there were jelly donuts taped to the bottom of some seats. People immediately raced to find them all and hurl them at the group on stage. Years later, I read an interview with Scott Thompson where he described being at that same show and said he was one of the donut tossers — and it was the day he joined the troupe.

Honestly, there weren't a lot of signs of what was to come. Shadowy Men were involved in our own thing, and I imagine the Kids sitting around one-upping each other with absurd ideas exactly as our band did. Shadowy Men caused an immediate reaction when we began playing, able to headline and do the shows we wanted to pretty much right away. The Rivoli, home of our first-ever show, was our place. We loved the space, the owners, everyone who worked there, and we easily played the club more times in our life as a band than anywhere. The Kids obviously saw the potential as a place where they could put on their own shows without the pressure of a traditional theatre or establishment comedy-club environment, kind of like a rock show. It felt natural for them to play there too, paving the way for the Rivoli to become the new comedy hot spot in town.

After providing original pre-recorded music, and them using tracks from our couple of singles, we made the leap to a full-on stage production in a "legit" theatre, one that regularly hosted festivals and hit plays. The Factory Theatre was a big old space, with a balcony and staff — a significant attempt at an upgrade from the spaces the Kids had worked in up until then. It was a big gamble, but so was everything at that point. It was 1986 and each of our groups had some kind of audience; together maybe we could make something exciting happen.

Shadowy Men rehearsed one block away from the theatre and took our gear over in a grocery cart and dolly. We'd rehearsed with combinations of the troupe in our space, tightening the loose ends with a couple of days of dress rehearsal in the theatre. One section on stage right was partitioned off with a scrim, us tucked in behind. When the theatre lights out front came up, we were invisible, but we'd magically appear from the darkness when the lights on our side of the screen came up.

Grave Robbers from Hipsville was announced with a poster drawn by Brian Connelly, really solidifying the aesthetic connections between us. The Kids are shown as being some kind of beatnik hybrid of the Spy vs. Spy guys from *Mad* magazine and the Shadowy Men characters that were increasingly becoming stand-ins for us, replacing boring trad-band pics. We played a few songs to start, and then, at the Kids' request, the song "Bennett Cerf" from our first single as their intro theme. During blackouts and set changes, which were minimal to nothing, we'd play from our then-smallish repertoire until the lights fell, our cue to fade out. In darkness, we watched the most refined version of the Kids' comedy we'd seen up until that point. John Hemphill, who was all over *SCTV* in their last few years, was directing. Something happened, and he was replaced by Andy Jones from Newfoundland comedy collective CODCO. The two of them really sharpened the chaos. The show featured some greatest hits of the Kids' repertoire at that point, mixed with a few new sketches — a fantastic, creative working experience.

It was originally scheduled to have a one-week run, part of the incentive being to showcase their comedy in a more rehearsed way. They were fishing for a produced broadcast show. Lorne Michaels was among the small handful of people who could make that happen. The run was held over when word came that Lorne wanted to come check them out. The first week had respectable attendance, but the extension was a harder sell. Factory had a lot of seats to fill. It was a bit of work to get the word out that the show was still running.

Midway through the second week, one Kid asked why we kept playing that song to open the show. "Well, that's 'Bennett Cerf,' the song you asked for." Oops, they meant "Having an Average Weekend," the song that followed it on the B-side of our first single. From that day forward, it became their signature song, opening the rest of the theatre run and becoming the theme for the TV special that led to their series, and then, of course, the series itself. When the *Kids in the Hall* series was briefly rebooted in 2022, it once again opened each episode. It's been a kick over the years to hear it played by people like Paul Shaffer and the David Letterman band, or other house acts when any of the Kids were guests on chat shows.

Back at Factory Theatre, the second week became a little looser. While we were unseen in our dark cavern, the *pfft* of beer cans opening cut through the acoustics of the space, even if we tried to mask them by waiting until a spot we knew was particularly loud. We were generally pretty responsible when we had a task to do, but the run was starting to feel a bit like summer camp, making music and laughs with our friends for hours every day. For me to even have one beer while playing was unheard of, my functionality diminishing exponentially. The Kids were improvising a little more freely, unexpectedly switching roles. One night near the end, Kevin made his entrance falling through the curtain, naked and giggling. Sketches like "The Seuss Bible" and "Running Faggot" were already fully realized; audiences would gasp and choke with laughter seeing those for the first time. It was years before those radical pieces showed up in the series, but every night it was clear the Kids were doing something exciting and unorthodox.

I don't think Lorne ever showed up, but he did poach Mark and

Bruce in 1987 to come write and perform for *Saturday Night Live*. It never sounded like that was a good fit for them, and it wasn't long before Lorne brought the whole troupe down to New York City to do a weekly residency, sharpening them up for the gruelling demands of a TV series.

A year and a half later, their resolve resulted in a one-hour special, co-produced by Michaels' company Broadway Video and the Canadian Broadcasting Corporation. The execs were mostly American, while the crew and facilities were in our home, Toronto. What was originally framed as a special then became known as the pilot, as the show was picked up for a series, running for five seasons.

We were tickled that we were invited along for the ride. Given our working history and friendship, it seemed natural to us, but not so much to daddy Lorne. We heard that he didn't want to take a chance on us, wanting something much more like the *Saturday Night Live* band. Someone in these meetings told us he'd described us as sounding like "cheap porno music," which we were definitely not insulted by. It was only because of the Kids' insistence that Lorne bent. We wouldn't have been there if it weren't for them pushing for us, and I'm always so grateful to them for doing that.

The pilot was directed by Robert Boyd. John Blanchard, who'd directed the extraordinary *SCTV* series, came on board to make a similar kind of group-chemistry magic work for the Kids series. Everything about it was in place to be something unique and quite exceptional for Canadian television. In so many ways, it felt inevitable despite being subversive. It was how TV comedy should be, but usually wasn't.

We three Shadowy Men got time off from our day jobs to record music for the special, and to play for the studio audience during the taping. Tapings would run pretty much exactly as the live show had: us to intro, then a sketch or three followed by a musical interlude from us again, and so on.

We recorded maybe fifteen ultra-short versions of our songs, and a few new instrumental zings used to soundtrack Super-8 interludes that bumpered sketches. We were sent to do our first recording session in the CBC Summerhill studio, although later we'd also record in one of many satellite locations they used when their studios were occupied. We re-recorded two versions of "Having an Average Weekend" to conform to the opening and closing credits, along with a few variations on flourishes excised from the song to lead into or out of commercial breaks. We didn't even really think of recording all-new music for the pilot because these were the songs that had been the soundtrack to KITH live performances so far, and it's not like very many people actually knew the cuts the pieces were snipped from.

The show was to be a mix of pre-taped video segments, shown to the audience to record their response, and sketches performed live with a multi-camera setup. The CBC studio on Mutual Street in downtown Toronto became our home for the next six years of taping. We had a considerable amount of real estate at the beginning, on a giant clamshell set that we built as our own backdrop. Given how picky unions can be, I'm now surprised that we got away with that, posing a potential threat to the carpenters working on the show. We were in prime sightlines for the audience, taking up one large end of the soundstage. Bruce asked Reid, "What's with the clamshell?" Reid replied with something like, "We have to put on a show too!"

As much as we were working, we were also the audience — few of us had seen a television show being produced on this scale. Everyone was effervescent with excitement about what was happening. Watching how cameras and sets were blocked, torn down, and moved around was fascinating. So many comedians we knew from the Kids' past were hired as writers and sometimes performers. Guys who'd been in the Audience troupe, like Norm Hiscock, Frank Van Keeken, and Garry Campbell, as well as Luciano Casimiri and Diane Flacks from earlier versions of the Kids, along with Brian Hartt and Paul Bellini, made up a dynamic writing team whose working history in the same venues had put them all at the same level to begin with.

It was a big thrill for the first show to broadcast. Not only was it our friends who were making this great thing, it was us too! I loved seeing Toronto represented from the opening second of the show, the locations being extremely familiar to any kid who got around in the city. The very first appearance of the Head Crusher, in the premiere, takes place in the park across from St. Lawrence Hall, right by the city's oldest farmers' market, and the interstitial film that leads into Buddy Cole's first monologue stops outside the old Yonge Street day-drinking gay bar, Trax. The "Naked for Jesus" sketch had scenes outside the office of the optometrist I've seen for more than forty years!

When the show was picked up as a series, it was extremely satisfying to give my notice at the job I'd worked since high school. No one knew how long the show would last or whether anyone would notice it, but after eight years in retail, I was definitely becoming cranky about dealing with people. The show started shooting in autumn, so I had a luxurious summer of going to my local pool every day, coming home to watch *I Love Lucy*, and having lunch before heading over to our Parkdale garage to work on music.

From day one there were a couple of things that made the production such a fantastic experience. First and foremost, the people who worked on *Kids in the Hall* were a real team in which it felt like everyone loved their job, and didn't just get along but were friends. At the beginning it felt non-hierarchical, everyone happy to see each other and to work in this unique environment. I'm sure a few people who were there would roll their eyes at that idea, but everyone I run into still talks about what a wonderful situation making that show was, that it was their favourite working circumstance ever. We all had a job to do, and people worked hard at their roles, but it was a rather loose environment. None of the union over-regulation and restrictive work guidelines were enforced in any heavy way. If someone needed help pulling a rope, they'd ask whoever was there, even if it was the cast. Each year changed slightly, but that was more about the removal of the Kids themselves from the camaraderie in the rest of the crew. As they became more known, more of their time was spent in their dressing rooms, while we had this vast playroom where we did our tasks.

One night, we were loaded into the back of a van and driven down into the abandoned Distillery District. In 1987, this area was completely deserted at night, vast swaths of land vacant except for rubble and other industrial and construction debris. The most active business seemed to be the scrapyard that looked part art installation, its hubcaps and bumpers displayed neatly as if in a gallery. I'm pretty sure no one had permits, another aspect of the show that really marks it as being from another era. Someone had scouted a freight railcar that provided a bit of visual shield while also making a scenic post-apocalyptic backdrop. A couple of lights went up and away we went, playing our theme song in the harshly lit darkness. Two or three takes and back into the van.

I was surprised at how much screen time we were given when the first season's credits were revealed. Perhaps feeling we'd been given too much of a visual cameo, each subsequent season's new credits cut us back a bit more until we weren't in them at all. One season's credits were shot in a "party" meant to visually twin with the party scene from *Midnight Cowboy*. Extras were paid to have fun and dance, while we did it for the bananas at the craft services table. At least it provided an opportunity to explore the disused former Simpsons Mail Order Building, built in 1910, a stunning cavernous space now renovated into lofts as the Merchandise Building. I'd been to a couple of raves there, but this credit shoot was legit, with much forced laughter and drinks, and was presumably shot with permits.

Shadowy Men on a Shadowy Planet played to the studio audience for every single taping. Realizing how precious every bit of floor space was, we were moved to one end of the studio, facing the audience's left side rather than head on. People had to crane their necks more to watch us — or not — as we were also shown on the studio TV monitors that pointed toward them so they could see pre-taped sketches. You could just watch us on TV, but there was no ignoring us. We were a loud rock band blasting the space as crew shouted over us to talk about the work they had to do. We'd play a longer set off the top, starting from when the audience were led to their seats.

In the pilot and at the beginning, Brian wore an earpiece to get instructions from the director, but that proved maddening and impossible. He'd be trying to play our songs while also having to pay close attention to every bit of non-stop information coming through his speaker. There was too much cross-chatter to decipher, and it wasn't long before we became light-sensitive, wind-up musical monkeys: turn the light on and we play, turn the light off and we stop.

Lorne Michaels came to visit now and then. There was always a tension when he was in the building. It felt like the boss was there because, well, he was. Early in the first season, the three of us were coming back to the studio for a late taping, walking across the big open parking lot that used to be across the road. We crossed paths with director John Blanchard and Lorne, returning from dinner. John introduced us to Lorne, and as he shook our hands, he said, "You'll find that this show makes you more popular." I wasn't sure if it was a warning or a blessing.

In each taping block, they'd shoot two shows a day, two days a week for two weeks, making a total of eight taping sessions every two weeks. The shows performed for the cameras weren't shot in chronological order, but were rather what worked together as a set, both content-wise and logistically — like how many and where the sets are going to be. The same set of sketches would be shot twice on each day of shooting, the best one used as the master take. Audience responses would reveal unexpected things about a piece, like the yucks being much greater, or less, than anticipated. The second set would have tweaks made to improve the subsequent performance. Once in a while, a sketch would reappear months later, having had a total rewrite. After the studio audience departed, pick-up shots were done to fix flubbed lines or to get particular shots not possible in the main shoot. Sometimes the redone shots were to create a more relaxed environment for, say, a dog to walk on set and eat a piece of fake poo.

We'd arrive after some of the crew had already been working for hours, receiving a shooting order and other notes as needed. We'd then make up a set list, overestimating because of the unpredictability of setup times between sketches.

The soundstage was an intricate puzzle of more detailed sets that remained in place for the shooting block, and a mapped-out collection of mobile sets that could be rapidly assembled as soon as there was time or room. Three elaborate panels forming the walls of a room would be rolled into place, with props like furniture and all the loose background details, along with extra actors, squeezed into the area. With all the lighting, sound, and camera crews, a wall of workers and equipment obscured the view for the studio audience.

For me and so many of the people I know who came to the tapings, watching the creative and technical production was as fascinating a part of the show as the comedy happening that moment. Our first stage during the series was elevated, but then, in the quest for ever more floor space, we went way up, a microcosm of how the city around us ended up growing. Onto a constructed platform — a structure rebuilt for every taping, made of interlocking bars and panels — we'd move our gear up, scaling a vertical ladder. It was ridiculously high, creating an entire room under us, which held craft services and the pass-through from backstage onto the soundstage. Dragging a bass drum or five-hundred-pound organ up onto that thing was hardly the safest situation, but they had to get up there. Like I've said before: once you're in a band, you're a furniture mover for life.

Because there were a few hours of break between the early and late shows, the crew would have dinner spread out on the soundstage and sets in groups, chatting and laughing. There were lots of laughs, not only from *The Kids in the Hall* at its best, but from the relaxed environment. In between shows we'd go for a walk or get groceries or something, and enjoy talking with the Kids and crew. The super-gay coffee shop that is portrayed in "The Steps" sketches was two blocks from where we shot, and always the destination for fancy-coffee runs. At the end of the night, after a taping block and as crew packed up sets and their work materials, a big plastic trash bin filled with beer and ice would be dragged onto the soundstage, people drinking as they finished their tasks. There were a few nights I left at 5 a.m. and was still not the last one to leave the office. People would sit around talking and laughing, someone would have something to play music on, and it would become an after-hours party.

Shadowy Men were nominated for two Juno awards. I was mostly against awards, unless we were winning them, which we did with one of our nominations. We rarely knew anyone at ceremonies like these. They were awkward, but sometimes silly fun. When I was in the band King Cobb Steelie, we were at a post-Juno party after we'd been nominated. And who did we know? One waiter working the event. The rap group Dream Warriors were slinking around the gathering, trying to find a comfortable place to be, them being in the same position as us as the odd ducks at the event. They spotted us, and like two sets of outcasts in the schoolyard, we were immediately drawn to one another.

One year when Shadowy Men were nominated, the Juno ceremony was broadcast live, with most of the TV crew being people we knew from *Kids* tapings. We knew who Barenaked Ladies were, but didn't know them. Seated in the same aisle, I waved hello and smiled to them as we made our way to our seats. Their drummer, Tyler, made a screw-you face, mouthing the words "fuck you" at me and giving me the finger! *Hiyee back!* When our name was called as the winner, all across the theatre the crew working the show jumped up and cheered for us. Honestly, that was as memorable to me as Reid kissing presenter Sylvia Tyson when he ran up to accept. Having the biggest applause coming from the crew working the show really meant something to us.

I feel like the Kids themselves missed some of the more fun parts of the tapings as time went on. They became distinctly the stars of the show, not just part of the working crew. They had to spend more time in hair and makeup and generally had greater demands on them, along with some ego that comes from being the stars of a popular TV series. Production in general, and the environments in which people make film and TV, especially within institutions like the CBC, have changed so dramatically over time that I can't imagine most of what we took for granted as an ideal working environment happening today. Imagine a drinking and dancing party happening on the set of *The National.* Security was so loose and barely there compared to any subsequent work I did in the CBC's Broadcast Centre. The security people were almost as much a part of the fun crew as anybody else.

There was nothing like *The Kids in the Hall.* They were so incredible, producing the most subversive and distinctly contemporary comedy on TV. And Shadowy Men got to enter into and be part of the tail end of a unique and now extinct period in the CBC's history, when they occupied beautiful old spaces spread throughout the city. Our complex on Mutual Street consisted of a large soundstage, with side rooms for assembly or staging, a series of dressing rooms, and a basement that felt like a private museum. *Kids* was alternating shooting with the last years of *The Tommy Hunter Show* in the same studio, so all his flats, sets, costumes, and longer-term dressing rooms were in the basement. It was a stunning place to investigate in the dark at 2 a.m. after a few drinks, the crepe paper "stained glass" windows of a church set looking real and holy, and Tommy's royal blue, rhinestoned suits looking like ritualistic robes in their plastic reliquaries.

Through a connecting courtyard, CBC radio and television operations occupied a gorgeous, stately, and huge historic office building facing onto the next street over. A massive old transmitter tower on the same property broadcast CBC and others. They were grand buildings that, like much of the most precious architecture in Toronto, were sacrificed for development, and for the consolidation of the CBC in their new Broadcast Centre. With that came a slickening of the shows they produced, much of the quirky and distinct regional character being lost in the process.

We were sent around to various CBC studios to record the stings we'd write for the show, and to do custom pieces like "Daves I Know" or "Premise Beach." Each of us took a line and sang the chorus of "Daves I Know," not imagining how unnerving it would later be to see our voices coming out of someone else's body. One of CBC's studios was at Yonge and Summerhill in a refurbished former Pierce-Arrow auto showroom. It was a treat getting to record in myriad facilities with so many great audio engineers, both casual and seasoned. These multipurpose spaces often had some kind of radio or TV production happening in the same building as the recording studio. This place had been home to *Front Page Challenge* before us.

We were somewhat awed to discover that this complex was also home to the *Mr. Dressup* children's television show, his modest set permanently in place, like a little village whose inhabitants had all gone away for the weekend. It was mind-bending to be at the treehouse where the show's puppet stars Casey and Finnegan played, and to see Mr. Dressup's Tickle Trunk and sketch board right next to it. Through thoughtful camera angles, they created the illusion of multiple spaces within this compact area. It was never one of my favourite shows, even when I was six at the show's beginning. It had cheap production values and a slow weirdness that characterized so many shows produced by the CBC.

Of course, those limitations are what made some of the CBC shows so iconic and everlasting in our minds, so ingrained in every Canadian's psyche, particularly in their earlier decades when there were fewer TV options. They were *it* in Canada, and so distinctly Canadian. I had much more appreciation for this and other shows as an adult, valuing their subtlety and gentleness compared with increasingly bombastic US dispositions. Retrospectively, it seems entirely fitting that the stunningly talented singer-composer Beverly Glenn-Copeland was introduced to Canada through his twenty-five-year residency on *Mr. Dressup*. It stung to see that particular building scrubbed of its history, turned into a chain store selling office supplies.

Lower production values weren't exclusively a Canadian TV trait. Take *The Friendly Giant*, for example. While we may think of it as not being anything but Canadian, it was nabbed from the US after running there for a few years, brought to Canada in 1958 along with host Bob Homme. These shows were so in our blood, such a formative part of a national identity through the 1960s and '70s as I grew up. Shadowy Men on a Shadowy Planet even did a cover of *The Friendly Giant* theme, "Early One Morning," for a cross-border themed compilation assembled by Nardwuar the Human Serviette. And one Halloween, we played a show in costume with Reid dressed as Rusty the Rooster, the puppet who lived in a bag on *Friendly Giant*.

It was at the live tapings where we met most of the *Kids in the Hall* crew, but among them were a few familiar faces: Chris and Terry, whose respective bands, the Love Brothers and the Dundrells, we'd played with often. Doing special effects on the show was a friend who I knew as Miss Gussy. Gus was housemates with another friend who also ended up working the show. Talking with him during tapings, I learned that he had made and operated the cow jumping over the moon on *Friendly Giant*! It was kind of weird to have this magic moment I looked forward to every episode be humanized, even more so when I was over at his place one day and he took out a large portfolio with a few versions of the cow pressed in it. He said he had to make new ones once in a while, and would be one of the people flying the cow through the air on the end of a stick or string, or drawing the bridge and closing the castle doors at the end of each episode.

Unbelievably, these amazing tangible pieces of history are not in the CBC Museum. Mr. Dressup's Tickle Trunk had once been there, but in an act of poor judgment, the CBC closed the museum in 2017. Even the star from Tommy Hunter's dressing-room door was put in the trash after his series ended, retrieved by me.

We had an assignment to record a hard-rock version of the Kids' theme song and were dispatched to a hidden laneway studio across from Allan Gardens, Studio 306. Brian shredded some exquisite Queen-like harmonies on guitar as we did our best to channel some of the arena bands we'd seen as kids. We crossed paths with Rush, as Geddy Lee and Alex Lifeson were working in the other studio in the same building. We said hi as we passed each other in the hallway, but it's hard to not be an awkward dork around Rush. Geddy popped his head in at one point, knowing we were recording music for *Kids in the Hall*. This was our second time encountering them in a studio complex where we were both working, verifying that they most certainly knew of our existence and strengthening many people's belief (including mine) that they'd borrowed a couple of riffs from us.

Another version of "Having an Average Weekend" hit us by surprise when one of the Kids' sketches featured a children's choir singing it, mouthing the melodies and harmonies with la la las. At the time, I thought, *This is the pinnacle, it doesn't get any better or weirder than this.*

So many people have asked me over the years if I'm sick of that song. Actually, they usually don't ask, it's more of a statement: "You must be really sick of that song." I'm not. There are certain TV shows where I watch the opening credits no matter how many times I've seen the show, so integral are they to the whole experience that they are inseparable. There aren't many, but *The Mary Tyler Moore Show*, *The Bob Newhart Show*, *Bewitched* and *The Sopranos* come to mind. The song has taken on a life of its own, and in some ways it feels like a cover song to play. It's so distinctly embedded in the *Kids in the Hall* show now, and the worlds they created, that it's hard to imagine the show without it. Every once in a while, some article or interviewer would refer to it as Canada's third national anthem, after the real one and the *Hockey Night in Canada* theme. It's definitely a song many people know and identify with us, but I think the Fabricland or Pizza Pizza jingles are dug far deeper into people's brains. I rarely heard the song played because I rarely watched the KITH show beyond its first broadcast. I mostly hear it in cover versions that bands send me.

It was very noticeable after the show began to air. From the first notes of "Having an Average Weekend," a roar would arise from the crowd. It was startling at first because it wasn't like we had a hit or anything; it was a song that people knew from TV, and that came with a conditioned response. If you like the Kids, your brain suddenly receives pleasure from the song. Playing it, like playing any song, is completely different from hearing it, and there are almost none of our songs I grew tired of playing, including that one. I somehow get extreme gratification from playing certain songs over and over again, refining and tightening in a never-ending reach for improvement.

We'd usually put it early in a set, just to release the anticipation, not give the song undue weight by saving it for last song, or worse, an encore. We knew from the response that it was unique in the set, but it wasn't a burden. Oh wait, we did put it into an encore! Toward the end of the band's first life, we started doing a medley of classic rock riffs that was like a vile soup. We named it "16 Encores" because when it began, it was something like that number — sixteen five- to ten-second snippets of the best-known riffs around. It was like a K-Tel encore: every single hit ever. We constantly added to it until it became a lumbering, massive memory exercise. It was super dumb, but ridiculously fun to play, and it left people speechless. Numbed by the dumb. At some point we dropped the opening bars of "Having an Average Weekend" into it. Cheers went up with every new movement, the song the riff was derived from distilled to its corniest essence. It's not even the hits, it's a whiff of them. The reaction was often loudest for our own song as we forced it into the pantheon of iconic riffs.

When we played to the studio audience, we drew from our own repertoire, which reached something like 144 songs by the last season of the series. Many weeks we'd learn something new, like the "Theme from Midnight Cowboy," or play a track like "It's a Gas" from the *Mad* magazine flexi-disc that we'd just learned for a film score. But like the title of the unauthorized bio about us, *The Songs All Sound the Same*, one day Scott Thompson came up the ladder to our perch and indelicately asked, "Don't you guys know any more songs? Why do you keep playing the same songs?" I can sort of understand how that many songs could sound like maybe only ten different ones, but we were trapped in the sound of our own voice. We excelled at our limitations.

The studio was open, and the Kids had no security for their dressing rooms. We were mostly free to come and go, and as friends, we'd spend breaks chatting or just checking in. Music was always blasting from their enclave. One day I heard Kevin McDonald playing something that immediately grabbed me. Asking him what it was, he said it was the just-released Nirvana album. I hadn't really loved a lot of the Sub Pop catalogue. This was different, and of course it was *Nevermind*. There are not many records that I can recall where I was the first time I heard them.

The Kids' rising popularity came with some tensions. Inevitably, the Kids' relationship to those working around them changed. We were on great terms with all of them, but our history with Bruce, who was most active in music decisions about the show, made us more connected with him in particular. One day Scott was raging to me about how the gay press was ignoring him, that he wasn't getting due credit for the radical gayness he brought to mainstream television. His Buddy Cole character was absolutely brilliant, and I looked forward to any new instalment of his monologues. Maybe my expectations were lower, but the month Scott said this, he was the cover star and feature in *The Advocate*, the biggest gay news magazine of the time. He may have even been on it twice, or maybe it was another magazine. There was a second cover, in which he has a painted-on T-shirt bearing a twist on the AIDS action graphic "Silence = Death" but reworked to read "Silence = Relaxation." It was so shocking and casually extreme, its rebranding from radical slogan for ACT UP's raging protests to a call for personal comfort. The only AIDS humour at this time came from homophobes, so it was excitingly dark to see Scott twist this very serious bit of rally-cry into breathtakingly black humour.

We appeared in a few sketches, including one scathing piece starring Bruce and Kevin about bass players. When we did the music for it, we hadn't heard the dialogue yet. The first time we heard it was as we were performing for the camera. We appear in silhouette behind a scrim and fade out as the dialogue starts, but continuing to mime as if we're still playing.

"Everyone hates the bass player, no one invites the bass player to the party after the show." I felt a twinge of self-consciousness, as one does when comedy hits too close to home. But then Bruce, as the bass player, asks, "Is Heather coming?" It couldn't be a coincidence that that was the name of *our* bass player's partner. Feeling the sting of that arrow, I turned to Reid and saw him wincing. He looked to me with a hurt and angry expression, unseen by the audience on the other side of our veil.

In our time away from the show, we carried on as bands do, writing songs, touring, playing shows, and making art. Various Kids joined us for our concerts. Kevin rescued us one night when the magician we'd hired to open the show suddenly couldn't make it. He stepped in as Keveen the Impossibilist, a bumbling magician who really didn't know any magic. Bruce opened another show, as Tramouth, a bitter but comical angry dad who seemed like the template for Cabbagehead. And we were enchanted to be joined by Scott as Buddy Cole for a Christmas show, in which we backed up him and our friend and Rivoli booker, Carson Foster, as they duetted to the classic Frank and Nancy Sinatra song "Somethin' Stupid."

Over time, a few people have jealously said pejoratively, "Oh, I guess it's who you know." To that I happily reply, *Yeah, fuck you!*

We did something really amazing together, and it happened because we were friends. We had a sympathetic chemistry from day one; it was never some auditioned thing. The TV show was actually the opposite. When Lorne didn't want us, it was the Kids who fought for us, insisting we were an essential ingredient in the thing. Collaborating on a big project together with people you love and trust is always more fun and positive, resulting in something better, or at least more idiosyncratic, than it would otherwise be. The show has aged well, as has the music we made for it, and I'm so proud and grateful to Bruce, Mark, Scott, Kevin and Dave for inviting us along for the ride.

TINA TURNER AT THE IMPERIAL ROOM

TWO YEARS BEFORE *PRIVATE DANCER* TURNED HER WHOLE LIFE around, Tina Turner played the Imperial Room, the 400-seat dinner theatre in the Royal York Hotel, in 1982. It was my first time in a venue like this, a ritzy spot decorated with more ruched curtains than Liberace has diamonds on his bracelets. Your seating and proximity to the stage were determined by the denomination of your discreet money-passing handshake with the maître d'. Ties were required, and at the entry desk, a cabinet of loaners for the evening displayed the available choices for those who showed up tie-less. My friend Bryan, who took me, must have tipped well because we had great seats, second table from the stage.

Of course, she was incredibly dynamic and in peak voice, but it seemed like this type of show was going to be Tina's future: two shows a night playing other people's hits, accompanied by the clink of forks on plates.

We must have seen her in the latter part of her residency, because three days after the first show, the album *Music of Quality and Distinction (Volume 1)* was released by the British Electric Foundation — members of the Human League and Heaven 17. Turner opened the album with her angular and bombastic cover of the Temptations' "Ball of Confusion." John McGeoch from Siouxsie and the Banshees played on it. This detonating song summoned her into the future, where there are synthesizers, and young people wanting to ascend her star. I naively thought, *Why is she playing here?* Obviously, a gal's got to work, and it's not always up to the performer what steps are next. It's the audience that determines your level of popularity.

We hoped she'd play "Ball of Confusion," but it was too radically different from the style her band was laying down. No '80s synth-stabs in this set.

She did her best-known songs from her time with Ike — "Nutbush City Limits" and "Proud Mary" — plus a bunch of middle-of-the-road cover versions, standard fare for a supper club. Her slow, pleading take on the Beatles' "Help!" seemed like a sincere call-out to those who'd loved her in the past; "help me get my feet back on the ground," indeed. The show was less than four years after her now well-known liberation from Ike. The public didn't yet know details about the violent split from her controlling husband, so it felt like these kinds of performances were Tina's chosen path. For as elegant as the Imperial Room was, it was not the launching pad for a youth-oriented career, but more where the decline happened.

Tina still moved with relentless fire, her shimmering dress made up of rows of beaded dangly bits that amplified her vibration, each strand moving in a different direction. She put her famous gams through the paces as she strutted, belting out Rod Stewart's "Hot Legs." Her two dancers were far more Solid Gold than Ikettes, the intense frenzy of her original backup troupe replaced with a more contemporary gliding style, waving arms and dancercising like the choreography in the popular hit-parade TV series. I was tickled to see the two dancers show up on the picture sleeve of her massive comeback single, "Let's Stay Together." They clutch at Tina's thighs while Tina beams that radiant smile that could so easily be read as triumphant. At the Imperial Room, Tina herself was an explosive powerhouse, but her choice of material was obviously holding her back. Her band were fairly sanitized compared to the nasty funk of Ike's ensemble.

After the show, most of the audience filed out politely. No one guarded the entrance to the backstage area, so we just walked through the curtain. Backstage, there was her pianist and Tina, still in her spangly stage dress but covered with a robe, leaning on a table outside her dressing room, her name written on its door. With huge grins, we said hi, told her how much we loved her and asked her to sign our table cards. She was very sweet and seemed happy to talk with us. We were the only ones who wanted to.

There were venues like the Imperial Room dotted throughout North America, classy overpriced joints serving up B-listers like Robert Goulet, or Broadway stars past their brightest days like Chita Rivera. Genuine stars like Ray Charles, Count Basie, and Ella Fitzgerald gave the grand room some extra dazzle. The only other time I went there was to see Peggy Lee, not long before she stopped performing. We thought it was glamorous that she'd go side stage every once in a while to take a hit of oxygen from a mask, the band vamping until she caught her breath and floated out in soft focus for more. Emboldened by Tina's lack of security, we tried the same thing with Peggy Lee, but this time her dressing room door was closed and guarded. What a different time.

I was genuinely thrilled that Tina Turner had such a spectacular second act. Everything that exploded out of her to the massive world stage was all right there in that tarted-up dinner theatre container, just waiting for the right ignition.

IT'S NOT JUST GOOD, IT'S DALLAS GOOD

I CAN BARELY REMEMBER A TIME WHEN I DIDN'T KNOW DALLAS Good. He must have been sixteen when he started coming to Shadowy Men on a Shadowy Planet shows, and he was in our orbit — friends with our friends, as it would be for the rest of time.

His early band, the Satanatras, played with us a couple of times, one of which was New Year's Eve at the pre-gentrification Drake Hotel, an outlier bar now cleaned up and posh-ified. Dallas performed wearing a full scuba suit and big, floppy garden hat, doing kicks and leaps with the brim of the lid seeming to keep him aloft longer than gravity would usually allow. I thought our early friendship might have ended that night when I told him he reminded me of Kim Mitchell, the hat being similar to one the Canadian rock star wore as baldness set in. Dallas grimaced while sweat poured from the leg bottoms of his rubber outfit. He was kind of ridiculous but so cute and charming, a real devilishly sweet kid. I think it was at this same show that future Sadie Sean Dean lay on the stage at Reid Diamond's feet, tripping on acid and watching the show upside down.

Our camaraderie solidified through evenings on the La Hacienda patio, and when he pitched me to buy a champagne-pink sparkle drum kit at Songbird, the music shop he worked at. From there, a deep friendship grew.

We started playing music together around 1994 when Shadowy Men wrote an album with Jad Fair. Brian didn't want to do it, so Reid and I asked Dallas to play guitar on the recording. We knew he was a Half Japanese fan and a fantastic player, so original and wild from an early age. He was young, smart and enthusiastic, and coincidentally had a quarter-inch eight-track machine, which we only knew about after asking him. He knew the basics of recording, so we really got to spend a lot of time learning and putting music together. Dallas recorded our songs in the warehouse space he shared with Sean Dean at Gerrard and River Street. Every day we'd arrive to find the two of them playing Jon Spencer Blues Explosion, Pussy Galore, and Bill Monroe records, the foundation of the first iteration of the Sadies. It was no surprise that Jad saw something special in Dallas too, and almost immediately after, Dallas joined Half Japanese for his first European tour. He played bass with them, foreshadowing of another future thing we'd do together.

Touring the Jad album, we opened shows as an instrumental trio before Jad joined us. It was easy to decide to keep going with the band — Phono-Comb — as Shadowy Men decided to split. Shadowy Men felt like it had narrowed to such a sharp point that there was nowhere to manoeuvre, nowhere new to go. Dallas's youthful positivity made it joyful and easy to leave behind the band that had been our life for the previous dozen years. He was in about seven bands, something he eased up on as the Sadies became more and more of a priority, so you had to get slices of time when you could.

Beverly Breckenridge joined us and we played our first show as a four-piece, opening for Yo La Tengo and the Pastels. Playing with him then was a mix of awe and frustration. He was always late and sometimes didn't show up at all — almost hilarious to think of now, as he became the most ruthlessly punctual person I know, with no patience for those who weren't. Every eight years or so he'd apologize for being late more than twenty-five years earlier, usually when we were waiting on someone else.

We recorded a single in my apartment together as a trio: two electric guitars, drums, and no bass. It felt like a perfect situation. Everything was open-ended and filled with possibility, made even more spectacular when our dream label, Touch and Go, agreed to put out our records. I'd acquired an eight-track recorder, a beautiful TEAC half-inch machine that I started fully utilizing with Phono-Comb. We'd try out different microphones and placements, learning on the fly how to get the best sound. There were lots of holes in our knowledge.

Phono-Comb did another album, an all-instrumental thing in which Dallas was the snaky counterpoint to Reid's melodic solidness. He played the most unpredictable parts and brought so much life to material Reid and I had been working out as a duo, making them so superior to the songs' skeletons. Years later, he cringed as he heard some of these, saying he wished he'd put more effort into them and worked out his parts more precisely. Dallas winging it was better than most people's articulated compositions, so I couldn't even imagine what else might have been there, what else he heard. I loved what he played.

We flew our pal Steve Albini over to Toronto to record the album at the Gas Station — a friend's joint in Liberty Village, right around the corner from the hillbilly loading dock inhabited by most of the musicians we did shows with. I think Dallas and Sean were living there too by this time, renovicted from their raw industrial space in the east side. These were warehouse units where you could pull a train right up to the door, tracks intact from the building's former life. A giant Kentucky Fried Chicken bucket cast a shadow over the area; other friends often used it as target practice, zinging slingshots full of garbage or paint balloons at it. And then we suddenly had an album! It was a really stimulating time.

We toured a bunch as Phono-Comb, doing a few fairly significant jaunts. On a tour east, we stayed with Rick White and Tara Landry in Moncton, playing shows with their band Elevator to Hell. Dallas was so hyper-productive, and loved nothing more than getting high and playing music. He was a perfect soulmate to Rick, as the two of them tried every one of Rick's collection of smoking devices (including pipe made from an apple for health), making music while we were out looking at thrift stores and waterfalls. We'd return home with little amps and music gear from junk shops, finding gems in the oddest places — before those stores were stripped once the internet ruined the thrill of the hunt. When we'd get back, they'd have half an album recorded. It was no surprise when Dallas also joined Elevator with Rick, Tara, and Mark Gaudet, indulging his cosmic psych stoner impulses.

The first couple versions of the Sadies were magnificent, a heavy trio with Sean playing electric and hard with a Fender bass and pick, more like he had in his previous band, Phleg Camp. I dragged my extremely heavy tape machine down to the Liberty Village warehouse and recorded the trio for a couple of days, with their second drummer Andrew Scott, of Sloan, splashing around the twisting progressions, keeping a rhythm that belied the melodic cadence of his guitar player. I imagine that somewhere there's a stash of tapes that Dallas must have recorded with the Sadies' original drummer, Ted Robinson, in the space where we recorded with

Jad. What I recorded was fantastic, but almost nothing from that period has seen the light of day.

Dallas had complete confidence in his abilities as a guitar player, and he played with ease, able to make up new parts on the spot. Singing was a different matter. Early in the Sadies' life, he hated the sound of his own voice, struggled with what to say, and treated the words as an afterthought. After doing the band tracks, we recorded vocals at my apartment, where the photo on page 267 was shot. Dallas had a few lyrics prepared and tried spontaneous composition for the rest, the text from a grass tapestry on my wall leaking into one song: "performing on a xylophone." He wanted to use the cheapest mic, almost as a shield to hide behind. The sound was gnarly, adding a harsh shrillness to the singing that sort of suited the raunch of these songs. But Dallas was already formulating next steps for the band.

The Sadies did their first tour opening for Phono-Comb, the first of many times Dallas would do double duty in bands. It was when his brother Travis joined the group, and the first time that drummer Mike Belitsky was a semi-full-time member. Andrew Scott and Belitsky had both been in Maker's Mark with Dallas and tag-teamed on drums with the Sadies, one covering for the other, subject to availability. Mike lived in the US, making things a bit of a challenge. The band donned cowboy hats, deepening their exploration of country music and Morricone's western film scores.

Travis had been in the Good Brothers, a popular good-time country band, with their dad and uncle; Dallas would do the odd tour as a fill-in when a member couldn't make it. There was a bit of a rescue happening, Dallas wanting to save Travis from a life of being back-up to their dad. As kids, Travis had been a mentor to Dallas, introducing him to punk rock and the downtown scenes Dallas stepped into as a kid. When I say kid, he was literally a child, and as such, bands like Bunchofuckingoofs took him in and watched over him when he went to hang out at their "fort."

Reacting to his family environment, I saw Dallas deliberately avoid overt country trappings for a long time. I was a bit bummed when Travis joined, which had nothing to do with Travis himself. The band's sound evolved and, for a while, I missed the heavy band they'd been. Like all brothers, they scrapped and called each other idiots, but they were stronger together. Dallas had a forming vision and direction for what he wanted, and was motivated as heck to make that happen. Travis had experience and supreme skill as a guitarist and fiddler. It wasn't long before I only saw what was in front of me, not what had been. Ultimately, the Sadies were superior with Travis.

Every one of Dallas and Travis's relatives was musical, and Christmas at the Good family home involved jamborees like I'd only ever seen on television. A family singing and playing together was so moving and anachronistic, so inspiring to see and hear, a far cry from anything I'd experienced in my family. The closest thing to that that I was exposed to was my childhood friend's uncle playing his on-the-road songs on acoustic guitar in their living room, or watching *The Pig and Whistle* on TV. It seems even more unique now, as almost everyone has abandoned singing together as a social activity when their friends and family come over. Besides the Good Brothers, Margaret — Dallas and Travis's mom — had been a singer on Ronnie Prophet's *Grand Old Country* TV show. Bruce and Margaret met when she was on her high school's entertainment committee and hired Bruce's band, Edgar Allan and the Poes, to play at her school. They instantly formed a singing group together, the Kinfolk. In one of their promo pics from 1967, Bruce looks uncannily like Dallas, while his twin brother Brian could easily be mistaken for Travis's twin.

Dallas and Travis's country knowledge was vast. As much as Dallas came of age as a punk kid in the city's hardcore scenes, the country rock that was in them was unavoidable. Dallas gravitated to Jerry Reed and his slick, high-speed picking, someone I knew little about and thought of only as a novelty artist, based on his hit singles like "When You're Hot, You're Hot." He and Reid shared a love for Roger Miller too, and his story songs that also often bordered on goofy. I didn't know the depth of those two artists.

His early guitar lessons from a family friend, the legendary country guitarist Red Shea, had him steeped in the sound that brought out the best in Gordon Lightfoot and Tommy Hunter. Red was an exquisite player who, until the end, Dallas talked about and aspired to emulate.

Phono-Comb's last tour was with label-mates the Delta 72. Singer/guitarist Gregg Foreman and Dallas clicked instantly, two wild creatures high on themselves and each other. They barely slept, raging at full speed. I think a few drugs may have been involved, but they were both "on" no matter what time of day it was. It was adorable seeing Dallas as rock star, Gregg and Dallas egging each other on in a competition with no losers of who could be most fabulous. They both played hard on stage and were stunningly elegant in their personal styles, two dandies catching a contact buzz from each other.

Dallas suddenly took an interest in coming around to see Reid and his wife Beccy on Florence Street. He would get all nervous and gentlemanly, and it was pretty obvious very quickly that the interesting young woman next door was his motivation. So we got to see the sweet and endearing first days of his meeting Amanda Schenk, who years later he would eventually marry and share a beautiful, loving, and long relationship. His love and caring for her was always on display, never coy. Like any sensitive person, I know he struggled with how often he was away, or not as present as he wanted to be in the relationship, because of his work.

Watching him investigate musical avenues and find his voice was so extraordinary. I recently saw a video clip from the first or second Sadies show, and Dallas was singing into a mic that was level with his hands as he played! It was way too far away to capture anything but the faintest of ghost vocals, but I see it now as Dallas exploring and experimenting with old recording and performance techniques, wherein a country band would all stand around one condenser microphone, the relative instrument volumes determined by proximity to the mic. Maybe he just couldn't stand hearing his own singing voice.

The first time I ever remember him being giddy and pleased with his vocals was when the Sadies worked with producer Gary Louris on 2007's *New Seasons*. He was learning how to best use the voice he had, and Gary had a significant part in guiding him. I am still stunned when I hear the Sadies' last few records with Dallas: how he actually learned to sing to his strengths, how confident and natural his singing is. Some of his last recordings, done with friend Richard Reed Parry, are also among his best vocally, honouring the inventive harmonies and movement of the Everly Brothers.

He was so young when we met that it was hard not to feel like the responsible adult with him. He lived on beer and cigarettes, and night was day. Being so incredibly skinny meant that everything he wore made him look like a model, and his height made him stand out, so he was a conspicuous target for insecure creeps looking for someone vulnerable to take their anger out on. Around 1994 he was mugged by a few jerks who beat him so badly that he ended up in hospital and had teeth knocked out. This awful situation really shook him up for a couple of years, making him anxious about being particular places at night. It muted his sunny but laceratingly devilish demeanour for a while — unsurprisingly. I can't imagine that you ever fully recover from that kind of break in the trust in your safety out in the world.

He had no patience for reductive questions like "Who's better, the Beatles or the Rolling Stones?" as I heard someone ask him once. He rolled his eyes and impatiently replied, "the Kinks." Dallas's passing has changed my relationship with my own record collection. He was the closest person in my life who also carried arcane knowledge like the order sequence of the first ten singles by the Damned, who else Stooges sax player Steve Mackay had played with, and why only Screaming Lord Sutch and Screamin'

Jay Hawkins could get away with wearing a top hat. We played records for each other all the time, knowing that the other would also hear the magic in something that excited one of us: like how the jug played on 13th Floor Elevator records made the whole song sound like it was oscillating, or how Generation X were the only punk band up until Discharge that could play metal engagingly. Without another nut to share them with, records lose some of the life they contain.

Dallas smoked more weed than anyone I've ever known. I don't know how he functioned; he's the only player I've ever known who didn't play worse while high. You could tell when Dallas needed a top-up, as he'd start to get cranky. Our mutual friend Damian Abraham, of Fucked Up, talks frequently about how discovering weed freed him from anti-depressants and other anxiety-related medications he was on. Neither Dallas nor I ever pathologized his weed intake, but from Damian's example, I saw that some of the same traits may have been regulated by weed for Dallas. He was such a renowned and prolific pot-smoker that whenever I travelled with him, people would be waiting to proudly share the award-winning hybrid they'd grown, or have a nicely wrapped tin of pot cookies for him, all grandma-like. I passed out once after ingesting one of Dallas's gift cookies, and it was his wide eyes looking down worriedly upon me when I opened mine again. "Omigod, you ate half a cookie? Those are for cancer patients!" Cancer patients — and Dallas. When he went overseas to play with hardcore band Career Suicide, who he was a part-time member of, it could only have been Dallas who'd score weed while in China for one day.

From that first eight-track recording on, I was recording and mixing Sadies sessions, working on many of their records. Most of the time, I worked *with* Dallas in the studio, collaborating on music, and I enormously preferred that to the days when I worked *for* him, mixing *Rat Fink* or the live album or whatever. It didn't matter if I was his friend, he'd get impatient and reprimand me for how long it took a tape to rewind to do another take. But just like that, he'd snap out of his cranky boss role at the end of the session and skip away while I held his irritation for a while longer, it being so unsettling and unfamiliar to me. But he was sensitive and caring, calling to apologize later when he knew he'd been a dick. How he treated others weighed on him.

It wasn't long before his amount of studio experience surpassed mine and, not surprisingly, his talents led to offers to produce others. On a TV Freaks album he produced and I mixed, I was puzzled when he would frequently ask me to do the opposite of what my instincts told me to do: compress things more, roll off more high end. Only after a while did I realize that he was making the sound be that of a vinyl record, not just a great-sounding mix. We had so much fun enacting our shared knowledge.

One session we worked on together was mixing the Sadies and Heavy Trash's collaboration with the legendary dirty old man of soul, Andre Williams. The machines were recording almost the entirety of the sessions, it being unpredictable when an improvised song or lyric would break out. Playing got sloppier and words became slurrier as day turned to night. I wondered later if they called the album *Night and Day* because there was a distinct before-and-after to the songs recorded straight and the ones soaked in booze and weed. The "night" songs required a bit more editing to make them salvageable, as Andre would leave more and more space between lines, the clacking of his dentures keeping time. We cracked up a lot putting that record together, cackling over Andre's non sequiturs. "Throw a brick at an ambalance! Get some shit going on!" became our call to action for years afterward, prime lines lifted for use in any situation.

I was always grateful when Dallas took me along for the ride on recordings I wasn't playing on, where he'd find a place for me as a recorder, mixer, editor. I got to be Steve Albini's assistant for the recording of the Sadies' live album *In Concert: Volume 1*, their career-spanning double set that brought together most of their collaborators up to that point. Dallas and I then mixed it together.

It was a treat to work with the audio tracks of so many brilliant performances, getting to hear what each of them was doing individually to make up the whole of the sound. We had some instruments muted as we worked on others. Eventually we listened through Garth Hudson's keyboard parts without accompaniment, hearing the ghosts of the other players bleeding through his mics. I felt so fortunate to hear this incredible performance on its own, to hear Garth play with such ease and beauty, weaving the most effervescently unpredictable lines through the song. But I was also startled that his performance sounded like a bit of a mess, the timing all over the place and not seeming to make sense in places. As we dropped each instrument back into the mix, Garth's brilliant spectral playing revealed how he constantly moved between leading and reacting to other players in the ensemble, creating a thread that wove around everyone and pulled them together. It was truly miraculous, and only because of Dallas did I get to experience that moment.

We had a couple of side "bands" at different times. We both loved the '80s German group Trio, particularly their fantastic debut album that we were both obsessed with for a period. We somehow thought it would be a good idea to start a Trio tribute band, but as a duo, naturally called Zwei — meaning "two" in Trio's native language. Part of the "concept" was to play two shows and then split up. Our first show was opening for Peaches and Gonzales as a duo, before they left Toronto and found the notoriety that was waiting for them — in, coincidentally enough, Germany.

Years later I had a couple of electronic tracks that I didn't know what to do with. I didn't know if they sounded complete or where they belonged. I played them for him, and he just said, "I'm in your band." His crazed guitar completed the instrumentals, and with a few friends recruited to sing, we had a new "band," Filthy Gaze of Europe. We released one seven-inch, and on the cover Dallas appears in a monstrous face made from a composite of all the participants. The creature that is the "band" photo features Dallas's open mouth, his silver caps gleaming. As much as the

Sadies were his primary objective, he loved the freedom to express something more manic or primal when the situation called for it, and FGOE was maximalist to the max. When he joined Shadowy Men and we played our first show in Toronto, I will never forget the multitude of reactions on his face when I introduced him. "You may recognize him from his other band" — scowl and glare from Dallas —"the Filthy Gaze of Europe!" That cracked him up, which cracked me up, and fulfilled our ultimate intent of entertaining each other.

He was aware that he was a charismatic magnet for others, that he attracted people with his "cool" persona. He loved it when he made the cover of a local paper as Toronto's "coolest" musician, appearing in shades and smoking a joint. He didn't put it on, he just was. With slightly embarrassed glee, he played me a phone message from Mary Hansen of Stereolab, a band I loved very much. They'd met through mutual friends, and she was clearly smitten with him. "Hello Dallas, it's Mary calling. Just thinking about you and wondering how you are." I equally loved seeing him in his slippers with a cup of tea, snuggling up to his kitties. He was a real gentleman, and the only person I ever saw who made a point of introducing himself to the staff at whatever forum he was working in, unselfconsciously eliminating the hierarchies often enforced between, say, bartenders and bands, or security guards and those on stage. He was considerate and empathic to others also doing their job, as he was doing his.

I loved when his withering bitch came out. Daniel Romano played some support shows for the Sadies early in Daniel's solo career. His style was amusingly and blatantly influenced by Dallas, not only by suddenly adopting a country-and-western twanged voice after playing in punk bands, but stylistically donning the Nudie suits Dallas and Travis had had passed down to them when their musician dad and uncles got too thick to wear theirs. Daniel also had a mother-of-pearl inlay of his name in the neck of his guitar, the same as Dallas's guitar. Dallas would tease him for copping his look, so when Daniel first showed him the guitar, he said, "That's nice but you spelled my name wrong."

Over time I saw him take what he was doing more seriously — and it sounds overly serious to even say that, because it was more that he had an incredible work ethic and drive. He wanted to work all the time, to do as much as he could with every day, which, when I think of it, included playing every day, in all senses of that word. Our local music families crossed over a lot, and with Dallas, I got to work on the first several Sadies albums, some soundtracks, Unintended recordings, their collaborations with John Doe, and the truly moving Good Family album with a band that included the Sadies, Travis and Dallas's parents Margaret and Bruce, their uncle Larry, and cousin D'Arcy. Observing the dynamic between Dallas and his dad Bruce was also hilarious, Dallas relishing being dad's boss for a change and delightedly cracking the whip until Bruce did exactly what Dallas wanted from him.

I was surprised to later hear, from Amanda, that Dallas regretted wasting so much time. This was completely opposite to how I saw it, but I guess everything is relative.

One of the overwhelming and emotional things I recognize now is how much of a family I shared with Dallas, how there were people all over North America that became my friends because they were Dallas's friends, and vice versa. Everywhere we went, people loved him and were drawn to his openness, his incredible playing, and his unavoidable charisma. It was natural for the Sadies to be swimming in the same waters as Shadowy Men. Brian Connelly ended up playing with Neko Case, a friend we first knew as a teenage go-go dancer with Girl Trouble, another band who made room for the Sadies as best-band-friends. The records the Sadies subsequently made with Neko were just so great; it was truly awesome to see and hear friends make such magic. Same with Young Fresh Fellows and Scott McCaughey, Yo La Tengo and Steve Albini. All our friends were theirs, and it almost felt like a part of Shadowy Men was carried on by the Sadies after we split.

I don't think Dallas knew what he was getting into when he agreed to join the reconstituted Shadowy Men for that one show in Calgary. We knew we had to be as good as before, so we rehearsed for seven months — for one show. We thought we couldn't put all that work in and not play Toronto, so one show became two, two became five, and eventually we'd played together as long as the original band had, almost ten years.

We never knew if there would be another show when we played, but it was just so incredible doing it with Dallas that we kept rolling. Gone was any tension or frustration that I experienced at the end of the original Shadowy Men's life. I had so much gratitude for being in the incredible position I was in. People were interested in seeing us, and we could do what we wanted, on our terms. I fucking loved watching two of my favourite players together from my seat behind the drum kit. I was probably more in awe than anyone watching Dallas and Brian play together, both of them making the most complex thing look easy, both of them so masterful and beautiful to take in as they made each other sound even better, if that was possible. Their greatness made *me* better.

Only now do I think that when we did play what were our last shows with him — a three-night run at the Monarch Tavern in Toronto just before Covid shut things down — we did it thinking there would be more. In a weird twist of fate, the only two photos the band posed for happened minutes before we played our first show with Dallas, a last-minute private preview show before a Boys and Girls Club group of children hopped up on sugar, and minutes after we played our last show with Dallas. There was some kind of cosmic fate at play, those pictures bookending what the universe somehow knew was going to be.

On stage with the Sadies, Dallas was in command and a conduit for the rest of the band to flow through, so at ease in turning on a whim, leading them to the cosmos as they lifted off. His playing often looked effortless: he knew where every nuance in his guitar resided as he closed his eyes and became one with it.

He'd probably hate that language, because it's so Grateful Dead–sounding, but he was consummate.

He was different as a bass player in Shadowy Men, the tone being more grounding, the kicks and bends happening in places that weren't as intuitive. He worked not harder, but differently. Like Reid, he played bass like a guitar, being the lead one second and rhythm the next. Even though I would often have adrenalized anxious anticipation before playing a show, I rarely felt what I'd call nervous. I was aware that I felt I was the observer, not the audience. I somehow thought they couldn't see me and was sometimes taken off guard when a person recognized me.

I don't think we would have continued with anyone else playing bass, including Reid. It was necessary for the dynamic to change in order to thrive and grow. At first it was weird — Reid's voice coming out of Dallas's hands, emphasized by Dallas actually playing Reid's Gibson Thunderbird bass — but eventually it became its own thing. Rehearsals almost always started with an hour of gabbing, talking about records, music, neighbourhood gossip, and what was going on in our worlds. There was always love and gratitude for the time we had together, and Dallas always had respect for Reid being at the forefront of everything he did in the band. I'm so grateful we got to have as much social time together as we did rehearsing, the bonding element that usually disappears when friends start a band together. We just became closer.

We were neighbours too, so during the Covid-restricted years, we got to see each other a lot and trade updates on neighbourhood cat activities and gardening. Dallas had a new interest in making his garden nice, so I started giving him plants and advice about his patch. He was so proud to show me the greenery he'd been nurturing in his front yard, how well they were doing. I laughed when I saw his biggest, healthiest ones were weeds! But that, too, was so Dallas. I don't think it was intentional, but he always saw the beauty in the mess, had a Wednesday Addams view of the thorn being as beautiful as the rose.

Dallas was a lover of kitties, the wild ones and the tame ones, helping out feral cats and those who just liked to hang out on his porch and get scratches while he smoked. They brought out the best in him, as he became a baby-talking nurturer, cooing at whatever feline crossed his path. Dallas was approached by strange cats on the street — always a good character reference. He was so supportive and sensitive when my kitty died.

We had a bunch of new songs I was so looking forward to recording with Dallas and Brian, but that was not to be. I imagined the songs we were stockpiling being part of a new album. Before we had a chance to get to that, we were brought out of the lockdown times to work together on new music for a reboot of the *Kids in the Hall* series. At last, a chance for us to be in a proper studio and record together. I can't tell you how sad it makes me to know I won't be able to do that with Dallas again.

Our assignment was, again, to produce interstitial music, short pieces that would accompany Super-8 clips that provided a breather between sketches. I always thought of the new Shadowy Men as being "reconstituted" rather than reformed. We were like that cheap concentrated orange juice brought to life with some water after being left in the freezer for too many years. "Reformed" made me wince, never feeling like it was really Shadowy Men on a Shadowy Planet without Reid Diamond. We even played with the idea of other names, but they were all too unwieldy, more explanations than band names, so the original band name it was.

Dallas and Brian were big mutual fans. In the past, I had seen the two of them get nervous around each other. I think there was a bit of intimidation when we began, but that fell away and they just became peers of the highest level — until it came time to write music for the show. We had to come up with a lot of music, a challenge as it was still the isolation phase of Covid. Each of us was assigned to come up with about twenty complete pieces of music. There was no opportunity to invent that much together, so we had to begin from an advanced place.

Brian and I emailed what we had come up with, but as our first date to rehearse together approached, nothing came from Dallas. After a few nervous reminders, Brian and I received a slew of basslines. Brian very succinctly replied, "Where's the rest of the song?" Dallas and I met, and he anxiously asked how he was supposed to write guitar lines for Brian — it was too disrespectful to him. I had to just say, "*Do it!* I had to write guitar and bass parts and I don't know how to play either one of those!" I knew they'd both translate my wonky piano pieces into something superior, and they did. Within two days, Dallas came up with finished pieces and we set about learning them all.

He was so good at making me and others laugh. At our last show together, we left the stage at the end of the set, and he disappeared somewhere. Not so unusual, but Brian and I went back onstage to play more songs and it was a few minutes before Dallas reappeared. He put the bass on in darkness at side stage and walked up to me with his back to the audience, with the hugest beautiful and bratty Dallas smile, to show me his shirt — emblazoned with big letters spelling "I HATE DALLAS." Sharing a name with a city led to a couple of choice double-entendre merch pieces, like the hat he had that read "It's Not Just Good, It's Dallas Good." We got good mileage out of that line.

Dallas is also one of only two people I know who I never, ever saw in shorts, no matter how stifling an oven you were in.

I regret that I have no pictures of us working in the studio, just one I shot of his dad Bruce and Dallas playing together at my place. I'm glad I asked to take that one. Most people who were in a studio with Dallas knew how unwelcome a camera was. Thankfully, others didn't know that rule of his, so some of those pictures do exist.

I see the Sadies referred to as the hardest-working band in showbiz. Dallas would pooh-pooh it, but it was only Dallas who would call me mere hours after arriving home from somewhere like Spain, and with only a short window before having to be at something that evening, ask to rehearse or just play together. He was so skilled, that rare person who could hear a chord or even a whole song once and play it by ear, knowing what all the correct notes were. He was gifted, but his real gift was his radiant personality. I loved playing with him so much. He and Brian could fake any song we thought of, and we'd spontaneously play everything from Wes Dakus B-sides to Lulu and Lee Hazlewood.

Phono-Comb once played a skatepark in Rockford, Illinois, to a disinterested bunch of skaters. Halfway through our set, Dallas just started playing Cars songs, and we proceeded to fake our way through their first album, Dallas knowing every note and word as we dragged along behind. He was practically a kid compared to us then, and I loved seeing him literally grow up and do such incredible things.

Musically, he worked really hard to be as good as he was. Actually, only some of it was work, because he just loved playing all the time. I always wished for Dallas and the Sadies to have that one big payday, one giant song that would set him up for life, but, like their audience, it all happened one person and one buck at a time. I'm so moved to see what the Sadies did on their own terms. They built a bond with a massive network of people who love, admire and respect them, and were left awestruck at every show. Every show mattered, and his gratitude for those that came and shared in the exchange was genuine.

The Sadies' love and respect from the mind-boggling collaborators they attracted was so awesome to see. It seemed totally natural that the Mekons should adopt them as mini-Mekons, because the Sadies are peers with the best. The legendary people they worked with were just future versions of who the Sadies were becoming. Dallas's glee as a fan was so wonderful to hear. He'd often come over after some crazy thing that happened and tell me about it, his disbelief being as much of the situation as anything. I can hear his laugh as he'd tell me about having to take the doors off the studio to get Neil Young's huge rig in before they recorded "This Wheel's on Fire" with Neil and Garth Hudson, or running to wake up Andre Williams in the van after he'd already been introduced from the stage, and the band were vamping as they waited. Or having dinner with Iggy Pop and being played and praised on his radio show. Getting to back up Roky Erickson — leader of Dallas's favourite band, the 13th Floor Elevators. Becoming friends with John Doe and Kid Congo. Buffy Sainte-Marie seeing him across a crowded room and crossing it with a big smile to hug him. Dallas as a fan was as in awe of what happened to him as everybody else was. So humble and sensitive too.

Reid Diamond was a master storyteller, a modeller of tales that weaved truth and fiction together into elaborate narratives that were as often designed to tell some exaggerated version of a true story as they were to suck in an unsuspecting listener. It was easy to turn the tables on Reid because he was as gullible as the most wowed listeners of his fabrications.

He once told us a long, implausible story of some young girl who had done the most absurd things, had the most unbelievable adventures, ran a post office, was the model for the Golden Boy statue atop the Manitoba Legislative Building in Winnipeg, and then ended up in some kind of parliamentary position. He paused at the end and said, "And that girl was Buffy Sainte-Marie," a nonsensical random line invented by Reid, and an implausible person to have done what he'd just told us.

For years afterward, whenever we'd hear some story that was too wild to believe, we'd conclude it with, "And that girl was Buffy Sainte-Marie." Others started doing it too after asking what we were talking about. Dallas loved Buffy and had tried for years to make a collaboration between her and the Sadies happen. On their 2013 album *Internal Sounds*, the Sadies went into the studio with a secret guest, and the next day he told me about the previous day's work: how they'd reworked a song written and recorded on an older record of this person's. He started to squirm, and his smile got bigger as he reached the punchline: "And that girl was Buffy Sainte-Marie!" At last, the exaggeration manifested into reality!

Two recent things I know he really loved were when Lenny Kaye, co-leader of the Patti Smith Group, was going crazy on the dance floor to a Sadies free-form medley that had to have included at least three songs from the 1972 *Nuggets* album Kaye put together. *Nuggets* was as formative to me as it was to Dallas. Every punk I knew when punk began had that record, it was foundational.

Dallas was really into psychological horror films when he was younger, so when he was immortalized, along with Travis, in Jim Jarmusch's 2019 film *The Dead Don't Die*, that was about as high a pinnacle as you could dream. Jarmusch borrowed their names for two zombie victims whose brains had been eaten. A character stumbles over their decapitated heads and says something like, "Oh man, it's Dallas and Travis. Those motherfuckers could play guitar like they came out the birthing canal doing it."

One day I told him how incredible I thought their 2010 song "Tell Her What I Said" was, how much I loved the magic this one particular part contained — a feeling of floating, of time standing still. He looked at me sort of scowling and deadpanned, "Yeah, Sean wrote that part."

I'm so grateful to have gotten to know his parents, Margaret and Bruce, and seen exactly where the beautiful things about him came from. You can always tell the kids who came from great parents by their manners. The Good Family band would sometimes almost move me to tears, just seeing and hearing a family playing and singing together so magnificently. I was always honoured to feel like I was part of the family. I remain connected to so many people and feel part of a family because of my friendship and love for Dallas: Amanda, Bruce and Margaret, cousin D'Arcy, Travis, his Sadies brothers Sean and Michael, Jude who helped guide the band's business, and Dallas's brothers in Career Suicide. I see and feel Dallas's spirit in others.

Dallas's sudden death in 2022 from an undiagnosed heart condition is still hard to reconcile. February seventeenth was already a day of private memorial for me, as it was the date Reid died. How could Dallas have possibly died on the same date? It's been three years as I write this, and that familiar feeling I've had when those closest to me have died has started to happen, that strange emptiness knowing no new experiences of being with that person will come again. Dallas was so full of life, so strong and unique in character, that his absence is hard to comprehend. I will never forget his beloved wife's voice when she called me and said, "Dallas is gone." Her voice sounded like I've never heard her, her words like dust or smoke, transparent and hard to attach meaning to, like *she* was the ghost. "Gone where?" I asked back.

When Sinead O'Connor and Patti Smith sang Nirvana's "All Apologies" and "Smells Like Teen Spirit," respectively, it was from the point of view of a wounded mother lamenting a child. I recognized that feeling because I had a paternal feeling for Dallas and felt the wound of a lost son/friend/partner.

Throughout your life, you sometimes imagine those you love the most dying. I've experienced a lot of death, as it gets to be when you reach my age. Some of them, like Reid Diamond, were about Dallas's age — Reid died at forty-three, Dallas at forty-nine — but with Reid there was knowledge of the inevitable, of terminal cancer that would one day take him. Likewise with my mother: She was elderly and in declining health, so my brain somehow prepared for what was going to happen. The pain of it was no less tangible or unfathomable, but it was a death I'd thought of many times, tried to prepare myself for. Dallas's wasn't like that.

Death is energy transformed, and when someone has an immeasurable amount of energy, they linger, the metamorphosis happening all around you, sometimes for years. That someone could be so full of life one minute and gone the next left me confused and with unresolvable anxiety. How could something that burned so brightly be just extinguished in a moment? It all felt like some sort of trick, a state of transformation that couldn't happen without Dallas's presence. It was all about him, so why wasn't he here? At times he felt so close that my body would feel an adrenaline rush, wanting to reach out and pull him back to this world. I asked out loud, "Dallas, where are you?" There was only silence in return.

How could something so intense not leave a residue, not be perceptible? Of course, the people we love do leave something behind. Their energy has to go somewhere, and we, the ones who loved him, become the receptacle for some of it. But his life was too big, too many things in motion that were building, unfinished work and love and places to go. When are we going to go to that cottage on the Pickerel River together, as we keep talking about?

I held my mother's hand as she died, my heightened awareness attuned to where her life energy would go. I felt none of it as the room suddenly fell silent, but for the whir of machines in the room, and the breathing of my sister and me as we looked at each other across my mother's still body, stunned. As we walked out into the early morning light, there was a quietude, but also a feeling of awakening as the world carried on indifferent to what had just happened in that hospital room. Birds sang their morning song, just as they did the morning after Dallas died, their song unchanged and unconcerned with the transformational loss that had happened. It was incomprehensible that my world could be so changed, but the world around me wasn't. It was me that was changed, Dallas's life in me, just as my mother's was in me on that morning and every day after.

None of us who knew him were ready for him to go. To this day, I can't explain what happened in the first couple of months after his passing. We have a salt lamp that glows constantly in our living room, always on, dim and barely perceptible in daylight but radiating a warm amber glow as day fades. It sits on a Victrola that had once been my great-grandmother's, next to the couch. The last time Dallas was at my place, he sat at the end of the couch, scratching the ears of the traumatized cat we had adopted. After seven months of her hiding in the basement, we started to think the specialists were wrong, she was not going to come up on her own. We had to take action and put her into the world we hoped she'd live in, with us. Her safe place to hide was under the Victrola, and Dallas wanted to make contact with her, to let her know that she was in a good place and there was more love to be received if she'd only let it happen. He pet her head and talked quietly, telling her everything was alright and she was being well taken care of. It was hard for that cat to receive that message, but in our home, it was the last thing he did.

Our perception plays so many tricks on us, like making us feel that a new day happens when the sun rises, when in fact it takes place in the dark of night.

A couple days after Dallas died, my partner asked why I'd turned the salt lamp off, was I tired of it? I hadn't, assuming he had shut it off. The switch had a rotary brightness dial on the power cord, between the Victrola and a wall, with nothing to bump into and turn it off by accident. He turned the lamp on and thought no more of it, until a few days later when the same thing happened again. As he brought the light level up, it was as if he were struck by an electric shock. "It's Dallas." I didn't believe this could be true, until the third time it happened. I realized that it was only shutting off after his wife, Amanda, had been here. It seemed so Dallas, kind of bratty and something you'd only notice if you were paying attention.

It occurred four times. The only time Amanda wasn't present was the day my sister stopped by and we talked about Dallas's estate, which she was helping Amanda deal with. The porch chair my sister sat in was three feet away from the lamp, literally on the other side of the wall it was against. As I came in, I turned and noticed the lamp was off once again.

I can't explain any of that, but I felt I experienced the energy transformation. It passed through in silent waves, not like a radio transmission but vaporous and intangible, not just passing through me but becoming part of me. With Dallas, I felt his life force all around me, centring on the last spot he had inhabited.

I still see him in the distance, walking toward me on our street in his green coat. I hear his voice as I answer the phone, greeted with one word: "Meow." Even with those who love him the most, I can't use that word to greet them, as they sometimes do in Dallas's honour. It's only with him and any cat that that word has weight. I feel him for a moment when I greet or say goodbye to someone, wiggling my index finger from the knuckle in the most minimal version of a wave, as he always did with me.

It's hard to even describe his not being here as an absence, for I feel his presence just out of reach. I've read enough things about other dimensions to believe they are real. Why not? Other things that are hard to make sense of happen all the time, like infinity or seeing the past. Every star we see in what we perceive as the present really exists in the past, the radiant light having originated a long time ago. Dallas's light leaks through from other dimensions all the time, but like a drop of colouring in water, it dissipates over time and becomes harder and harder to perceive, diluted in the vastness of the world we live in.

Dallas's death came with many levels of grief. It was a while before I realized that one of those was for the end of Shadowy Men. Those of us who loved him shared in a strong communal connection of sadness; my love and heartbreak for his family and the Sadies was intense. But my bereavement over the end of Shadowy Men came with very little acknowledgement, and it was painful to contain that loss, along with feelings of selfishness for having feelings about *my* loss. While so many people reached out and expressed condolences for Dallas's death, only a few did so for the end of the band. I had to remind myself of my own conflicted rationale: It's only a band, its form isn't precious. But it was. I imagined Shadowy Men and Career Suicide being Dallas's mistresses to the Sadies, the place he went for relief and fun away from his "job." He was a different person with us than he was with the Sadies.

It was kind of miraculous that our reanimation with Dallas lasted as long as our first life with Reid. The band had become something precious again, a privilege I rarely took for granted. Occasionally I wondered how our time together might end. The final days of any band are rarely good. The first iteration had ended badly, but we'd managed to heal a lot of the damage done to our care for each other. Dallas was the bridge, the through line from Reid and Phono-Comb to our renewed life as Shadowy Men on a Shadowy Planet.

I could never have imagined that the end would come as it did. There's some security in knowing when an album, a movie, a book, or a season is going to end. The predictability prepares us. At the end of a book, the feel of the number of pages in our right hand is a measure of time. The tenuous fragility of our own duration is something else.

We become the soil from which a breathtaking flower grows, a home for every little insect to scurry about, moving grains of sand from one place to another. In an instant we transcend into that same light we see shining in the night sky.

CREDITS AND THANK-YOUS

Quote regarding Louie Beeson used by permission of Kid Congo Powers.

Quote of text from Reid Diamond's art used by kind permission of Rebecca Diederichs.

"Steel Rail Blue"
Words and Music written by Robin Masyk and performed by Handsome Ned. Lyrics reproduced by generous permission of Jim Masyk.

"Ode to a Gym Teacher"
Words and Music by Meg Christian. Olivia Records, 1974. Used by generous permission of Meg Christian.

"View from Gay Head"
Words and Music by Alix Dobkin. Women's Wax Works, 1973. Lyrics reproduced by generous permission from Adrian Hood and the Alix Dobkin estate.

"Angry Atthis"
Words and Music by Maxine Feldman. Harrison and Tyler Productions, 1972.

I am indebted to the documentary *Radical Harmonies* for some information in "The Menacing Threat of Self-Determination," directed by Dee Mosbacher, 2002.

Interior photographs by Don Pyle, except "The Menacing Threat of Self-Determination" by Lisa Kannakko. Used by kind permission of Allyson Mitchell and Deirdre Logue.

Thank you to Rik Emmett for being such a prince and drawing my portrait.

Rough Description was supported by Toronto Arts Council with funding from the City of Toronto, and would not have been possible without their support. I thank them.

Rough Description was supported by the Ontario Arts Council Recommender Grants for Writers program and I am grateful for their assistance.

Thank you to the following people:
Michael Barclay, Daniel Bowden, Beverly Breckenridge and Dave Rosencrans, Joanne Brigmantas, Neko Case, Meg Christian, Brian Connelly and Michelle McPhee, Jack David, Dallas Diamond, Grant Diamond, Beccy Diederichs, Alix Dobkin and family, Rik Emmett, Matt Finner, David Gee, Bruce and Margaret Good, D'Arcy Good, Michael Holmes, Calvin Johnson, Ira Kaplan, KP Kendall, Bon von Wheelie, Dale Philips, Bill Henderson aka Girl Trouble, The Kids in the Hall, Kirby, Alex Koch, Steve Koch, Laura, Lisa and Sally, Stevie Manning, Jim Masyk and Handsome Ned, Jason McBride, Bruce McCulloch, Allyson Mitchell and Deirdre Logue, Mohamed Nagdee, Kathy Pennington, Kid Congo Powers, Rob and Pamela Pyle, Johnny, Joey, Dee Dee, Tommy, Damian Rogers, Amanda Schenk, Patti Schmidt, Sandi and Michael Smith, Gary Topp and Gary Cormier, Sandra and Walter Winkler, Sean, Michael and Travis, Jason Winkler, Yo La Tengo, and everyone at ECW Press.

RIK EMMETT

Don Pyle is a Toronto artist, working primarily in music, sound, photography, and writing. Author of two books, including *Trouble in the Camera Club*, he's released fifteen albums, has shot photos for the covers of numerous books and records, and has scored music for feature films and TV series.

thedonpyle.com